How to Hire and Develop Your Next Top Performer

The Five Qualities That Make Salespeople Great

Herb Greenberg

Harold Weinstein

Patrick Sweeney

McGraw-Hill

New York   San Francisco   Washington, D C   Auckland   Bogotá
Caracas   Lisbon   London   Madrid   Mexico City   Milan
Montreal   New Delhi   San Juan   Singapore
Sydney   Tokyo   Toronto

The McGraw·Hill Companies

3 4 5 6 7 8 9 0   DOC/DOC   0 9 8 7 6 5 4 3 (HC)

2 3 4 5 6 7 8 9 0   DSH/DSH   0 1 0 9 8 7 6 5 4 3 (PBK)

ISBN 0-07-136244-4 (HC)

ISBN 0-07-142219-6 (PBK)

To our parents, our foundation,
our wives, our inspiration,
and our children, our future.

Contents

the exact same product for the same company—both playing to completely different strengths.

Acknowledgements

Given Caliper's history of four decades, it is virtually impossible to acknowledge all of the people who are responsible for the experience and knowledge that the authors have acquired that we are presenting in this book.

This having been said, however, there are a few people and a few institutions that must be singled out, given the fact that without their contribution, Caliper would never be the company it is today.

First and foremost, we want to acknowledge our nearly two hundred employees who have made Caliper what it is and who teach us so much every day. Their voices ring loudly in this book.

We also must mention the late David G. Mayer. It was David who spent four years with Herb Greenberg conducting the research that led to the development of the Caliper Profile. It was David who, together with Herb, borrowed $15,000 to found Caliper, and it was David who traveled to Boston, Hartford, Detroit, and many other places in attempting to sell the idea that there was, in fact, a test that could predict sales success. It was also David in the early years of Caliper who would pick up on the other telephone extension with Herb so that both of them would have something to do on the rare occasion that a client called. And, of course, it was David who with Herb co-authored the landmark article in the July/August 1964 issue of the *Harvard Business Review*, "What Makes a Good Salesman?," which contributed so enormously to Caliper's success. It is certainly safe to say that without David, Caliper would not be here.

Caliper also would not exist were it not for the confidence of the late Gayle Smith. Gayle, an executive at General Motors, had enough confidence to say, "Let me see which division is hurting badly enough to try this." And it was he who called one day in late December, when there was literally no money left to continue the business, to ask David and Herb to come to Detroit and to start a program with Buick Motor Division. All of us feel the enormous debt of gratitude to this executive with the vision and courage to try something new.

We will also never forget the contribution of Leon Levy and Jack Nash, who in 1962 were senior partners with Oppenheimer and Company. They believed in Caliper when we were virtually unknown, and we are proud to say that Oppenheimer remains a valued client to this day.

Joan Brown, who in 1964, was an executive at the Office of Economic Opportunity in Washington, D.C., and Gerry Sentari, an executive at Sales and Marketing Executives International, should also be acknowledged. Together they provided Caliper with the opportunity to embark on our ongoing efforts to help people rise from poverty and join the mainstream of productive society. They, along with the United States Department of Welfare and the National Alliance of Business, were responsible for Caliper working for two years in Puerto Rico in what was called the New Opportunities Program, which led to the large New York City program that resulted in the placement of over thirty-five-hundred unemployed individuals. This program provided us with the experience to continue our efforts today in a number of Welfare-to-Work programs.

It was Gordon Gund who gave us the opportunity to demonstrate that our job-matching concepts, so successful in business, could translate to the sports arena. He had enough confidence in us to ask for our help with his Minnesota Northstars hockey team and his Cleveland Cavaliers basketball team. It was our success with these two teams that made it possible for us to expand to the 23 major league teams with which we currently work.

We also would like to acknowledge the obvious contribution of Philip Ruppel, McGraw-Hill's vice president and group publisher, and Mary Glenn, our editor. Again, people and projects can only move forward when other people show confidence, and Philip and Mary, first, expressed their belief in this project and, second, helped enormously with its completion on time — particularly given the procrastinating nature of these authors. We have necessarily left out so many people who have taught us so much and people who have provided us with so many opportunities to learn what is in this book. The reader can only imagine the numbers of people that could be mentioned if we simply say "thank you" to all of the executives of the some 25,000 companies with which we've worked, "thank you" to the owners and general managers of the 23 major league sports teams, and "thank you" to the executives of some one hundred trade associations, all of whom taught us at least as much as hopefully we taught them.

1

The Sales Enigma

Why is it that some people succeed in sales, while others, who work just as hard, seem to get nowhere? What do the best have that others do not? What does it really take to succeed in sales?

Sales is a career with enormous opportunity. For those who are ambitious and too impatient to inch their way up the career ladder, sales is an extremely attractive profession—if they have what it takes. With a sales career's high income, personal freedom, and limitless opportunities for recognition and advancement, why is there any problem recruiting and retaining highly productive professional-level salespeople?

1

The Opportunity and the Challenge

In striking contrast to most corporate positions, sales provides an opportunity for those who want to operate with a good degree of autonomy and independence. It remains the only profession where individuals are judged according to a dollar-and-cents standard. And for those willing to sacrifice the security of a consistent paycheck, sales can be extremely lucrative.

For fast trackers, who are looking to make more money than their peers, are seeking increased responsibility, and are too impatient to slowly climb their way up the corporate ladder, there is only one option: sales. But as inviting as all this sounds, sales is not for everyone.

It takes a special kind of person to succeed in sales. First of all, salespeople have a different way of looking at the world. They sense opportunities where others fear rejection. Frowns are not signs of discouragement; they are something to be changed. Where others see obstacles, salespeople see challenges.

That is why, more than anything else, salespeople must believe in themselves. And the best salespeople we have encountered know themselves very well—they know how to play to their strengths.

And because of who they are, as salespeople grow in their positions, they are constantly seeking new opportunities. In a recent study, we found that most top executives have come up through the sales and marketing ranks. This is because the best salespeople and the most effective corporate executives share many of the same qualities, including initiative, drive, imagination, and a willingness to work hard.

But what attracts successful people to sales? What do they have that others do not? What, ultimately, does it take to succeed in sales?

We intend to give you a clearer picture of exactly who the best salespeople are. We will explore what drives successful salespeople, what differentiates them from people in other professions, and perhaps most importantly, what distinguishes the best salespeople from the rest of the salespeople. In addition, we'll explore why some people excel in sales, while others, who seem to work just as hard and enthusiastically, fall short of meeting goals.

We have counseled over 25,000 firms on these questions throughout the past four decades. And in this book, we will share our findings.

As our service economy shifts into high gear, what it takes to succeed in sales has become a little more complex than it once was. One certainty is that there is a growing need for the human touch. As the Internet opens new doors, the nature of sales is changing. Customers find themselves looking for someone to guide them through the labyrinth of possibilities they face. Many products and services today are difficult to distinguish from the competition. So, above all, this sales process depends upon trust. This trend underscores the growing importance of truly professional salespeople.

That is because what is being sold in today's economy is not really products or even services. What the best salespeople truly sell are solutions—solutions that uniquely meet the particular needs of each client.

Throughout this book, we will be taking out our psychological pens and sketching portraits for you of the kinds of individuals who have what it takes to make it in this game—a game where there are few clear-cut rules and where the odds are inextricably stacked against success, but where the opportunities and challenges are virtually limitless.

What we are about to describe for you are rare individuals, but they are not impossible to find. In our work, we have found that approximately one out of every four individuals today has what it takes to succeed in some form of sales, either consultative, or relationship building, or display sales, or the hard and fast-driving closers. However, only a few of those select individuals with sales ability end up using their innate talent. And as we are all well aware, far too many people who are completely lacking in sales ability wind up selling. The result is that sales has received a professional black eye. But more about that later.

For now, we would like to concentrate on those who do best in sales. For starters, they do very well—make that exceedingly well—financially. The truth of the matter is that it is not uncommon for top salespeople to earn more money than their sales managers. Sales superstars sometimes earn even more than the owners of their companies. Some of our clients have salespeople earning $500,000, $750,000, even $1 million annually. All these head-spinning figures prompt the question: What special skills or motivations explain why many salespeople earn more than we pay the President of the country?

Sales, perhaps more than any other profession, is a psychological testing ground. Ten years ago, a survey rated product knowledge as a salesperson's most important attribute. But now a similar survey has found that product knowledge has been surpassed by honesty, integrity, and professionalism.

The best salespeople unanimously say that they would leave their jobs if they did not wholeheartedly believe in their product or service.

Prospects, meanwhile, go through a precise psychological order when making a buying decision. First, they judge the salesperson's integrity. People today simply will not do business with someone unless they are sure they can depend upon the person. Then, prospects will determine whether the salesperson's company can back up its product or claims. Next, they determine whether what is being offered, regardless of price, will take care of their needs. Price becomes the final determinant of whether they will place an order.

The salesperson who succeeds is the one who works as an assistant to customers, helping them do their jobs better. To accomplish this, salespeople bring several qualities to the table, including empathy, persuasiveness, persistence, patience, and resilience.

And the very best salespeople make it look so easy, so . . . natural. While thoroughly understanding the advantages of the products or services they represent, they are also well versed in the weakness of their competitors— and they seem to anticipate their customer's evolving needs. To top it off, they make it look as though they could do it all while walking in their sleep.

Supersalespeople are extremely attentive to each client's needs and totally intent upon seeking an ideal solution to each client's unique problems. In the end, such individuals are problem solvers. They are the ones who solve problems better and more quickly than their competitors.

For such work, salespeople enjoy an unusual degree of independence, a chance to make money commensurate with their abilities, and limitless opportunities. They are, in many ways, their own bosses. When it comes down to it, few individuals in other professions can say the same.

The picture that develops is of highly paid, independent professionals who are often the sole representatives of their company and are trusted confidants to their clients. Such individuals are out there proving themselves every day. They are on the cutting edge, in a black and white world, where either they make it or they do not. There are really few jobs that hold that level of continual suspense. But that is what the best salespeople thrive on.

So for all its advantages, why has sales, historically, received such a bad rap? Why are there so many jokes about the traveling salesman? Why are there so many negative phrases about the profession, such as "selling you a bill of goods," "selling you down the river," and "selling out"?

Our studies show that the real reason the sales profession has suffered in terms of prestige is because four out of every five people now selling should be doing something else—for themselves, for their company, for the profession, and certainly for the sake of the prospects they encounter. Because these salespeople do not have a natural talent, they try to fake it and, in the fast-talking process, sell themselves, and all the rest of us, short.

Unfortunately, these are the kind of salespeople whom we all seem to come across more frequently than we encounter the true professionals. They are the type that make you want to ask, "Why don't you do all of us a favor and get another job?"

We hope this book will help eliminate the hackers and pave the way for true sales professionals. We hope to provide insights that will enable managers to uncover people with natural sales ability and that will help individuals to determine whether they have what it takes to succeed. If we can contribute in the slightest way toward this goal, we feel we will be providing an enormous service to the business world and to the unfortunate customers who unwittingly come across the lion's share of mismatched and ill-equipped salespeople.

Why, you might ask, is it so difficult for executives to find talented salespeople? We believe it is because most recruiting practices start out by looking in the wrong places for the wrong things. In the hiring process, we have found there is, almost universally, entirely too much concern with external superficialities (what salespeople are supposed to look like), and not enough concern with what is inside (whether they are motivated to succeed in sales). This seems to have been the case throughout time. For instance, an article in the premiere issue of *Sales and Marketing Management* 80 years ago noted, "Large men command attention, providing that they are physically well-organized and their muscle tone and health is all that it should be. Large salesmen are most likely to depend upon their size and bluff to succeed than they are to make use of every ounce of their gray matter. Smaller salesmen must make up for this deficiency in height and brawn by using their minds more effectively. They must either have more courage and self-reliance, more tactfulness and friendliness, or more intellectual resourcefulness."

Recently, the editor of that magazine related, "I got a letter from a plastic surgeon who avows 'more salespeople than ever before are utilizing plastic surgery to improve their sales.' Then, he proceeds to outline just what he can do for a salesperson who needs a lift (face, that is) to shore up sagging neck skin, a sure sign of . . . aging. Particularly striking, in the words of the good doctor, are thin lips ('not trustworthy') and weak chin ('not reliable')." The editor goes on to ask, "Is the suggestion of plastic surgery just another version of the old wheeze that looks and patter are more important than product?"

Sometimes, the more things change, the more they seem to remain the same. We can only assume that the continued emphasis on external factors, such as size and appearance, is due to a lack of understanding that sales is fundamentally a game of motivation.

If we can convey one thing in this book, it is that succeeding in sales has to do with what is inside of you. When push comes to shove, no one can give a salesperson the desire to succeed, the need to persuade, the ability to bounce back from rejection, the ability to understand the needs of others, or any other qualities that are needed to succeed in sales. These are all inherent gifts that some of us have in larger quantities than others. But they are not gifts that we can neatly package and give to someone else.

In addition, we have found that the best salespeople, regardless of their field, share one other characteristic. Ben Feldman, one of the most successful life insurance salespeople in the world, summed it up best when he was asked, "What is the best shortcut you've discovered for getting to the top?'" "Shortcut?" Feldman repeated. "I've never been able to discover any shortcut around hard work."

It is important to keep in mind that both a piece of coal and a diamond consist mostly of carbon. But it would be fruitless to give a jeweler a piece of coal and ask him to polish it until it becomes a precious gem. That, however, is what many sales executives are asked to do every day—to create salespeople out of individuals who are not fundamentally suited to the task.

Having assessed over a million individuals, we are convinced that the majority of people have the potential to be winners in this world. What it takes is understanding our inherent strengths and then getting ourselves into positions where our limitations are not of consequence and our strengths are allowed to shine.

With this in mind, we will examine why, with all its advantages, the sales profession continues to suffer from high turnover and poor productivity. Then we will look at the key motivations and personality dynamics critical to sales success. After that, we will try to provide you with a clear understanding of the specific internal motivations that distinguish the best salespeople.

Next, we will show you how to develop a thorough understanding of the specific requirements of a sales job and how to determine whether an individual possesses the necessary qualities to succeed. We will then deal with the "how to." We will discuss ways to maximize the productivity of a company's existing sales team, recruit sufficient numbers of applicants, and identify individuals who have what it takes to make it in sales.

With this backdrop, we will examine, in depth, the qualities needed to be a successful salesperson in six industries: life insurance, property and casualty insurance, automotive, real estate, banking, and high technology. We are using these industries—a representative cross section—as a way of explaining the differences to be found among successful salespeople in varying sales situations. We will conclude by examining how sales has changed and how the profession may develop into the next decade.

It is our hope that this book will help executives improve their ability to upgrade the productivity of their sales team and help them to bring into sales the kind of high-quality individuals that the profession deserves. We also hope that the information contained in this book will help individuals to objectively determine whether sales is for them and, if so, in what area.

Ultimately, for people who have what it takes, sales can be a very lucrative profession, offering many opportunities.

2

So Why the Revolving Door?

If the sales profession is indeed so attractive, offering the high income, personal freedom, and limitless opportunities discussed in the previous chapter, why is there any problem in recruiting and retaining highly productive, professional-level salespeople?

Whenever sales and marketing executives get together, poor productivity and high turnover are invariably key topics for discussion. These executives are constantly seeking ways to reduce the incredibly high cost, in both time and money, of recruiting, selecting, and training salespeople, only to have the majority leave, be terminated, or, at best, turn out to be mediocre producers. While striving to solve these problems, they nevertheless seem to accept, as a fact of business life, that 80 percent of all sales are made by only 20 percent of the sales force. The staggering, wasteful costs stemming from this situation are endured because they are thought to be inevitable. The resulting high turnover among those 80 percent who are fumbling along is, in turn, accepted as a necessary cost of managing a sales force. The fact is that neither the universally accepted poor productivity among sales forces nor the high turnover need be inevitable.

Our studies show that 55 percent of the people earning their living in sales should be doing something else. Quite simply, they do not have the personality attributes that are needed to succeed in sales. Another 20 to 25 percent have what it takes to sell, but they should be selling something else. These individuals could be successful in some selling situations, but they are only marginal performers in their current sales position. This leaves only 20 percent of salespeople selling the products or services best suited to their personality. The same studies indicate that this 20 percent of properly placed people is precisely the same group of individuals responsible for selling 80 percent of what is sold.

So a small percentage of each sales force is overwhelmingly successful, while the vast majority barely hang on, leave, or are terminated. But it need not be this way. A realistic goal can be that a majority of a company's sales force can consist of people as effective as the highly productive 20 percent. The benefits of having such a sales force are exciting to think about. Just imagine two-thirds of a company's sales force selling at the level of the current top 20 percent. We leave it to you to do the math. That final figure would not even include the reduced costs that would result from less turnover, recruiting, training, and managing of novices.

A more objective approach to recruiting and selecting sales personnel can result in significantly increasing the percentage of productive people. It is a matter of looking at the sales profession in a new way.

But before looking at the way to dig out of this hole in which the sales profession finds itself, let us try to understand how we got there. Why is it so difficult to identify people who have what it takes to succeed in sales?

Our studies show that most salespeople are hired for the wrong reasons. Most hiring approaches do not predict whether someone has what it takes to succeed in sales.

Depending upon the industry, there are two prevalent hiring approaches, both completely different—and both predominantly doomed to failure. First there are the traditional, but invalid, hiring criteria. There are companies and industries in which the hiring process is selective, but their hiring criteria have absolutely nothing to do with predicting whether someone has what it takes to succeed in sales. Second, there is what we term the "warm-body approach." These companies and industries just need someone to fill some empty shoes, so they take their chances with anyone who walks through the door.

Invalid Criteria

Regardless of how selective companies might be, they cannot hope to make correct hiring decisions if their selective criteria are incorrect from the start. These companies often use extensive application forms, have multiple interviews, check references carefully, and, in short, take many of the steps that are required in making logical, thoughtful hiring decisions. This process is often costly, but is considered worth it, again because of the importance of the decision. As most human resource executives and sales managers will confess, despite all the time, money, and effort, wrong decisions are the norm, and so the poor productivity and high turnover endure.

When we speak to groups, we jokingly describe the candidate typically sought, legalities aside, as the young, white male 25 to 35 years of age, who has 20 years of experience, has multiple, advanced degrees, is earning $60,000 a year, but will go to work for you for $20,000. We go on to say that even if you could find this paragon, who commenced his working career at age 4, the likelihood is that you would be hiring another inappropriate person. In fact, our studies have revealed that the odds are about 4 to 1 that you would be hiring the wrong person. The reason is that these same studies, which we will describe later, have proved that age, sex, race, formal education, and even experience are invalid predictors of sales success. Most people today will at least agree that sex and race are inappropriate criteria. Besides, the law is very clear that these criteria cannot be used. But we have found that in presenting our findings to managers, there is much argument about the other three criteria. Let's look at the arguments and see where they go.

Age

There are two specific views relating to the question of age. The predominate one is that management wants young people who will make a career with the company. Somehow, for management, youth becomes equated with longevity, energy, openness, and a willingness to learn. Of course, the arbitrary age cutoff varies, but the desire for youth predominates. Yet have not we all interviewed recent graduates who, among their first questions, ask, "What is your pension plan?" Do you really want 40 years' longevity with a young person who is worried about his or her pension plan?

Our studies show that young people are no more or no less willing to learn than their older colleagues, and the likelihood of longevity may be even less because they have not thought through their career choices. Your job may be part of their experimentation, and they may simply not be appropriate for a career in sales.

On the other side, there are those companies who seek "older, more stable people." Part of that thinking relates to the image of stability or reliability thought to be projected by an older candidate. Age is also associated with experience, which we will talk about next. Again, the situation comes down to the individual. There are some 50-year-olds who are less mature than many teenagers, and do indeed, over the long run, manage to convey that lack of maturity. On the other hand, we have all met 22- and 23-year-olds who in bearing, demeanor, and knowledge convey a far older and very definite professional image. The issue, as in so much that will be discussed in this book, comes down to the qualities possessed by each person regardless of age. In the long run, there is no magic formula.

Would it not be better to hire a 50-year-old who is appropriate for a job and who will give 10, 15, or perhaps 20 years of high productivity, rather than that 22-year-old waiting for his or her pension, who will provide 40 years of mediocrity? Similarly, would that same firm not prefer to hire a young person who is mature, open, and anxious to learn rather than an older so-called mature person who has floundered around through life and now comes to that company on the road to mediocre retirement? Simply put, it is not how old a person is, but who that person is.

Experience

Of all the invalid hiring criteria that managers use or misuse, experience has been the most difficult for us to debunk. It is much easier to hire someone with knowledge of your product or service or a person with a "long-term track record." Someone with this kind of experience can be up and running quickly, and does not require the kind of basic training that is required by someone without experience. Yet the price is high for taking this easy road.

First, we should look at who this "experienced person" is who is being pirated from a competitor. Why is this individual willing to give up all the benefits of seniority and customer relations in order to start all over with you? The reality is that this is probably an individual who has performed just well enough not to get fired—classic mediocrity—and who is looking to find an elusive pot of gold at the end of a nonexistent rainbow with another firm. The widespread practice of pirating from one's competitors has almost always resulted in nothing but the recirculation of mediocrity.

Perhaps an unrelated and yet appropriate example might help to make this point. Let us pretend that you are a coach of a professional football team—and it is not really important in this fantasy whether you actually know or care anything about football. You are looking to recruit players. You now have two candidates to consider. The first is 5 feet 7 inches tall, weighs 135 pounds, and has excellent credentials in playing high school football. He also has encyclopedic knowledge of the game. He can quote statistics and discuss strategies of every past football game, and so he brings to his candidacy every value of the experienced person. The other candidate is 6 feet 4 inches tall, weighs 270 pounds, and can run the 40-yard dash in 4.5 seconds. However, he does not know the difference between a punt and a pass. If you are that coach, would you hire the experienced young man or would you be willing to put the time and effort necessary into the exceptional physical specimen? In other words, would you not rather teach the second man football than have the little expert attempt to put his expertise into practice on the field?

The hurdle we face in conveying this point to managers is that although we know that this comparison is apt, it is not nearly as visible in the job situation. The difference is as pronounced, but exists within the individual's psyche, rather than being manifested externally. The ability to sell is not demonstrated visibly as is the 6 feet, 4-inch tall, 270-pound frame, nor is the obvious lack of such ability clearly visible. Yet hiring the so-called experienced person who lacks the fundamental dynamics permitting him or her to succeed in sales is just as inappropriate as trying to make a pro football player out of a knowledgeable, but slightly built, young man.

It is important to add that there are, obviously, some situations in which a firm will find individuals possessing the necessary sales dynamics qualifying them to sell its products or services who have experience to boot. That obviously presents a "best of all worlds" situation. Perhaps someone has done a brilliant sales job in California and is moving to New York. So the company has someone with the talent, who can be up and running immediately with little effort. Unfortunately, the real world does not normally present these wonderful situations.

Most things in life involve trade-offs, and what we are suggesting, in the strongest possible terms, is that a manager should be willing to trade lack of experience and lack of product knowledge for real dynamic ability to sell. The lack of knowledge can be overcome by training, but the lack of fundamental ability to do the job cannot. Just as we discussed in regard to age, it is still the individual's inherent abilities that must be the focus.

Education

It is amazing how many managers believe a college degree is an essential requirement for their sales positions. In many instances, when this requirement is questioned, it becomes obvious that there is actually no connection between having a college degree and selling their specific product or service. Of course, a number of technical sales situations do require a college degree, as well as extensive knowledge in a particular field (computers, electronics, etc.). For the most part, however, we have found little relationship between a diploma and an individual's ability to learn. The ability to quickly obtain product knowledge and learn effective sales techniques is fundamental to selling effectively. But that ability is not necessarily proven by the fact that an individual possesses a college degree. By equating a college degree with intelligence, and more importantly growth potential, managers are effectively eliminating many excellent candidates who are more than sufficiently intelligent, but who do not happen to have a degree.

Again, what is critical here is that the individual must be the primary focus. The manager should ask, "Is the content involved in obtaining a degree really important to this sales situation?" If the answer is yes, then, of course, a specific degree should be required. On the other hand, if the answer is no, then the manager should seek other means of determining whether an individual possesses the ability to acquire the product knowledge and sales technique needed to succeed in that specific job. While it might be convenient to use the lack of college degree as a simplistic screener in the selection process, our studies reveal that a college education has little to do with sales success in many industries. Of most importance, the possession of a college degree, in and of itself, clearly cannot assist in predicting sales success.

The Warm-Body Approach

At the opposite end of the spectrum are those thousands of companies and many industries which, though they certainly do not call it that, rely on what we term the "warm-body approach" in their hiring of salespeople. The way it works is that little or no salary is paid in lieu of sky-high commission rates for people who "are willing to meet the challenge," "will work hard," "are career-minded," "have real ambition," and "want to get ahead." Since no salary is paid, the theory is that anyone who wants the job, and can earn a license where necessary, should be brought aboard. People who hire on this basis figure, "What do I have to lose?" If the individual sells one property or one life insurance policy, "I'm ahead of the game." The result is that a continual slew of recruitment advertisements are run in the newspapers, and a revolving door is set up for masses of people who figure they'll take a shot at these "great opportunities." But since four out of five of them have no sales ability, most of them only last long enough to bother their relatives, friends, and a few unsuspecting prospects. And so the turnover carousel continues. This warm-body approach has, in fact, damaged the image of many industries, while creating huge, though often hidden, costs for the companies employing it.

When we focus later on the real estate and life insurance industries, we will deal with the real costs of this warm-body approach in these specific industries. For now, suffice it to say that the costs of conducting an ongoing recruitment and selection process, training incapable individuals, and then supervising them until they realize that they are in the wrong place at the wrong time are virtually incalculable. On top of this, these inappropriate people will inadvertently burn a company's precious prospects. Once these figures are added up, it becomes clear that the mere fact that salaries are not paid does not offset the true cost of hiring inept salespeople.

Another unfortunate result of this approach is the direct, negative impact on sales as a profession. If it is so easy to obtain one of these sales jobs in a warm-body–oriented industry, then what kind of status can be accorded to someone who holds such a job? Job status is derived from the fact that it takes a particular expertise to be a member of the profession. Engineers, physicians, lawyers, and accountants all hold their jobs because of recognized professional skills, knowledge, and training. But salespeople in one of the warm-body industries know that almost anyone walking the street could be filling their shoes.

An even more serious result of the warm-body approach is the fact that four out of five salespeople with whom the public comes in contact are essentially incompetent. Thus, most people grow up with an exceedingly negative view of salespeople. Many of us remember that very pushy life insurance salesman who called at an inappropriate time and would not take no for an answer. We all, of course, look askance at the tire-kicking used car salesperson, and we have all heard stories of swindles conducted by fast talkers. So why would anyone want to join a profession with such a negative image?

Of course, not all companies or industries use this warm-body approach. There are many cases where the selection of salespeople is more judicious. Many sales positions pay substantial bases, plus incentives; and many companies, due to the nature of their specific sales situation, are keenly aware of the enormous cost involved in the training required to even begin to sell the particular product or service. And, of course, in this high-tech era, there are increasing numbers of companies and industries in which specific technical know-how is a prerequisite to selling. The problem is that, even in situations where there is emphasis on carefully selecting the right person for the right job, in most cases, the wrong criteria are employed for making that final hiring decision.

In this chapter, we have attempted to answer the fundamental question, why, given all the opportunities in the sales profession, is there difficulty in finding and retaining highly productive people? The high turnover rate, the lack of status caused by large numbers of inappropriate salespeople currently selling, the use of the warm-body approach, and decisions about hiring made for the wrong reasons go a long way, we feel, toward explaining why professional sales is not one of the most important and most sought-after positions in the business hierarchy.

The real sales professionals, on the other hand, are an exciting, dynamic group of people. After getting to know them, as we have, you quickly realize why they are the leading life insurance people, why they win national awards for computer sales, and the like. It is these professionals who should be representative of the sales profession, but unfortunately they only represent approximately 20 percent of that profession.

We will next delve into the personality attributes that are shared by the top 20 percent of salespeople (those who sell 80 percent of what is sold). Then we will look at ways to replace the old, outmoded, invalid hiring criteria, and, of course, the warm-body approach, with recruiting and hiring methods that can attract productive people. We will explore how to select, develop, and manage those individuals who are best suited to a company, selling a particular product or service. Ultimately, we will describe an approach that will help you reach, or at least come close to, the situation where 50 percent of what is sold is sold by 50 percent of your salespeople. Just imagine if your sales force more closely approached, in its totality, the level of productivity currently represented by that magical 20 percent.

2

What It Takes to Succeed in Sales

Successful salespeople possess special personality attributes enabling them to succeed. Unlike many jobs where mediocre performance can be disguised and an individual is able to get by despite intensely disliking a job, a salesperson's success or failure is revealed immediately by bottom-line numbers. The very nature of the sales job precludes success for those who do not possess the fundamental motivation to sell.

In this part, we will first talk about motivation in general and then discuss the five central qualities that are key to success in sales. As we discuss these qualities—these key motivational forces—it should be kept in mind that though possession of these qualities is essential to sales success, simply possessing them by no means ensures success in a specific sales job. Part 2 of this book is devoted to examining the basic foundations of the question, What does it takes to succeed in sales?

3

The Motivation to Succeed

The key element that separates the top 20 percent of all salespeople—the 20 percent who sell 80 percent of all that is sold—from the rest is their motivation to excel in a very special way. Only by understanding what motivates an individual from within can we know what it really takes to succeed in sales or any other occupation.

Companies are continually looking for ways to motivate their people. Motivational speakers are featured at company meetings and industry conventions. Incentive plans are developed, and contests are held. In most companies there is an endless sequence of carrot and/or stick programs designed to motivate. Unfortunately, virtually all this attention to motivation deals with external factors rather than internal motivation. Our work over the past 40 years has proved beyond question that the real key to productivity is not external motivation but, rather, that which is generated from within the individual—what we term "internal motivation."

Motivation is commonly defined as an incentive that persuades someone to do something. We pay salespeople commissions to motivate them to sell—a positive motivation. On the other hand, there is the threat of being fired if people do not come to work on time or if they fail to work diligently. The annual review serves as another motivator, theoretically driving people to do their best for the purpose of earning salary increases or promotions. These are the classic carrots and sticks.

But it is our view that entirely too much emphasis is placed on these externals, and not nearly enough on what is the critical key to effective job performance—internal motivation. In the long run, the external motivations have little bearing on how well, or how poorly, an individual will perform. Of course, people want promotions. Of course, they want the highest commissions they can receive. And, of course, they do not want to be fired. However, these carrots and sticks do not lead to effective, productive work.

The true motivation that causes individuals to excel comes from within. It is this inner motivation that distinguishes the 20 percent of those who succeed in the sales profession.

Internal motivation relates to what drives us from within to act. We need no one to tell us to eat when we are hungry. Similarly, when we are tired, we sleep because of our internal feeling of fatigue. When we are thirsty, we drink. We need no one to motivate us to enjoy the sunshine, or to listen to a symphony (if we love music). Whether inner motivation is physiologically based (hunger, thirst, fatigue) or based on learned motivation (music, golf, fishing, sports, etc.), we are driven to satisfy those motivations from within, and often we will even fight external resistance to satisfy these motivations.

When we look at internal motivations driving us toward specific job functions, we are dealing with needs of far more complexity than the easily described motivations of hunger and thirst. It is a simple matter for people to recognize that they are hungry, just as it is simple for someone else to understand when an individual says, "I want to eat because I am hungry." When, on the other hand, one is dealing with job-related motivations, there is neither the individual's own clear-cut recognition of these motivations, nor the simple possibility of revealing these to another. When we talk about ego-drive in Chapter 5, we will be looking at one specific example of an internal motivation—the need to persuade. Yet can you imagine an individual saying to someone else, "I want to sell because I get specific ego-gratification from having someone else say yes to me"? Not likely. But, as we will see, that is precisely what is occurring. It should be added that even here the matter becomes more complicated, because some people are much more in touch with their inner motivations than others.

Without belaboring the point, it is important to understand that while all inner motivations spur us to action as clearly as hunger and thirst, we are not always aware of these motivations. Still, there is nothing more important in determining the effectiveness of an individual in a job than to understand his or her basic inner motivations, and to gear the job placement, training, compensation, and supervision to those motivations. There is nothing more basic to the individual than those inner forces—those inner needs—driving that individual.

However, because inner motivation seems so difficult to understand, many managers focus on the more obvious, but less effective, external motivations. For instance, many sales organizations set aside a particular month as "super sales month." All the salespeople are listed on a board, and each person's sales are noted on a daily basis. This public display is, of course, designed to motivate everyone to compete. At the end of the month, the top producer will receive an all-expense-paid trip for two to Hawaii with all the frills.

As expected, everyone works hard during that month, sales increase, and someone wins the glamorous trip. Aside from the wonderful time the top producer has in Hawaii, however, the story does not have such a happy ending. Two results somehow tarnish the luster of the exercise in external motivation. First, to no one's surprise, the winner of the contest has been the top producer consistently for 2 years. Second, and much more important to the success of the company, although sales increased during the contest month, they dropped substantially over the next couple of months, and the year's final results were the same as they would have been without the contest. What the external incentive did was generate some additional activity for a short period of time and cause people to either delay sales in order to close them in that month or hurry to push them into that month. But the overall totals were not affected. Simply put, sales, and individuals, found their level.

It is much easier to hire motivational speakers or to set up contests of this kind in the hope that such external processes will increase productivity. Externals, whether incentives or threats, are tangible, and so we reach toward them as solutions. Everyone walks out of a room feeling wonderful after being exposed to a dramatic, motivational speaker. Still, we cannot help but wonder whether the productivity increase is any better than it would be if the participants had gone to a Broadway play or a special concert, after which there is also a wonderful feeling.

The truth is, although it is much more difficult to uncover, it is the inner motivation that determines how well an individual will do in a specific job. These inner motivations are much harder to deal with because you have to delve below the surface to uncover and understand them. Interviewing, conducting psychological testing, and checking résumés and references are all focused on uncovering some of these motivations. How effective we are in this quest determines how successful we will be in our hiring. The plain truth is that if we hire people whose motivation and abilities suit them to the position, then and only then can some of these external motivational approaches have a long-lasting, positive effect on productivity. Without the proper internal motivation, the externals can create motion but not consistent achievements.

We should add here that as strongly as we deny the power of externals to create productivity, we have seen situations where externals can place serious limits on that productivity. It is certainly possible, for example, to set up a compensation system that runs counter to the motivation of the people receiving that compensation. If highly driven salespeople, with tremendous persuasive motivation and entrepreneurial orientation, are placed on a salary, even a high salary, with little upward mobility, this will demotivate them. The incentives—the commissions—will not in and of themselves act as a motivation, but their absence, for certain individuals who need enormous up-end potential, can act as a disincentive.

A number of years ago, we ran into a classic case of this disincentive with one of our clients. We were asked to do a study on the company's sales operation in order to solve a problem that had plagued the company for more than a decade. The company felt it was hiring effective salespeople. Most of the new hires started quickly and over the first couple of years were highly productive. However, counter to the experience of most companies that lose salespeople early in their careers, this company found that there was a high level of turnover between the third and fifth years of its salespeople's careers, and a parallel flattening out of sales productivity.

When we tested the sales force, we found that the company did have an unusually high number of strongly driven, highly motivated people. Instead of the usual 20 percent of effective salespeople, the staff consisted of more than 50 percent whom we would have recommended for hire on the basis of their sales dynamics. When we investigated further, we found another unusual fact: The high turnover rate in the third to fifth year was largely among the salespeople with strong dynamics. The marginal people, those who were just getting by, were hanging on and were making a career of their mediocrity. This was puzzling. Normally, people leave because they are not succeeding. Here it was the productive people who were leaving.

As we studied the situation further, the reasons became clear. All signs pointed to the company's sales compensation plan. What occurred simply was that when a salesperson's level of sales became "too high," the person's sales territory would be split. The reasoning, as we found out from interviewing management, was that a salesperson could not possibly handle too large a territory since there was continuous follow-up involved in most sales. Thus, once a salesperson had too many clients, the reasoning went, that person could not possibly service all those additional clients.

As rational as this sounds, the net result of splitting the territories was to totally remove the most productive salespeople's incentive to do well. People with drive are normally willing to work for little or no money at the beginning, but they cannot tolerate limits on their top potential. This splitting of territories created an absolute upward limit and therefore destroyed the motivation of those people the company counted on to be most productive. On the other hand, the mediocre salespeople probably never reached a high enough production level to require a split of their territory, and so they hung on with their mediocrity.

We suggested that rather than split the territory of the highly productive people, the company provide these top producers—these inner-motivated people—with a service assistant whose job would be to help in the ongoing servicing and follow-up of accounts. Rather than destroying up-end incentives, we felt it was important to give the top salespeople the ability to deal competently with their ever-expanding book of business. The result was that, within a year, the turnover among the productive salespeople was reduced by two-thirds. As might be expected, productivity substantially increased in proportion to the increased tenure of the effective salespeople. Within one more year, the company was able to affect important savings through reducing the number of "senior account representatives" and supporting its talented sales staff with lower-paid service assistants.

This is not to suggest that one compensation plan can fit all situations. Far from it. There are other cases where an individual's major motivational pull is toward security, consistency, and stability. In these instances, an up-end incentive system, regardless of its potential, could be viewed as too risky and therefore clearly demotivating.

We will discuss compensation in more detail later. Suffice it to say here that while we should look at externals to make certain that they do not demotivate, we should not look toward them as a key factor in increasing individual or overall productivity.

We should underscore the point that money motivates virtually everyone to some degree, but truly effective individuals in any field of endeavor are motivated by more than money. For them, money is a symbol of achievement, not a motivational factor in and of itself.

The case of George provides a classic example of how internal motivation is the dominant factor, regardless of how positive the external motivation is thought to be. George was an operations manager for one of our corporate clients, and he was well on his way toward a vice president of operations position. He had been on the job for 10 years, received substantial salary increases each year, and enjoyed all the requisite perks that go along with being the rising star.

We were contacted by the vice president of operations, whom George was destined to replace due to that vice president's imminent retirement. He was concerned because, during the last 6 months, George's work had fallen off and he had confided to friends that he was thinking of leaving the company. The vice president asked us to test and interview George to determine what the problem might be, since the last thing the company wanted was to lose this exceptional employee.

After evaluating George's test, the problem became apparent to us, though it took several in-depth interviews to convince George that the problem was, in reality, what we thought it to be. As an operations manager, George was obviously involved with a great deal of detail, much coordinative work, and substantial overall administrative skills. Within this operational function, there was little or no opportunity to persuade. Our test showed, however, is that George possessed enormous persuasive motivation. For George, convincing people was a key means of gaining personal gratification. Lacking this opportunity on the job, he exercised his desire to persuade through a substantial degree of political involvement and some fund-raising activity for the alumni association of the university from which he had graduated. But as his job made increasing demands on him, in terms of both responsibility and time, the opportunity for these external persuasive outlets diminished. And with the vice presidency and the demands that it would impose, the chance to exercise his powers of persuasion might disappear entirely. Added to this was the fact that although George was able to cope with the detail required in the operations job, his inner motivation was not that of a detail-oriented individual. He could tolerate detail but did not really enjoy it. Thus, despite the fact that George was successful in his job, the job demanded that he do things he was not motivated to do. Thus, success and the intended externals that go with it were not enough to provide George with satisfaction. Rather, the deprivation of his inner motivations was causing him to want to leave his job despite all the external trappings.

When we shared this with George, he was totally astounded. To paraphrase, "I really believed in your test until now. But when you say to me that I have sales ability, you lose your credibility." He continued by telling us that he had never sold anything in his life and that the last thing in the world he would want to do would be to sell. He backed that up by pointing to his degree in finance and to his 10 years of exceptional success in operations.

After a while, however, George began to see how his involvement in politics and his fund-raising activities really provided him with more personal gratification than his day-in and day-out work. He also began to connect both intellectually and emotionally the fact that these activities were in effect sales and that it was the sales process that he enjoyed so much. It then became clear to him how the lack of this sales process created his primary frustration with his operations job.

The result of this was our startling suggestion to corporate management that George make a mid-career change right within the company. To make a long and happy story short, this change was made and within 2 years, George was one of the company's top sales producers, again heading toward a vice presidency—this time vice president of sales, a position directly attuned to his internal motivation.

Despite all the external motivations that could have been provided, George would have left his job and sacrificed his fast career track just because his more basic internal motivations were not being fulfilled. This is true even though George was not consciously aware that it was sales that really excited him. Despite this lack of conscious awareness, he would have given up the externals because of the internals. And this is the key to everything we are saying. If the internal motivation is there, and the externals do nothing to inhibit it, but, rather, act to enhance it, people will succeed on the job. External motivation can never get the job done if the internal motivation is absent.

To help better understand internal motivation, think for a moment of the laziest person you know. Most likely, that individual is working for your company. When you look at this "lazy person," ask yourself if he or she is too lazy to get up at 4:00 in the morning to go fishing, or to stand in the hot sun swinging a golf club, or to work in the garden, or to play bridge, or to do one of a hundred other enjoyable things. The answer is "of course not." What you are really saying when you think about that "lazy person" is that the person is too lazy to do what you want him or her to do. The reality is that this so-called laziness, with few exceptions, is really a lack of inner motivation. Provide people with an activity that connects with their inner motivation, and they will work as hard as anyone else.

This is our basic thesis. If an individual possesses the inner motivation to do a job and is given the proper training and supervision, he or she will succeed. On the other hand, if an individual does not possess the proper inner motivation required to perform successfully in a specific job, all the training and incentives in the world will not make that individual highly productive. That "lazy person's" willingness to work hard at fishing, golf, or bridge is really typical of all human beings. We will work at what is fun for us—at what we enjoy. If we enjoy our work because that work satisfies our inner motivations, we need no one to tell us to work harder—we will do it because we want to, because it is rewarding. If, on the other hand, we hate what we are doing because it runs counter to our basic motivational forces, we might go through the motions, we might do our best because it is our responsibility, but we will never really be happy and will never really achieve at a top level, regardless of the external motivations.

Before discussing the key motivational factors essential to sales success, it is important to underscore that while we have found that it is extremely difficult for an individual who does not possess these dynamics to be successful in sales, the mere possession of these by no means ensures success in a specific sales job. It is vital to begin by possessing these dynamics—empathy, ego-drive, ego-strength, service motivation, and conscientiousness. The possession of many other attributes, however (which we will discuss later), determines whether an individual will succeed in a specific sales job. With this in mind, we can turn to a discussion of these central dynamics. Before doing so, we will briefly review the events leading to our discovery of these dynamics.

In the late fifties, we were asked by an insurance company to determine what could be done to reduce the enormous turnover among its agents. That company, like so many in the life insurance industry, was experiencing a 60 percent annual turnover of new agents and a nearly 90 percent turnover in 3 years. If it could find a test, a structured interview, or any other method of reducing its turnover, even by 5 percent, the economic impact would be enormous.

We spent 3 months exploring hundreds of tests, interview guides, biographical and demographic appraisals, and even handwriting analysis to uncover a way to identify people with the potential to succeed in sales. The result of our 3-month effort was a very short memo, which essentially read: "There is nothing we can find worth the paper it is written on."

We found it amazing that at a time when the boundaries of outer space were being explored, there was still very little understanding of what goes on inside of us. Why was it conceivable to plot a lunar landing, but so difficult to predict whether someone had the qualities needed to succeed in sales? So we spent the next 4 years exploring what kind of people are motivated to put themselves on the line, day in and day out. What kind of people feel a need to persuade others? What does it take to endure the enormous amount of rejection that characterizes the sales profession? From this research we discovered the central dynamics needed to succeed in sales.

4

Empathy: The Guidance System

The first key quality we found to be of critical importance to sales success is empathy. We define empathy as the ability to sense the reactions of other people. It is the ability to pick up the subtle clues and cues provided by others in order to accurately assess what they are thinking and feeling. Empathy does not necessarily involve agreeing with the feelings of others, but it does involve knowing what their feelings or ideas are.

Empathy is not sympathy. Objectivity is lost in sympathy. Someone once said that "empathy is placing oneself in the other person's shoes, but sympathy is putting them on and feeling the pinch." Sympathy involves a feeling of loyalty to another person and, thus, the loss of objectivity. If you identify with and feel the emotions of others, you cannot view them in a dispassionate, objective, and helpful manner. Thus, in order to sell effectively, you must understand how a prospect or client is feeling while still maintaining your own sense of identity, your own purpose, and your own objectives. A salesperson simply cannot sell without this invaluable and irreplaceable ability.

Because sales involves evasions, objections, and changing of course by the prospect, salespeople need to be empathic and flexible enough to adjust their presentation and approach. Understanding the needs of individual customers and selling them an appropriate solution is part of a building-block process that starts with someone who is empathic enough to really hear what is being said and really feel the needs of the prospects, including clear recognition of hidden agendas and hidden objections, not the clearly stated ones. More often than not, these hidden agendas and objections defeat a sale. Only with sufficient empathy to recognize the real needs of a prospect can those needs be met through the product or services being sold.

During the course of our early research, we identified empathy as the single basic ingredient common to all good salespeople. Please note, however, that empathizing with a prospect is not the same as identifying with the prospect.

The successful salesperson, while he or she may genuinely like the prospect and sincerely wants to serve the prospect well through the product or service, nevertheless sees that prospect as a means of achieving the end of making the sale and, therefore, as a means of gratifying that salesperson's ego-needs. A salesperson who loses sight of this goal, though he or she may be well liked, will be less effective in overcoming objections and close sales.

We overheard a conversation in the office of one of our clients that well illustrates this point. The sales manager was berating one of her salespeople for failing to close an important prospect. The sales process had evidently been going on for more than 3 months.

In response to the manager's criticism, the salesman explained that the president of the prospect firm was extremely busy. He went on to describe the absolutely staggering schedule the president followed and how difficult he found it to add to the president's pressure. He explained, "When I did get to see him, I felt I only had part of his attention, and that he always had one foot out the door."

What was happening here was that the salesman so identified with the customer's pressures that he failed to keep his objective in mind, which included providing a service that would in the long run actually help alleviate some of those very pressures.

The overidentification with one element of the customer's problem—the busy schedule—prevented the salesman from meeting his own objective—making the sale—and simultaneously prevented him from really providing an important service to the customer.

In order to understand how empathy functions, it is important to realize that one's capacity to empathize relates entirely to an individual's motivation to do so. No one really knows whether an individual is born with a certain capacity for empathy. What we do know, and what is critical to all our discussions about what it takes to succeed in sales, is that in a behavioral sense, people vary widely in their ability to make use of their empathy. The point we are making here is that whether or not there is a built-in empathic capacity within an individual, the key factor relates to the motivation of people to use their empathy.

There are many people who choose to perform on the surface of life. They deal with what is tangibly in front of them and tend to accept what is said and what is done at face value. They are not interested in exploring what might lie behind a statement or action and spend little of their energy thinking about the motivations or needs of others. These individuals might be perfectly nice, friendly, outgoing individuals, who, if given other personality attributes, might literally be the life of the party. They might even be right there when someone needed help, especially physical help. The key, however, is that they do not probe beneath the readily recognizable aspects of life. If someone falls and is injured, they will respond to this, but they are not likely to recognize the psychic pain that another might be experiencing. Simply put, these people do not think about reading another and so are not motivated to do so.

There is also another kind of "blockage" to empathy. It envolves the inability to change or to perceive reality through the eyes of others. There are those individuals who might be extraordinarily intelligent and might even possess some motivation to understand others. They might, however, be so rigid that they use their intelligence to defend their preconceptions and screen out empathic feedback that might be contrary to their own ideas or attitudes.

On the other side of the coin, there are those individuals who are motivated to read and understand others. They probe beneath the surface and are constantly examining situations and individuals in terms of underlying, rather than surface, factors. These people are motivated to use their empathy—to open up their receivers—and to take in the feedback from others. You can almost relate these three groups to a hi-fi receiver. The first does not bother to buy one. The second might own a fine receiver, but either does not turn it on or, at best, permits it to function defectively through a great deal of static. The third turns it on and makes sure it functions at its fullest capacity.

This brings us to another significant point: There are no moral values attached to empathy. Salespeople who are providing a product or service that is genuinely needed by a prospect use their empathy as a key tool in persuading the prospect to make the right decision. On the other hand, the con man will use empathy to find the weaknesses in victims that will cause them to act in a way that will injure themselves but help the con man. Empathy itself does not determine the ways in which it will be used. Other factors influence this determination.

When we first started exploring the qualities needed to succeed in sales, we felt that empathy was the sole key to predicting sales success, and indeed there proved to be a high correlation. However, as we ran studies in company after company, a pattern emerged indicating that although empathy was clearly essential empathy alone was not enough. Invariably situations would arise in which top management agreed that certain individuals possessed empathy, but nevertheless were producing poor sales results. A case from our files illustrates the problem in these situations.

Sara, a real estate salesperson whom we tested at her manager's request, appeared to perform her sales role perfectly, but, mysteriously, she rarely closed a sale. She educated buyers about local real estate values, worked with great energy to find available properties at the right price and style, and expertly guided potential buyers toward the best financing arrangements and mortgage institutions. Throughout the process, she cultivated her customers to the point where she was deluged with golf and tennis invitations. But when the customers signed on the proverbial dotted line, it was usually with another salesperson, frequently from another broker.

Sara, like so many people following this pattern, was empathic enough to develop excellent relationships with customers and associates and to maintain existing accounts. But she rarely brought in new business. The simple fact was that she could not close the sale.

So often, as in Sara's case, we were told that these individuals presented a product or service well, developed excellent relationships with customers and associates, maintained existing accounts, but rarely brought in new business.

It became clear, from studying hundreds of cases such as Sara's, that while the irreplaceable feedback provided by empathy is absolutely essential to sales success, empathy by itself is not enough. What is needed is the motivation to use the empathic feedback as a tool for persuasion. We call this motivation "ego-drive."

5

Ego-Drive: The Motivational Force

What is there about salespeople that sets them apart from other professionals? Why don't they look for jobs in which they can drop an anchor in calmer waters and face a judgment of their abilities only when it comes time for an annual salary review? Why do they endure rejections even though they could be avoided? Actually, the answers to these questions are one and the same—ego-drive.

Ego-drive is a special quality that makes the salesperson want and need to make a sale in a very personal way. Individuals with ego-drive feel that the sale has to be made. So the prospect is there to help fulfill a personal need. To the top salesperson, getting a prospect to say yes provides a powerful means for ego enhancement. His or her self-image improves dramatically by virtue of achieving that yes and diminishes with each sales failure. Whether the yes involves commission is far less relevant than the yes itself. To the ego-driven individual, "Yes, I will go out with you," or "Yes, I will join your club," or "Yes, I will vote for your candidate," or "Yes, I agree with you" is just as satisfying as "Yes, I will buy your product or service." If an individual really has ego-drive, he or she needs that yes—regardless of what the yes is—as a key means of satisfying the ego-drive.

How people view themselves underlies most of their ambition and motivation. We seek approval; we want acceptance; we enjoy our associates' acclamation for a job well done. For the fortunate among us, the path we choose in search of self-enhancement becomes our career.

Engineers are gratified by designing complex equipment, building bridges, or planning a dam. Artists achieve gratification by expressing themselves creatively. Teachers achieve gratification through the accomplishments of their students. Carpenters, tailors, and repairmen achieve gratification by exercising their craftsmanship. In the same way, top salespeople enhance their egos through persuading others, frequently in a face-to-face, one-to-one situation.

What salespeople seek is an opportunity to turn others around to their point of view. That is why top salespeople never really retire. Characteristically, after reaching the mandatory retirement age, they may head a local fund drive, or put their energy to work fighting for one civic cause or another, or perhaps even enter into politics for the first time. Even when he or she no longer needs the money earned in a lifelong process of persuasion, the person is still strongly driven to persuade. Persuading is like breathing for the ego-driven individual.

The strongly motivated career salespeople or sales managers who retire at the company's compulsory retirement age seem young, fresh, and vigorous, virtually until their last day on the job. If they find other ways to channel their energy, they appear to maintain youth and vigor for years. However, if they spend their postretirement months and years puttering around the house or relaxing in the classic retirement community style, their former associates are frequently shocked to note how much they seem to age in only a year or two.

Ego-drive should not be confused with the usual perceptions of drive, willingness to work, or aggressiveness. For example, a bank president may be extremely ambitious, driven, hardworking, and aggressive but still not have an inner need to persuade. Ego-drive is a particular means of gaining self-enhancement through persuasion of another person; it is not to be confused with a general desire to get ahead or to achieve.

Strong ego-drive alone does not ensure success in selling. Ironically, unless it is properly balanced with empathy and other key personality characteristics, strong ego-drive alone can spell disaster in selling. The reason is simple: Salespeople whose ego-drive is in overdrive are "too hungry" for the close. They are so driven to conquer in a one-to-one situation that they tend to bowl customers over, rushing toward a close without listening to possible objections or not even relating the product or service to the prospect's needs. Such a salesperson, by the sheer force of his or her personality, may produce some sales. But he or she will miss many sales that a more sensitive, more balanced salesperson would have achieved in similar circumstances. Such salespeople often offend or alienate potential customers and, in the process, burn territory for their company.

Clearly, a balance must exist between ego-drive and other basic personality characteristics if a salesperson is to be genuinely successful. We can illustrate our point here by considering the case of Jack, a salesman for a major computer firm. On first appearance, Jack would impress any potential employer with his prototypical sales abilities. Yet he was among the least productive members of the sales force. When we examined his personality dynamics in detail and then checked his personality profile against his job, the reason for his low productivity was clear: Jack's job was to sell large computer installations to the government. Success was defined as selling two major installations per year. The financial rewards for these two sales were enormous, but Jack's ego-drive was so intense that he simply could not tolerate the infrequency of closings. In his desperation to achieve a quick sale, his need for the close impelled him to push too hard, so he met with failure.

This does not mean that Jack had no value as a salesperson. It simply means that his personality dynamics were wrong for the particular sales job in which he was slotted. He was transferred to another division of the company which provides time-shared computer services—payroll, accounting, and the like—primarily to small- and medium-sized businesses. His success was almost immediate. The reason was that he had several closing opportunities per day and, given his level of ego-drive, was able to convert more than his share. The reality for Jack was that his up-end financial opportunity was somewhat less in the new situation, but the opportunity for satisfying his ego-drive was greater.

We have learned from dealing with thousands of Jacks and their employers that the salesperson with an overabundance of ego-drive can, if his or her drive is tempered by other qualities, be exceptionally successful with essentially hard-sell and small-ticket products.

The evidence is clear that no single salesperson would be equally effective in all sales jobs. (This is one of the most critical, and often overlooked, factors in attempting to build a sales force.) Some people's personality dynamics suit them to a particular kind of selling, but no person is ideally suited to all kinds of selling.

With that fact in mind, we will in later chapters discuss the various personality characteristics that are needed to succeed in different types of selling. Nevertheless, empathy and ego-drive are the two most important characteristics for identifying the basic sales personality.

The question that invariably arises in discussions about the dynamics of a successful salesperson is this: Are these abilities inborn, or are they developed? Is ego-drive something—a genetic quality, perhaps—that exists in the individual from birth, or is it something that can be developed in anyone through training and motivation?

There is no way to know the exact role genetics or socialization plays in any behavioral trait. As it does in most human functions, the answer probably lies somewhere between nature and nurture. Undoubtedly, there are some inherited qualities that provide the kind of climate in which ego-drive is more likely to develop. Yet there is not sufficient evidence to prove that genetics alone is responsible for ego-drive. What appears to be the predominant factor in the existence of ego-drive—as in the development of other personality characteristics—is childhood and early adolescent experience.

For example, a young boy may be well endowed with physical strength as a result of heredity, exercise, good nutrition, and other environmental factors. As he develops, he finds through athletic accomplishment and feats of strength that he receives a great deal of approval. He is able to throw and catch a ball better than his 5-year-old peers. At age 6, he may be praised for defeating an 8-year-old bully in a fight. At age 9, he becomes the leading pitcher for his Little League team and helps win a championship. All these things have brought him ego-gratification, the self-enhancement we all seek. Is it surprising, then, that as a teenager he goes out for his high school baseball and football teams and yearns for a major league baseball career or a starting slot with the Chicago Bears or the New York Giants? Since he has achieved his gratification primarily through athletic prowess, he would hardly be likely to anticipate adult gratification in a sales career. Physical accomplishment, rather than persuasion, would be his likely means of achievement.

In this example, as in most, it is almost impossible to separate the roles of nature and nurture. Certainly the boy could not have achieved his primary ego-gratification through physical accomplishment were it not for the potential with which he was born; but neither could he have achieved this satisfaction if he did not have appropriate nutrition, motivation, care, and a conditioning environment. What is clear is that by the time this young man is 20 or 21 years old, his motivational pattern will be set. He is what he is, and his means of receiving gratification are what they are, regardless of the nature-nurture balance.

Ego-drive develops in the same way. For example, another youngster's early gratification is gained through talking and interacting with people. Because of either genetics or the stimulation of her environment, or perhaps a combination of both, she is an early talker, and at 18 months she has a surprisingly broad vocabulary, for which she is praised and commended by parents and other adults. Early in her childhood, she learns that she can accomplish more by persuasion than by temper tantrums, and gradually she comes to enjoy the process of persuasion as much as she does the ultimate goal of persuading someone. This learned response strengthens as she matures, converting a simple childhood lesson into a direction and a career—sales—that allows her to profit from a gratifying pursuit.

The development of the ego-driven personality does not appear to follow a classic pattern. People develop the desire to persuade for many reasons. But it is quite certain that these reasons are rooted in childhood experience. Putting aside "born" or "made" theories, we know that ego-drive exists in young adults to the precise degree that it will continue to exist for the rest of their lives. A person who is not basically motivated to persuade others cannot be trained to derive primary satisfaction from selling. You cannot train people to use what they do not have. Only a person with ego-drive can be trained to use what he or she has in a maximally effective way.

Ego-drive is to the salesperson what fuel is to an automobile engine. Without fuel, the automobile engine cannot move forward. With fuel, but without steering, the automobile constitutes a hazard and is valueless. In selling, ego-drive is that fuel, while empathy provides the steering.

6

Service Motivation:
The Emerging Factor

For many sales positions, there is a motivational force parallel to ego-drive that can be as important to success as ego-drive itself. While the ego-driven individual derives personal gratification from getting the yes, the service-motivated individual derives the same gratification from receiving the "thank you," "you did a good job," I appreciate that," and so on. The feeling of approval provides the same gratification to the service-motivated person as the closed sale does to the individual with ego-drive.

More often than not, these two motivational forces do not exist in the same individual, and yet on first impression, for example in a job interview, the two may easily be confused with one another. We will discuss the reasons for this confusion later, but suffice it to say this confusion leads to many hiring mistakes and many wrong decisions relating to training and developmental approaches to improve individual productivity.

What is becoming more and more true, is the fact that success in selling increasingly demands that an individual possess at least some degree of both of these motivations. Where both are demanded but only one exists, failure is likely to be the result.

This situation is illustrated by one of our multinational client companies, which acquired a medium-sized U.S. company whose products fit extremely well into our client's overall product mix. The smaller company was purchased at an extremely advantageous price because, for several years, it had lost market share and in the last couple of years had lost substantial sums of money. This was in spite of the fact that the company's product was at least as good as, and perhaps better than, that of most of its competitors. We were asked to conduct an audit of the sales and management team to see how much of the problem rested with the quality of that team.

After assessing nearly 500 salespeople and their managers, we were able to diagnose the problem easily. Simply put, some 90 percent of the salespeople did not possess sufficient ego-drive to allow them to sell successfully. Many had empathy, and a good many more possessed qualities that permitted them to do an exceptionally good service job. Thus, these "salespeople" were in reality very good servicers.

Early in its history, the company held a prominent position in its market because its product was novel, was in great demand, and virtually sold itself, and so the "salespeople" were able to "get away with it." They literally took orders for the product, and the most selling they had to do involved getting retailers to push the product just a bit more. As the situation changed, however, and competition, with aggressive salespeople, entered the market in increasing numbers, these so-called salespeople were swept away by their more effective competitors. It was clear that nothing changed in terms of the nature of the people, but with newfound competition the nature of the job changed radically. Most of the company's existing salespeople did not possess the personality attributes that would allow them to change with the situation, and the result was accelerating failure.

When we presented these findings to people in management, they expressed no surprise. They, too, felt that many of their people, especially the long-tenured ones, were more order takers than real salespeople. Yet they correctly said that the nature of their product absolutely required service as well as sales. We agreed that the job could not simply involve closing sales but had to include effective, outstanding, ongoing service as a follow-up to each closed sale. What was clear, then, is that this company indeed needed salespeople with empathy and sufficiently strong ego-drive to close more effectively if it was to be able to compete. The salespeople had to be motivated to persuade, to get the yes, as a means of gaining personal satisfaction—but while also being motivated to come through and enjoy being told, "Thank you. You did a good job" and "I appreciate that," as a parallel key means of deriving ego-gratification. This need we term "service motivation."

Service-motivated people have a strong inner motivation to come through and a strong need for approval and appreciation. As we mentioned earlier, all people find means of making themselves feel good. For the ego-driven person, getting someone to say yes provides enormous personal gratification. For the service-motivated person, "Thank you. You did a good job" provides the same kind of gratification. It is critical to service-motivated people that they be liked, and they work as hard to accomplish that as the ego-driven person does to achieve the yes.

Service-motivated people need to have the ability to get things done in a timely manner. They must have the attitude and conviction that if they have committed to do something, they will get it done, and it will be done right. Their word is their bond.

Certain qualities are critical if an individual is to fulfill his or her service motivation—to do a good service job. Obviously, people skills are essential together with a strong sense of responsibility. Yet it is not good enough to "yes" someone to death or smile in the most ingratiating way. Strong personal organization and the ability to handle detail well, without being absorbed in it or using detail as an excuse for delay, are key tools for service effectiveness. Service people have to judge the legitimacy of a customer complaint and be willing to take the responsibility for making a decision about the best way to resolve the situation. But here lies a common problem: If you are motivated to look good, to receive approval, you do not want to make a mistake and risk looking bad. Thus, indecisiveness and inaction are endemic among too many people in service roles. What they tend to do is take what they consider the safe way and do nothing, rather than take the chance of being wrong. Also, in an effort to be liked, the service person may tend to promise anything, but unless he or she possesses the wherewithal, both practically and in terms of personality, to fulfill the promise, bad service will obviously be the result.

As we indicated earlier, many people who possess strong service motivation lack strong ego-drive. Thus, finding people who possess both is not an easy task, given the inherent contradiction between the two motivational forces. More often than not, companies find they have salespeople with one or the other, but not the combination. Ego-driven people typically tend to be impulsive and individualistic, they have less of a need to please or seek approval, and they dislike detail and follow-up. Service-motivated people, on the other hand, tend to be cautious team players who are oriented toward detail work and are good at follow-up; they have a strong need to be liked and approved of. These service-motivated individuals are essential to the good functioning of most companies. Selling without quality service will guarantee eventual failure, as certainly as failure to sell the product in the first place. Most successful salespeople will be the first ones to emphasize how critical the sales support provided by service people is to their own success. In fact, service as a profession is becoming an increasingly important and respected role in our changing society.

The problem only occurs where service motivation is confused with, and so substituted for, persuasive motivation or ego-drive. The dilemma arises when the service-motivated person with little ego-drive attempts to sell, or the ego-driven person with little service motivation attempts to provide service.

The potential to confuse ego-drive with service motivation can wrongly impact hiring decisions. We can recall a situation that illustrates this point. A couple of years ago one of our senior account executives recommended that a client not hire a particular applicant for a sales position. There was a heavy moment of silence followed by, "But she came across so well in the interview. What is wrong?" Our account executive replied, "From our analysis, I can see that this individual is very intelligent and probably made a pleasant impression. The right questions were asked, and a warm, friendly, and genuinely likable demeanor was conveyed. In fact, the applicant probably came right out and said that the interview was enjoyable and your firm was impressive. She may have even written you a thank-you note or called to express her continuing interest." The client thought a moment and then said, "That is exactly right. That is exactly what happened. Even the thank-you letter. So, what is wrong?"

What is wrong, and what our account executive tried to explain to our client, is that the applicant's motivations were not what the client needed for that specific sales role. The applicant made a good impression because she was strongly motivated to do so. She possessed service motivation. Thus, during and after the interview, she worked very hard to be liked, to come across as nice, and to do everything in her power to create a positive impression. Making that impression might have gotten her the job, because the impression was condensed into a 1-hour interview. That impression, however, rarely is sufficient to allow an individual to succeed in sales, in an ongoing way, without the motivation to sell (ego-drive). Simply put, selling is far more difficult than simply making a good impression. Yet how many people have been wrongly hired because of that first impression and then let go 6 months or a year later? "But he or she looked so good in the interview." In the hiring process, it is necessary to distinguish first impressions from inherent personality qualities.

It is particularly important for managers to separate ego-drive and service motivation, which may on the surface, over a short time span, look similar, but which are in reality very different dynamics. In most instances, despite the good impression that the strongly service-motivated person conveys, such persons simply are not sufficiently motivated to sell, nor, again typically, can they or do they want to take the rejection involved in sales. So most purely service-motivated people will be sales failures.

Of course increasing numbers of sales roles require people who possess both of these motivations to a rather strong degree. And it is important to reemphasize that there are those individuals (though they are difficult to find because of some of these inherent contradictions) who do possess both motivational forces in sufficient degree to succeed in sales roles requiring good service follow-up. We were in fact able to assess a number of these individuals for our client, who is slowly replacing the pure servicepeople as they either change jobs or retire. Our client will, in fact, end up with a smaller sales force, but with people who can both close sales and do the servicing that continues to be a vital aspect of the job.

7

Conscientiousness:
The Discipline from Within

To Sigmund Freud, the psyche is separated into three parts: the id, ego, and superego. Putting it simply, the id is the "I want"—all the physical drives—hunger, thirst, and so on, that create the "I want." The ego is that part of the psyche that's in touch with reality—that determines behavior. And the superego—the "I should"—is that part of the psyche which society imposes as limitations to the "I want." In other words, people cannot always get exactly what they want when they want it, and the superego prevents us from thinking that constant pleasure is even possible.

The reader might ask why this lesson in Psychology 101 appears in a book focusing on what it takes for an individual to succeed in sales. The simple answer is that the motivation to succeed in sales all comes back to basic psychological issues. When, in fact, we look at empathy, for example, we're looking at an individual whose ego possesses the capacity to read people. When we look at ego-drive—the need to persuade others—we're looking at gratification or an id issue. What, however, we have not looked at is the superego—that's why the foregoing explanation was included.

What Freud failed to describe as he discussed the superego is the fact that we should look at the superego as both an external and an internal function. That view is extremely relevant to the job-matching process, which will be discussed in Part 3, but is also highly relevant to sales success in general, particularly when it comes to exploring the quality of conscientiousness.

We all know individuals whose personality is clearly geared to the external aspects of the superego. Such individuals, when told to jump, say, "How high?" We all know such good soldiers, people who will do exactly as told and will worry if their work is not carried out precisely as it has been expected. These people desperately want structure. The more they can be told exactly what to do and when to do it, the happier they are. In short, these are people who depend on the external to constantly create their "should" system. In the extreme, even the least amount of ambiguity makes

38

them uncomfortable. You will hear such complaints as, "But you didn't tell me to do that" or "How was I supposed to know that that's what you expected?"

While this good soldier—this externally driven, rules-oriented individual—may not jibe with the stereotypical description of the sales personality, we're certain that the reader can think of some sales jobs for which this attribute could be an important asset. We will go into this further in the next section, but suffice it to say that whether employers want to admit it or not, they will often hire good soldiers because they are so gratifying to interview and will obviously be compliant with the rules of the organization. Again, this could be a correct hire in some instances, but could be a catastrophic mistake in many others. This is because good soldiers may be totally inappropriate for many sales situations.

Two Types of Conscientiousness

Essentially, we have found there are two different types of conscientiousness. They can both produce the same results. People with either type can be outcome-oriented, tenacious, responsible, adept at follow-through, and good at their word.

But the two types of conscientiousness we have identified begin with very different motivations. The one form of conscientiousness we call "externally driven," and the other we have dubbed "internally driven."

People whose conscientiousness is internally driven accomplish goals and complete tasks as an expression of themselves. They have an inner compass that points them in the direction of achievement. Conscientious individuals are purposeful, strong-willed, and determined. As you would imagine, almost all exceptional professionals—from musicians to athletes—have a very high level of conscientiousness. They have an inner drive to practice for an extra hour every day—an hour they don't even notice goes by. This kind of conscientiousness embodies the kind of self-control that results in actively planning, organizing, and carrying out tasks. In this way, conscientiousness is the task master that drives an individual to complete what has to be done—without the need for external sticks or carrots. Individuals whose conscientiousness is internally driven combine high levels of "self-drive" with a high degree of responsibility.

A high level of responsibility is also a key factor for individuals whose conscientiousness is externally driven. But the similarity ends there. Externally driven individuals are very cautious and anxious. They worry about things being done to accepted standards. Ultimately, they are driven by rules and expectations laid down by others. This type of conscientious individual has to be told what to do and then reminded when to do it. Inside these people's heads, they hear words like "should" and "ought to." Professional coaches are all too familiar with exceptionally talented star athletes who have to constantly be reminded to do their drills. They are conscientious, they will come through, but it is because of that external voice, that constant reminder from an authority figure.

What is always a plus for sales, and for that matter for most occupations, is the internal type of conscientiousness. Certainly, these individuals are much easier to manage, as they are more demanding of themselves than you could ever be.

When you are trying to manage someone whose conscientiousness is externally driven—the good soldier—your job becomes much tougher. Such individuals will do the right thing, but need to be reminded of expectations.

How does conscientiousness manifest itself in day-to-day behavior? The athlete, for example, who exemplifies external superego is coachable. He or she will do exactly what the coach says to do. If the coach says, "Shoot a hundred foul shots," the athlete will shoot a hundred foul shots. If the coach says, "Let me see you practice bunting," the athlete will do that. But the "Let me see you do it" is the operative language. The externally conscientious athlete will be given an exercise regime and will be told to stay in condition and will do so if he or she is observed.

Internally conscientious athletes, however, will practice foul shots on their own. They will be annoyed at their inability to bunt well enough and will practice after the team is long gone. The internally conscientious athlete will come to camp in good condition because he or she "wants to" and is driven to, even if not observed.

The difference in behavior in the sales area is just as clear. Externally conscientious salespeople will read the script extremely well. They will make the requisite number of calls. They will present the product or service precisely how they are directed, and will never deviate from the prescribed rules. They will also follow the action plan laid out by the sales manager.

Internally directed salespeople, on the other hand, will organize their time on their own, and may, in fact, resent too much interference by the manager. They will organize their presentations, and may even take some liberties, depending on other factors, in bending rules where appropriate. In other words, internally directed individuals simply need less management than their externally directed colleagues.

Here is one example of how the chemistry between the salesperson and the manager can have a profound impact on the success of the salesperson. If the manager needs to control, he or she had better work with an externally driven salesperson who will welcome that control. On the other hand, if a manager wants independent functionaries and lacks patience to tell someone what to do all the time, he or she had better choose internally motivated people.

This manager-salesperson relationship will be discussed further in many of its aspects, but it's touched on here as one means of making the important point that these two aspects of superego—or conscientiouness—both play a critical role in the understanding of what it takes to succeed in sales.

Perhaps the most relevant behavior to drive this point home relates to a salesperson's ability to stay with a prospect or a customer. Individuals who lack self-discipline may make a great sales presentation, and if they possess enough ego-drive and empathy they may close their share of sales. However, if that first or second presentation is unsuccessful, will the salesperson continue following up as long as it might make sense, or will he or she simply lose patience and go on to the next prospect? Similarly, once a sale is made, will the salesperson essentially forget about the new customer and go on to new fields to conquer, or will the salesperson work to service that new customer as a key means of developing continuing business from that customer? Again, conscientious salespeople, particularly if their motivation is internal, will follow up and will provide service.

A senior vice president of sales and marketing for one of the country's largest brokerage houses recently told us: "Conscientiousness is a key factor for us in identifying the best salespeople. In fact, I have come to believe that conscientiousness can even make up for deficiencies in other areas. In our business, I can think of several successful salespeople whose strong level of conscientiousness and attention to detail offset their tendency to be less persuasion-oriented than their peers. Particularly when selling financial services, if you have a strong work ethic and a solid sense of responsibility, you will not disappoint people. And that will go a long way toward success. Our business, like so many others, depends so much on developing relationships and trust with clients. And gaining referrals is very important. I have seen more salespeople fail because they did not keep track of what they were doing than because they didn't make the sale."

A recent case history may serve to make the point of when self-discipline can be as vital a consideration as empathy, ego-drive, and ego-strength. We evaluated a young woman for one of our clients who possessed every talent in the world. She was smart, assertive, aggressive, and proactive; she had ego-drive; and she could make quick decisions—basically a terrific salesperson. Yet we still recommended that our client not hire her.

Why? Because the job was going to take place in a small town about 500 miles away from headquarters where she would only have contact with the sales manager about once a week on the phone. The job would entail not just closing sales, which she could do extraordinarily well, but also putting together a marketing plan and organizing her work and time, which she could not do so well.

She had no patience for going through telephone books and lists to plot out a program. She just wanted to sell, sell, sell. I told this manager, "If you bring her into the home office and have her work under you where you could structure her time and expose her to a number of prospects a day, she'll be a closing machine. But if you put her out there where self-starting is as important as sales ability, she'll waste most of her time spinning her wheels." For that position, self-discipline was very important, and she just didn't possess it.

In summary, the stereotypical view of sales does not mesh with the term "conscientious" or "self-discipline." The stereotype, in fact, is quite the opposite. However, more and more sales situations depend as much on this factor as on empathy, persuasiveness, service motivation, and the ability to bounce back from rejection. As a result, more and more attention will have to be paid to conscientiousness if we're really going to understand what it takes to succeed in different sales situations, and if we're going to avoid the mistakes often based on stereotypical thinking.

8

Ego-Strength: The Key to Resilience

When all is said and done, selling is a game of trying to beat the odds of rejection. Rare indeed is the salesperson who can close a sale in two contacts. Regardless of the industry involved, the person who is attempting to persuade another individual is more likely to be rejected than to be accepted. What happens then to the persuader (the individual who likes himself or herself better as a result of getting someone else to say yes) when the inevitable rejection occurs? The individual feels diminished. But the key here is that the salesperson must never feel totally diminished. When one fails, he or she obviously does not feel too good, but the essential question is, does that person have the resiliency—or what we call "ego-strength"—to bounce back from rejection?

Ego-strength is the degree to which an individual basically likes himself or herself. If an individual possesses a high level of ego-strength, then failure can motivate the person toward the next try.

Persons with ego-strength feel as bad as anyone else would when they encounter failure, but they react to that failure much as the hungry person does to missing a meal: they are that much hungrier for the next opportunity.

The failure, though disappointing, does not destroy their positive view of themselves. The failure is not personalized, but, rather, creates a disappointment—a lack of fulfillment—that the next opportunity will correct. On the other hand, when people do not have sufficient ego-strength to react with resiliency, if they don't have enough positive feelings about themselves, they take the rejection personally. They feel that the no is a no to them personally, and is further proof that they are indeed not very good, not really worthwhile. They are, therefore, very hesitant to seek another situation that could incur yet another rejection, because even if they have a desire to persuade (the ego-drive), the pain of the potential rejection is simply too great to run the risk.

Another serious problem where there is a lack of ego-strength results from the sheer intensity of the conflict within the individual. As we said, people work very hard to like themselves, and so the individual who inherently lacks a good sense of self (ego-strength) is putting forth enormous effort inwardly

43

to find ways to like himself or herself better. This inner conflict takes up so much of the individual's energy that there is literally no time and certainly no energy to invest fully in a job. The preoccupation is with self, and anything external must of necessity take a back seat. This preoccupation makes it difficult to work in a consistent way, particularly when there is a good deal of pressure or confrontation involved.

Many years ago, when we were only vaguely aware of the importance of ego-strength, we ran into a situation that taught us, in a most dramatic fashion, its importance. We evaluated a sales applicant for a client and strongly recommended that the client hire the individual. He had outstanding empathy and possessed more than enough ego-drive to close sales effectively in that company's situation. He also had a strong sense of responsibility and clearly possessed the desire to succeed.

Sure enough, the young man started out like a whirlwind. Within a month after the training period, he was in the top 10 percent of the sales force and to say the least, we had a very happy client.

Three months later, we received a panicked call from the sales manager. To paraphrase, the manager said to us: "Jim simply stopped producing about a month ago. As you know, we thought he would be the best person we ever hired. But all of a sudden it all seemed to come apart. He has not made a sale in the last month, and what is making it worse is that he is beginning to come in late and take long lunches, and some days he does not even show up at all. He obviously has the ability. But what do you think could have happened?"

We reevaluated his personality test and determined, again, that Jim had all the ego-drive and empathy that we originally thought he did. But what we began to see as we examined the results of his behavioral test was that he really did not have positive feelings about himself. His ego-strength was clearly lacking. As we discussed the situation in more detail with the manager and interviewed Jim several times, the picture became clear. Given his ability, Jim successfully closed a number of sales in succession. Someone with less ability would never have made those sales, but anyone, regardless of ability, could not continue at that sales pace. Inevitably, rejection pushed Jim out of the supersales level. Statistics being what they are, those rejections came in three out of every four sales attempts, and simply put, Jim's lack of ego-strength made it impossible for him to deal with such rejection. He was not able to simply look at the rejections as statistics inevitably catching up with him, but saw them as a truth finally being told. The early successes he viewed as simply a fluke, and the real Jim was represented by the failures.

As a means of desperately trying to turn his situation around, Jim pressed too hard, acted inappropriately, and literally drove away prospects whom he would have sold earlier. The more he pressed, the more he failed, and the more he failed, the more he came down on himself. Finally, despite his obvious sales talent, Jim was terminated.

Jim and thousands like him remind us of a baseball player who is the spring phenom. He tears the cover off the ball during spring training and continues at this almost impossible pace into the first week or two of the season. But within a couple of months, he is back in the minors and soon after has faded out of memory. Why? Obviously, if he could hit over .400 even for a couple of days in the majors, he had hitting talent. However, nobody hits .400 steadily. So, like Jim, the phenom falls into the inevitable slump that is going to bring him down to a lofty .333 batting average. If he had ego-strength, he might maintain this average through a Hall of Fame career. However, again like Jim, lacking ego-strength, the phenom comes quickly down on himself. He presses, changes his swing and, in his desperation not to fail, guarantees failure by doing things differently—by getting away from the natural talent that brought him his success.

The case of Cathy illustrates the role of ego-strength in quite a different way. When we evaluated her personality attributes, we saw an individual who had excellent empathy, was highly intelligent, and possessed both a strong sense of responsibility and fine personal organizational skills. Our only doubt related to her ego-drive. She definitely had some persuasive motivation, but she lacked the intense need to persuade that characterizes most highly productive salespeople. She got pleasure from the close—from getting the yes—but not the typical kind of intense satisfaction that strongly ego-driven people receive. Thus, we felt that she might miss some closes because of this lack of intense drive.

Given her other strong qualities, especially her strong sense of self (her good ego-strength), we suggested to our client that Cathy be hired. We also suggested that if at all possible, she be provided with training in the area of closing skills to try to bolster her moderate ego-drive.

Cathy was hired, and for the first month or 2 we and our client were concerned because she started extremely slowly. In the first 2 months she only made one sale—although, as our client described it, she did have a number of prospects on the line.

Slowly, however, the situation began changing. A few of the prospects became customers, and her number of prospects steadily increased. Within 6 months, Cathy was functioning in the middle of the sales force, and by the end of the first year, she was high in the second quartile. At this writing, 4 years later, Cathy is still functioning well in the second quartile of the sales force, and though not a top producer, she is well above average and an important, strong contributor to the company's bottom line.

Unlike Jim, Cathy's rejections came early. Because of her lack of intense ego-drive, she did not close sales early and often. Rather, she experienced the rejections and failures that are so typical of novices. But again unlike Jim, because of her strong sense of self (her good ego-strength), she did not view the rejections in a personal way. She saw her failures as the inevitable result of inexperience and of the price she had to pay to gain that experience. Because of many other strong personality attributes, she would not accept no as a final answer, but continued to consider her prospects as potential customers in need of follow-up. And of equal importance, she was able to continue looking for more prospects without fearing their rejection. In the long run, she had enough ego-drive to convert some of those initial rejections to closings and, with increasing know-how, to slowly but steadily improve her initial conversion ratio.

The difference between Jim and Cathy can be summed up this way: Jim obviously had more drive and possessed the potential to function near the very top of the sales force. His lack of ego-strength, however, made it impossible for him to actualize that talent because he could not deal with the inevitable rejection that even a superstar must experience. On the other hand, Cathy, with less inherent persuasive talent, could function near the top of her potential because she felt good enough about herself, and strong enough within herself, to do so.

Ego-strength is then, quite simply, an individual's ability to feel good enough about himself or herself to accept rejection, not as a personal affront, but as part of life. The individual with ego-strength has the ability to leave the rejection behind and go on from there. Those who accept themselves, who possess ego-strength, operate freely and fully, allowing themselves to function at or near the top of their capacity.

Integrating the Dynamics
for Success

There is an enduring stereotype of the successful salesman. He stands 6 feet tall with a halfback's physique and a bone-crushing handshake. He is an incurable extrovert with an unending supply of hilarious jokes. He likes people in groups and is dependably the life of any party. He is great on the golf course and is ready to converse, at least superficially, on almost any subject.

Recognize him? Of course. The legend has survived for generations, and today is so thoroughly ingrained in our culture that it appears not to be subject to change. In fact, it is so much a part of our heritage that an entire branch of folk humor—the traveling salesman joke—is rooted in it.

In truth, the typical top salesperson is often strikingly dissimilar to this idealized portrait, a fact that can be verified at any number of annual sales meetings, where the "salesperson of the year" award often goes to a middle-aged, somewhat balding fellow who is 5 feet, 6 inches, has a slight paunch, and wears rimless glasses; or to a petite, soft-spoken, young woman who might remind you more of an effective teacher than a gregarious salesperson.

In working with thousands of companies throughout the world, we have found that hiring people who fit the sales stereotype is as expensive as it is fanciful. Salesperson after salesperson is offered a job because he or she conforms to the superficial stereotype, only to fail in the field. (We have seen more sales vice presidents surrounded by gregarious, athletic-looking failures than we care to remember.)

The fact is, sales success is only remotely related to external characteristics. The stereotypical attributes of the successful salesperson are demonstrable nonsense.

Two primary observations should be made on the subject of what makes a good salesperson: (1) As we have emphasized in earlier chapters, determining factors are internal, related almost entirely to the individual's personality; and (2) No one person, regardless of his or her personality dynamics, can be equally successful in all types of sales situations.

Let us look at why this is so. The five major personality characteristics that we have been discussing—empathy, ego-drive, service motivation, conscientiousness, and ego-strength—do not exist independently. They affect one another—sometimes positively, sometimes negatively.

In the inherently successful salesperson, empathy and ego-drive exist in a dynamic relationship, where both combine to reinforce and fulfill the potential of each characteristic. People with strong ego-drive have maximum motivation to use whatever empathy they possess. People with fine empathy are equipped to direct and temper their ego-drive,

Naturally, there are a number of possible combinations of empathy and ego-drive. A person may have a high degree of both empathy and ego-drive (ED), little of either (ed), or a mixed combination (either Ed or eD). For example:

ED: Salespeople who have a great deal of both empathy and ego-drive will almost invariably be at or near the top of the sales force as long as they have sufficient ego-strength and other qualities needed for the specific position.

Ed: Salespeople with fine empathy but too little drive may be splendid human beings, but in many cases will be unable to close effectively. They are usually well liked and, from all appearances, should be among the best salespeople on the staff. But they never quite make it. While they develop very good relationships with prospects, they never convert these prospects to clients. Salespeople with fine empathy but very little drive get along with and understand their prospects, but they lack enough inner hunger to move those final few inches to a completed sale. This is not to say that such individuals will never sell anything. In fact, there are some sales situations in which these individuals may perform reasonably well. They may succeed in detailing doctors for a pharmaceutical house, for example, or in selling the government a large-scale computer installation. These are instances where service and relationship building are more vital than the close. But where fast and frequent closes are the requirement, such individuals will not succeed, despite their congeniality, personableness, and sensitivity.

eD: A salesperson with much drive but too little empathy will, by sheer force of personality, bulldoze his or her way through to some sales, but also will miss a great many. In the process of making an occasional sale, such salespeople may cause enormous damage to their employers' professional reputation. Again, there are some specific sales situations in which these bulldozers can be reasonably effective. For instance, they may do well selling used cars in a metropolitan auto dealership. Or they may be effective selling debit life insurance. In other words, they may succeed in situations where the immediate close is the name of the game, the potential market is unlimited, and the likelihood of repeat business is minute. But their strength begins to wane as soon as the sales situation requires follow-up, service, relationship building—in short, where repeat business and the development of a stable market are important. Then, even if their number of sales seems acceptable, they can be like termites, causing unseen harm to the firm's professional reputation.

ed: Someone without much empathy or ego-drive simply should not be in sales. A potential employer would save much time and money by determining this in advance, before hiring, training, and then losing him or her. This, of course, does not mean that such individuals are failures as human beings. They might be excellent at hundreds of other pursuits: engineers, accountants, computer programmers, technicians, operations personnel, or any number of non-selling activities. But they are destined to fail at selling. It is tragic that many such individuals, with little or no chance to succeed in selling, nonetheless carry on a perennial and futile quest for success. This makes for a double waste. First, they fail their employers at the job they have chosen, and, second, they fail themselves by not choosing a profession at which they could succeed. Our studies have shown that these individuals without sufficient empathy and ego-drive account for 55 percent of the individuals now attempting to earn a living in sales. Ironically, within the same companies in which they work, there might be any number of openings for jobs they could fill with distinction and profit.

An individual cannot sell successfully without possessing empathy, ego-drive, service motivation, conscientiousness, and ego-strength. However, it is not a case of all or nothing. It is not as though someone has, for example, ego-strength or is totally devoid of it. People function on a continuum. As we look at their ability to sell, we have to look at how much or how little of each quality they possess and how these qualities integrate with the strengths of their other qualities. For certain sales jobs there can be too much ego-drive, while others need as much as possible. Certain jobs require only moderately strong persuasive motivation, but a high degree of service must go along with it. Many sales jobs can tolerate somewhat reduced levels of ego-strength, but others demand very high degrees of that quality.

In short, few people possess optimum amounts of all these essential qualities. The human condition involves trade-offs. As we look at an individual and determine whether that person is suited to a particular sales job, we need to look at how much of each of these central qualities he or she possesses and how these attributes may interact with one another to produce a motivational pattern within that individual. Next, we need to look at the real requirements of the sales job to see how that pattern fits those requirements. Then, we still must go to the next step and look at additional qualities beyond these central dynamics that might be required for success in the specific sales role. Then and only then can we predict with some confidence whether an individual is indeed suited to the specific sales job and would most likely succeed.

In Part 3, we will turn to the process by which the individual's unique personality attributes are matched to the job as a key means of predicting success on that job.

3

Job Matching

As we discussed in Chapter 2, one of the key reasons for high turnover, poor productivity, and the fact that 20 percent of salespeople sell 80 percent of what is sold is the inappropriate approach management takes to hiring salespeople. Both the warm-body approach and the use of invalid hiring criteria lead directly to hiring inappropriate people, virtually guaranteed to be unproductive, who will turn over quickly at great cost to themselves and to their employers.

In this part we present job matching as an alternative to these two invalid approaches to hiring. In Chapter 10 we will talk about step 1 in the job-matching process—understanding the job. Chapters 11 and 12 will deal with step 2—understanding the personality attributes required for the job. Here we will deal with qualities beyond the central dynamics that determine whether or not an individual can succeed in a specific sales job. Then we will talk about matching the strengths of an individual to the functional requirements of the job and examine the role that a fatal flaw might play in preventing effective job performance, even if there is a match between personality strengths and the job requirements. Finally, in Chapter 13, we will discuss the bottom-line results of substituting job matching for the traditional approaches to hiring.

10

Understanding the Sales Job

As we indicated in the last chapter, the fact that an individual possesses all the key sales dynamics central to success—empathy, ego-drive, service motivation, conscientiousness, and ego-strength—does not mean that the individual will be effective in your specific sales job. If we look at that individual from the perspective of vocational guidance, we would certainly suggest that the driven, empathic individual possessing ego-strength should be in a career in which successful persuasion is central to success. That does not mean, however, that a person's persuasive ability alone will ensure that he or she has the other key attributes necessary to succeed at a highly productive level in a particular sales position. It is for this reason that we have never simply looked at the central sales dynamics to help our corporate clients determine whether or not an individual is suited to a particular sales job. Rather, we look at what we term the "job match" to make that decision. This section will be devoted to the job match, which begins with an understanding of the job for which an individual is being considered.

Though it is obvious that all sales jobs involve, at their core, the ability to persuade, the breadth of these jobs is virtually limitless. Sales jobs range from quick-closing, hard-selling, short-term, commission-only positions to the opposite extreme where the persuasive element is camouflaged and only takes place once or twice a year at the end of a long process. This same range of sales jobs can include positions requiring numerous closes per day to positions in which one or two closes in a year could produce as much, or more, income. Similarly, many sales positions require little or no technical background or skill, while others require the salesperson to be a technical expert in a particular product or service. Some sales jobs presume that the individual customer will buy once and likely never again, while in most other sales situations, a one-time-only buyer would be disastrous.

Numerous additional examples of these extremes could be cited, but we hope these serve to make the point that saying a position involves sales is far from adequate for understanding the nature of that position. As we begin to look at the job-matching process, let's review some of the key elements that are necessary and some of the key questions that must be asked to develop an understanding of the specific sales role, and the personality attributes required for an individual to fill that role successfully.

Product or Service

The first question to be asked is, what is the nature of the product or service to be sold? It is not enough to say, for example, computers, or automobiles, or real estate, or pharmaceuticals. Within these broad categories of products and services are numerous subdivisions, each of which requires many differing individual qualities and work processes to sell successfully. For example, it is a far different job to sell personal computers over the counter in a retail store than it is to sell large mainframes directly to business and government. Both can be technically categorized as computer sales, but there the similarity ends. Thus, as simplistic as it may sound on the surface, it is important to understand, and to convey to potential jobholders, the full nature of the product or service being sold. Along the same line, and as part of understanding this product or service, the potential customer base must also be understood. Personal computers may be sold to business, incidentally, but they are sold over the counter to many personal users as well. We know of few mainframes that are sold directly to individuals. Residential real estate is obviously sold to individual home buyers, while commercial real estate is sold for business purposes. The purchaser of a Mercedes, Porsche, BMW, or Rolls Royce is likely to be a totally different customer than the buyer of a Honda, Plymouth, or Ford. Selling proprietary drugs to pharmacies is far different from detailing pharmaceutical sales.

This critical difference was brought home to us a few years ago. A pharmaceutical firm expressed interest in working with us and began by having us evaluate a substantial cross section of its "pharmaceutical" sales force. Since this was in part a test of our accuracy, it did not provide us with production data or explicit job descriptions until we had already made judgments about the productivity of its salespeople.

Given this lack of information—the impossibility of making a real job match as part of our analysis—all we could do was evaluate people on the basis of their empathy, ego-drive, and ego-strength and assume that people who were strong in these dynamics would, in fact, be the best salespeople. It turned out, however, that our predictions landed far from the mark, and in fact, in many instances, people with strong ego-drive were at the bottom, while people with moderate to extremely mild ego-drive were performing exceptionally well. Empathy seemed to hold up as a predictor, but ego-drive and ego-strength failed, and so our overall judgments did not prove out.

After we were provided with job descriptions, we were able to explore the reason for our lack of predictive accuracy. What we discovered exemplified the critical importance of defining the job before making a decision about whether or not an individual is really suited to that job.

What we found was that the sales force we evaluated in reality should have been broken down into two sales forces: proprietary sales and medical detailers. The job for proprietary salespeople was to visit pharmacies, present the company's proprietary products, and sell the pharmacy on purchasing more of those products. The salesperson literally was charged with walking out with an order from each visit. The sale was tangible, and success or failure was determined by the dollar value of the contract with each pharmacy. Several closes a day was the name of the game.

On the other hand, the medical detailers literally never closed a sale. They would visit doctors, leave samples of various prescription drugs, and talk with the doctors about the value of the drugs. They would leave the doctor's office hoping that they made a sufficiently good impression so that the doctor would think of their particular antibiotic or blood pressure pill when they prescribed to patients. Since they never closed sales, they only got feedback about whether or not they had succeeded in general by quarterly, semi-annual, or annual reviews of how their area was doing. Thus, when we fully understood the nature of these two radically different jobs, both called "pharmaceutical sales," we were able to quickly determine why our earlier analyses, absent this information, had to be incorrect. If an individual had too much ego-drive, he or she simply could not tolerate the lack of closing involved in the detailer position. He or she would have no opportunity to gain the satisfaction that an ego-driven person needs from hearing a yes. Thus, it was not at all accidental that the very people we would have predicted, on the basis of ego-drive, as being successful in this detailer position did, in fact, fail.

On the other side of the coin, we would have predicted failure on the basis of moderately low ego-strength, which is correct in most sales situations. However, in the detailer position, the potential for rejection is relatively low. The detailer with empathy is providing the doctors with samples, with information, and with a pleasant break from a highly stressful day. The lack of ego-strength, therefore, might not, unless it is too serious, reduce the ability of a detailer to do a good job. On the other hand, the lack of both ego-drive and ego-strength would be totally destructive in proprietary sales.

The list of similar titles with drastically different job functions goes on, and some of these differences will be studied in later chapters. Suffice it to say here that to make a rational judgment on who can fill a particular sales job, we need to understand the product being sold, the nature of the prospects being solicited, and the very process through which success can be attained.

Frequency of Close

Related closely to the foregoing is the issue of how many opportunities are present for closing the sale. As we said earlier, many sales jobs require multiple closings per day in order to be successful, while many others offer relatively few, but all extremely important, closing opportunities. If, for example, an individual has extraordinarily intense ego-drive, and perhaps possesses the impatience that frequently goes along with that kind of drive, that individual hungers for closes as a key means of satisfying that drive. Thus, regardless of the compensation, a sales situation that provides two or three closing opportunities per year would simply not satisfy that individual's ego-drive. He or she would not have sufficient fun; there would just not be enough closings to keep that person happy. On the other hand, for the individual who has moderate drive but possesses great consultative skills, service motivation, persistence, etc., the job requiring frequent closes might prove too taxing, while the ability to slowly develop an account with two or three closes over the year would be ideal. Thus, it is critical to determine the frequency of closing opportunities so that an individual geared to that level of close could be properly matched to the specific job.

Lead Production

It is a far more difficult sale when cold calling is required. The cold caller must, out of necessity, experience far more frequent rejection, often of a far more abrupt, even nasty, kind, than the individual who follows up leads that have been furnished. The warmth of those leads also determines, in large measure, who can or cannot be successful in their conversions of prospects to customers. Thus, a very clear definition of the job must be made internally and presented honestly to the candidate about the nature of customer conversion, cold leads, cool leads, well-screened leads, etc. Very different people will be successful depending on an accurate definition of this aspect of the sales role.

Nature of Customer

We touched on this subject when we talked about differences between the buyers of a Rolls Royce and the buyers of a Honda, as well as the differences between the residential and the commercial real estate customer. It is extremely important to thoroughly understand who the customer is. Many people would be highly successful at selling individual consumers a tangible product but would fail totally if faced with the necessity of making a full-scale, well-developed presentation to a committee or a board of directors. Others could deal extraordinarily well at a middle-echelon level (e.g., with a purchasing agent, branch manager, or office manager), but would find it extremely difficult to make presentations on the board room or CEO level. Still others would be effective in selling to one person but would lose effectiveness if that individual has to work his or her way up the chain of command in order to get the final sign-off. Thus, it is critical to know not only to whom we are selling (companies, individuals, etc.), but on what level the sale is initially made, and on what level the final purchase can be approved.

Technical Background

The technical background required for a specific sales job relates closely to the question of who plays the final part in the decision to purchase. If microcomputers are being sold to office managers who know little about the technical aspects of the machine, somewhat less technical proficiency will probably be sufficient for the salesperson, so long as that salesperson can speak accurately about the machine's capabilities and its potential benefits to the customer. On the other hand, if the buyers are engineers, heads of data processing divisions, MIS specialists, etc., that salesperson had better be exceptionally proficient in the technology, or his or her credibility, and the credibility of the product, will quickly be lost.

Thus, as we look at the specific customer, we must at the same time make a determination, given the nature of that customer, of how much technical know-how the salesperson must have, or at least how much technical ability that salesperson fundamentally possesses so that he or she can quickly and expertly acquire sufficient knowledge.

Support

There are large numbers of salespeople who relish their positions because they are able to function in a totally independent manner. This is one of the great attractions of the sales profession to many people. Being a salesperson to some is the closest possible thing to being an entrepreneur, without the risks inherent in investing in your own business. These are people who want, and need, little support, and who function best in situations where they are left on their own. On the other hand, there are equally successful salespeople who need support and, perhaps, the structure and the security that go along with such support.

They want to know that if they lack information, a technical apparatus is ready to come into the situation and help them. They want to have that sales manager who will help them close that critical deal, or writers and research people who will help them develop that all-important presentation. These are the team players—the people who work effectively in an integrated team approach, each member doing his or her part.

This support requirement relates closely (although it is not identical) to another key part of a valid job description: How much travel is needed? Does the job require working in the home or a branch office, or is there a great deal of individual field work? The more that people are in the field (the more that their jobs take them away from the home office), the less secure that they are, and the farther away their support system is. Also, since they are far away, there is no sales manager to say, "Here is what to do today, and here are your plans for tomorrow." Such a salesperson must do it all.

Perhaps a case from our files might serve to illustrate these two, as well as some earlier, aspects of the critical job description.

Several years ago, we helped place an individual in a large metropolitan auto dealership in the East. He had the empathy, ego-drive, and ego-strength necessary to sell, plus some other important qualities that allowed him to succeed in that highly competitive, metropolitan dealership. Indeed, the individual turned out to be as successful as we had hoped, becoming the dealership's leading salesperson in less than 2 years. A sales recruiter, knowing of that individual's success, recruited that young man for another dealership selling the same make of car. When we received permission from the first client to discuss this individual, we suggested to our other client, in the strongest possible terms, that it not hire this highly successful salesman. The second client was in the Midwest and was located on a state highway away from any large metropolitan area. The second client was surprised at our nonrecommendation, and given the fact of his past success, plus the obvious sales dynamics he possessed, they made him the offer anyway. Six months later, our second client contacted us and asked if there was anything we could suggest before they had to face the unpleasant, but necessary, task of firing the young man.

Why did we urge that client not to hire the individual, and why did this highly successful salesman fail miserably in the new situation? The reason certainly could not be found in understanding the product, since the product being sold was identical. Nor could the answer be found in the nature of the customer, because the customers were virtually the same. Rather, the answer came from an understanding of the way the leads were produced and, perhaps more importantly, the nature of the structure and support system provided.

In the first case, our strongly driven salesman got his leads in one very simple way—people walked through the door. Being located in the center of a large city, the dealership had no lack of walk-in traffic. True, many of these were simply browsers, but some were serious buyers, and others, once they were in the showroom, could be converted into customers if the salesperson was effective enough. The leads were there; they would buy now or probably not at all, and so it remained only for the salesperson with strong sales dynamics to close those prospects on the spot. Further, the metropolitan area dealership had a strong sales management team to approve deals, as well as finance and insurance people to handle those aspects of the sale. In general, there was a strong support system to help the salesman, in terms of closing approaches and, more importantly, in terms of the myriad details necessary to maximize the deal, both for the dealership and for the customer.

In the Midwest situation, on the other hand, the job called for the salesman/assistant sales manager to leave the dealership to produce prospects. Relatively few individuals casually entered the showroom, and so prospects had to be created through country club memberships, solicitation of businesses, referral programs, etc. Not only did a structured outside system have to be developed to create prospects, but that system had to be fully implemented by the salesperson in a structured way, and the total deal had to be carried through from beginning to final contract by that salesperson. Thus, the support system so badly needed by that individual was absent, and though the prospects (the potential customers) were essentially the same, the process of securing these customers was radically different.

Oh yes, the story had a moderately happy ending, though by no means in the grand old Hollywood tradition. We were able to save this man's job by suggesting that he be brought back into the dealership and begin functioning as a real assistant sales manager. We suggested that other salespeople go out to generate the leads, to do the country club work, to solicit the business, etc., and bring the prospects they generated into our "hero." Then he could use his enormous closing ability and other sales talents to help close the deal. That provided him with some of the team play he needed, and, at the same time, substantially reduced those aspects of the job for which he was totally unsuited. Then after a couple of years of this, he returned to work for another metropolitan area dealership, where he is currently the leading salesman.

This case really serves as an excellent example of the vital importance of a clear, specific job description. The way prospects are provided, the support system, the need to travel, and the nature of the sale itself all played a role in defining an individual's success in one situation and abject failure in another. The simple fact that the Eastern metropolitan dealership could do very well with its thousands of potential one-time buyers, while the Midwestern situation demanded repetitive buys, could have, by itself, explained the entire saga; but when you add the multiplicity of factors we discussed, it was no great feat on our part to have predicted failure in the

Midwestern situation. Our Midwestern client made the mistake of thinking selling is selling, and that selling its particular product equaled selling the same product in a metropolitan area. The client was not willing to examine the different natures of the two positions. Had it done so, it could have avoided a great deal of pain, time, money, and effort, on its part, and on the part of the individual involved.

To conclude, there are a number of other questions that should be dealt with in defining a specific sales job. These include:

To whom does the salesperson report?

Does the salesperson have any secretarial or administrative help?

What is the compensation plan—salary, salary plus bonus, commission only, etc? (We touched on the implications of this question earlier.)

What is the career path of the position? (Does it lead to bigger and better sales, or is the next step management? If so, management potential should be part of the consideration.)

Are we dealing with tangible or intangible sales?

Are we dealing with small-ticket or big-ticket items?

Are sales cyclical or consistent through the year?

On average, how many contacts does it take to close a sale?

Is the job in a big city, suburb, town, or rural area?

How large is the sales force?

Is the company known in the market, or is part of the sale selling the company name?

There are more questions to consider. But if companies and sales managers do no more than develop their job description using the questions outlined here, they will have taken a major step toward achieving the job match that is the key to sales success. The exercise of putting together such a job description for their own edification will substantially improve their ability to make judgments concerning who can fill the job. In addition, presenting a job description of this kind to individuals in line for promotion, or to applicants, will help these individuals immeasurably to determine whether they really want the particular sales position, given a clear description of all its aspects.

So now, it is hoped, we have a better understanding of the "job" part—of our sales job. The next aspect to consider is whether you are looking for a "hunter" or a "farmer."

11

Hunters and Farmers

In virtually every study we have conducted of successful salespeople, we have found that the best succeed when they have a combination of the five qualities we've been discussing so far—ego-drive, empathy, ego-strength, service motivation, and conscientiousness.

By way of a quick example, when we combine all our studies of salespeople, we find that the mean score of the top performers is at the 68th percentile of ego-drive. Simply put, top salespeople have more ego-drive than 68 percent of the population at large. This figure clearly validates the importance of ego-drive as a predictor of sales success. There is, however, a dilemma created by this figure. What about the 32 percent of successful salespeople that may not have the strongest ego-drive? How, despite this lack, were they able to be numbered among the top salespeople in their company?

Our research points to one answer. The sales role can be broken down into two broad categories—"hunters" and "farmers."

On a very simplistic level, hunters are the classically driven, highly persuasive, fast-closing salespeople. Then there are the farmers, who slowly cultivate clients, build long-lasting relationships, and close less frequent, but have larger sales. It would be easy to say that both of these sales types succeed when they are matched to a product or service that requires such abilities.

What about situations in which hunters and farmers succeed side by side, selling the exact same product or service? If there is one ideal profile of a top salesperson, how do we account for these two completely different types of salespeople succeeding? How do we account for the one-third of the top salespeople within the same company—theoretically in the same sales role—who have only a moderate need to persuade?

We have come to identify two very distinct personality profiles—both of which can be extremely successful in sales, for entirely different reasons. Working side by side, these individuals succeed by playing to their core

strengths. Allow us to share with you how hunters and farmers succeed—
in completely different ways—by recounting the success stories of two top
performers from our studies.

Hunters

Karen was last year's account manager of the year for a leading
manufacturer of computer software. Throughout the past 3 years, this recent
college graduate has consistently surpassed her sales target. With no prior
selling experience, we would describe Karen as "motivated to persuade and
come through for clients."

She describes herself as "highly driven and very competitive." Karen
started off doing 40 cold calls each day. She now has 250 accounts.

She says her greatest thrill comes from converting a dormant account into
an active one. She particularly gets a kick out of getting a really big order,
"especially when the effort is solely attributable to your own efforts."
Preferring to work as a solo performer, she admits to getting frustrated when
customers call on other people to help make the final decision.

Karen adds that it is "vital to establish and build relationships." She says
she hates losing a sale. When it happens, she says, "It is usually because I
haven't grasped the opportunity quickly enough."

One of the things she likes about her company is that "a healthy
competition is encouraged within the team, and our compensation is based
on individual achievement." In fact, she has just returned from Greece, a trip
she won for being Account Manager of the Year.

What were the results when we assessed Karen's personality strengths? It
is hard to describe Karen without using words like "very." Exemplary of the
composite profile of hunters, she is very persuasive, extremely confident,
definitely willing to take risks when necessary, and very assertive,
disciplined, and gregarious.

Karen comes across as a truly outgoing, engaging individual who
genuinely enjoys opportunities to meet new people and to transfer her
knowledge. She enjoys persuading others or "guiding" them to what she
believes is the best solution for them. And because of her confidence and
assertiveness, she won't hesitate to share her point of view—which, because
of her discipline and focus, is usually very well considered. Underlying all
these qualities is a fundamental urgency, or a need to get things done
"now." This sense of urgency enables her to capitalize on opportunities and
not allow commitments to go unfulfilled.

Karen's approach impresses customers because she conveys a definite
perspective, in a confident manner, and wants to make sure her solution is
thorough and, ideally, delivered before it is even expected.

Farmers

Saul conveys a completely different demeanor and approach to selling—which has enabled him to be very successful for the same computer software company for which Karen works. He used to work in the company's customer service department, so he brings a thorough knowledge and understanding of the needs of his 185 accounts.

In one particular instance, after only 6 months in his new position as a salesperson, Saul turned a negative situation into a growth opportunity, and the company involved has gone on to become one of the firm's largest clients.

He has maintained and grown his business by keeping close to customers and understanding their business. As Saul says, "Succeeding in sales starts with demonstrating awareness and understanding of each customer's needs." In order to do this, he "has to build trust and deliver on each and every promise."

Saul's personality profile is exemplary of the composite profile of farmers. He is very outgoing, highly engaging, enormously accommodating, with a consistently conscientious approach toward servicing his clients' needs. Not a risk taker, Saul is the kind of individual who worries about whether or not his clients are satisfied. Clearly, this results in customer loyalty, account retention, and a client base that continually refers new opportunities.

He is, above all else, a service-oriented salesperson. His motivation to come through for others comes across loud and clear. He works with his customers as a partner—seeking to provide the best possible solutions. He has a need to "come through." Two terms—"conscientious" and "service-minded"—best describe Saul's character and behavior.

The Best of Both Worlds

This poses an interesting dilemma for owners and sales managers who are trying to hire salespeople with the potential to build their business. Do you bring on hard-driven salespeople to convert sales quickly? Or do you invest the time necessary to hire salespeople with more of a consultant's demeanor, who will not necessarily bring in new business immediately, but may, in time, set new records?

If you lean toward the more thorough and accommodating model, how do you know that such individuals will be able to survive through the first several years that it typically takes for them to build their base of business? Or if you are looking for the more classically driven salesperson, you have to ask yourself, "Why is it that top salespeople who have been around for a long time seem to come across more as consultants?"

The ideal would be to find someone who is a combination of these two profiles—a hunter and a farmer. The perfect applicant would be empathic, driven to persuade, assertive, able to bounce back from rejection, *and* thorough, conscientious, sociable, and accommodating. Such an individual would be able to close sales early on *and* know how to build long-term relationships.

But we are rarely in a position to take advantage of the best of both worlds—particularly when trying to make quick hiring decisions. Usually, some trade-offs are necessary.

So while you might set your sights on finding individuals who are a combination of these two ideal profiles, the truth of the matter is that you will usually have to decide on someone who tips toward either the more consultative or the more driven profile. The question is, how do you decide which profile is best for your situation?

Coming up with just the right mix of sales talent depends upon first determining the specific needs of your company and then assessing the potential of your sales candidates. You can start out by asking yourself what is most important. Selling more units? Increasing profit? Satisfying customers? Or bringing in repeat business? The answers to these questions and the order in which you prioritize them will point the way toward defining the profile of the next salesperson you are seeking. Other questions to consider are: Does the location of your company require an enormous amount of prospecting? Are you trying to alter the public's perception of your company? Are you more concerned about your clients or your competition? And what is the mix of salespeople currently on your staff?

From a practical matter, trade-offs are necessary more often than not. We may find a candidate for a sales job who possesses the requisite amount of empathy, ego-drive, and ego-strength, but who lacks self-discipline. Do you hire this candidate? The answer might be yes if it's determined that he or she can be managed tightly enough to impose enough structure externally to overcome that particular lack of self-discipline. Similarly, another driven individual might lack of self motivation. Is he or she worth hiring? Perhaps, if there is a sufficiently well-organized service function in the company to provide the needed ongoing service. And so it goes.

As one of our clients put it so well, "Especially in sales, which is very much a people game, there is no one answer to what will work and what will not work. We have a very diverse group of salespeople, some who are more persuasive, others who are more service-oriented, and everywhere in between. You need that mix to keep your organization running."

In the next chapter, we will explore a series of additional qualities, the understanding of which will allow us to make a better job match based on a range of issues beyond the five basic dynamics. Beyond exploring whether an individual can sell, we'll delve into the many additional attributes needed by farmers and hunters.

12

Other Personality Qualities and the Job Match

As we indicated when discussing the central qualities required for sales success, the possession of empathy, ego-drive, ego-strength, conscientiousness, and even service motivation does not ensure success in a particular sales position. When people possess these qualities, they should certainly be in a position in which persuasion is central to success. What that specific position is, however, depends upon the possession of a number of other attributes. Once the nature of the specific sales job is understood, as we discussed in the previous chapter, the personality attributes needed to succeed in that job can be determined.

Let us look at some of these qualities that can be as crucial to success in specific sales jobs as the central dynamics themselves. These attributes include the ability to grow on the job; to be an effective decision maker; to be good at, or at least tolerate, some degree of detail; to organize work and time; to communicate effectively; to work as a team member; to be willing to risk, to try new things; to be assertive and aggressive where necessary; to be shrewd in sizing up situations; to possess a sense of urgency, driving the individual to get things done; and more.

Growth

Whether an individual has the ability to grow in a job should be a major concern. The ability to grow, which is closely related to the ability to learn, is a necessity in most sales jobs and in virtually all management jobs. But while growth is related to one's ability to acquire new information and view situations from a fresh perspective, it is not merely a reflection of IQ. Some individuals, while possessing an outstanding IQ, are so opinionated, rigid, and dogmatic that they use their intelligence to reinforce and defend preconceptions. In other words, they use their intelligence to build a wall around themselves, selecting evidence supportive of what they already believe to be correct and ignoring all conflicting ideas and facts. Such individuals use their intelligence to keep themselves from growing. More than once, we have discovered an individual with an IQ of 165 who was incapable of growth, even in simple job situations.

Growth involves intellectual capacity, of course, but it truly manifests itself in empathy, sensitivity, and the flexibility of mind that receives and ponders—and sometimes accepts—new ideas and methods.

Decision Making

In many situations, the ability to make quick, correct decisions can save a sale from being lost. In some ways, this ability surpasses in importance the salesperson's need for intelligence. Should the price be cut? Should a special guarantee be offered? Should the close be pushed for? Should another meeting be scheduled at which technical assistance can be brought in? Is this customer a genuine prospect that should be pursued, or one that is just looking for diversion, enjoying the attention that hopeful salespeople lavish? Is the customer picking the salesperson's brains for technical information without any real interest in buying? What should the salesperson do when the purchasing agent wants to refer him or her to the vice president? How does the salesperson react when a customer accuses his or her company of giving poor service?

Even with generous shares of empathy and ego-drive, a poor decision maker can fail as a salesperson by acting too impulsively and be even more destructive by not acting at all, out of fear of making a mistake.

An overly impulsive salesperson may immediately cut price, wildly promise extravagant benefits, accuse competitors of outlandish practices, and behave in a way that is irredeemably embarrassing and totally unprofessional. This hasty, impulsive, impatient decision maker tends to be poor on follow-up. Yet given empathy and the ability to grow, such individuals may learn from mistakes. With experience and a course in time planning, such impulsive salespeople may partially or even fully overcome this tendency.

But the non-decision maker has less opportunity to learn from mistakes, because those mistakes are due to inaction, rather than judgmental error. Consequently, the results are difficult either to trace or to measure. Because such overly cautious individuals cannot decide to make a fractional price cut, they may fail to secure a million-dollar order, but still no one can accuse them of having made a "mistake."

It is hard for anyone to learn from mistakes that are camouflaged or rationalized out of existence. It is this failure to learn that poses the largest problem for the overly cautious decision maker. Overly cautious people fear the possible results of their actions and, therefore, never act decisively. So they lose critical opportunities and rarely sell effectively.

Shrewdness and judgment are also critical attributes that play a part in the decision-making process. As we want to balance willingness to act with a strong sense of responsibility in order to temper hastiness, we also want to include the shrewdness, insight, and good judgment components of good decision making. We look for an individual who will take a risk, learn from whatever mistakes are made, and, by and large, make astute decisions.

Detail

The ability to handle some degree of detail work is also important in many sales jobs in spite of the stereotypical view that salespeople despise and, indeed, cannot cope with even the smallest amount of detail. And many salespeople do, indeed, exemplify this stereotype. To the hard-driving, impulsive salesperson, detail is an abomination; it is a form of torture to write a sales report.

Yet there are thousands of good salespeople who are capable of coping with detail adequately, and some of them are even good at it. In thousands of sales jobs, detail is an inescapable part of the operation. For example, how could a real estate salesperson sell a house, a commercial property, or an investment program without involving himself or herself in detail? How could a person begin to sell complex equipment and machinery and stay clear of detail? Without the ability to handle details, is there any way, even with an abundance of drive and empathy, that a registered representative could sell securities, a wholesaler sell mutual funds, or an agent sell estate planning programs?

Of course, some sales jobs require less ability to handle detail than others. Car salespeople, if they have a sales manager to back them up, need only moderate detail ability. The telemarketer, retail salesperson, and soft drink route person all have the required details built directly into their canned presentations, and they need relatively little inherent detail ability. All this clearly indicates why knowledge of an individual's ability to handle detail is critical in assessing potential in any given sales job.

Organization of Work and Time

The ability to organize one's own work, in combination with initiative, also needs to be considered in determining a person's sales potential. Many sales jobs, by their very nature, bring customer and salesperson together and so permit the salesperson with significant ego-drive a reasonable number of customers, regardless of whether he or she has done preparatory work. But in many other sales jobs, even outstanding salespeople could starve while they waited for the customer to come to them.

The nature of those sales jobs requires that salespeople find customers and then use their ego-drive to close sales. In these sales situations, individuals without the ability to organize their work are likely to sit all day waiting in vain for a prospect to persuade. They are like the lonely person on a Saturday night who wishes for a date but cannot quite manage to dial the number to get one.

The case of Sandra exemplifies this point. An insurance agency asked us to test its entire sales and management staff. Sandra, we found, possessed outstanding empathy and ego-drive, exceptional intelligence, and all the prerequisites of an outstanding salesperson. Yet she was not succeeding.

Why, in view of Sandra's strong central dynamics, was she failing? She was an impulsive, driven salesperson who intensely disliked detail, had little or no capacity for self-starting, and had a low level of organizing talent. She was simply incapable of going through customer cards or prospect lists with painstaking care or engaging in routine follow-up activities.

Though the job was called sales, the primary means of retaining and expanding business was through what is known in the industry as "x-dating." What this means is that the salespeople had to keep close tabs on their account files so as to be aware of when their policies were coming up for renewal (the "x-date"). It was at that point that the salespeople were supposed to contact the customers, discuss their current insurance, and look to opportunities for increasing amounts or broadening coverage. Sandra's lack of detail ability and personal organization made such careful record keeping and follow-up virtually impossible. She much preferred the rejections involved in looking for new customers to the painstaking detail work involved in working through customer record cards.

We advised the CEO that Sandra would never be appropriate if her job continued to involve detailed follow-up. Yet we did not want our client to lose an individual possessing Sandra's high degree of sales dynamics. Sandra was installed in a purely outside sales role, and she was replaced by one of the agency's customer service representatives who had too much ego-drive for a purely service role. The customer service representative possessed the detail ability and personal organization skills needed to follow up on x-dates, but still had sufficient ego-drive to take advantage of the sales opportunities presented during these follow-ups.

Without these job shifts, the agency would have lost a valuable salesperson in Sandra because she was attempting to fill a sales role with a job description not suited to her personality. The agency also would have lost a customer service representative who had too much drive to function in a purely service capacity. With these shifts, both people were retained, and both were made more productive. Sandra filled a role not requiring so much detail ability, while the customer service representative was placed in a role using her detail ability and personal organization skills, while also allowing her to satisfy her persuasive motivation.

Communication

The ability to communicate is also critical. Empathy, a vital component of communicative power, makes it possible to receive a message from the customer and understand it correctly. However, having empathy is no guarantee of being able to communicate ideas effectively and clearly to the customer. Some sales situations require no more than standard forms of communication, but other situations require as high a degree of communicative ability as that needed by a top sales trainer or a first-rate teacher.

Clearly, selling is communicating in one form or another. In virtually all one-to-one sales situations, the effectiveness with which the desirability of the product or service is communicated determines whether or not the sale will be made. The ability to receive accurate feedback from a customer, coupled with effective presentation skills that address the customer's reaction, is, at least in selling, two-way communication at its best. Where the salesperson lacks empathy, the conversation that is thought to be a meaningful sales dialogue is in reality several alternating monologues: The salesperson is talking at the customer, the customer is talking at the salesperson, and no real communication is taking place. On the other hand, if the salesperson has empathy, and so genuinely understands what the customer is thinking and feeling, but is unable to translate that understanding into good presentation skills, the empathy could be wasted and the sales failure would be just as complete as if the empathy did not exist in the first place. Thus, real communication involves both the ability to gather vital feedback from the customer and the ability to use that feedback in order to effectively communicate the product or service in terms of how it will meet that customer's needs.

Team Player: The Ability to Delegate

One of the most overlooked attributes of the successful salesperson is the ability to function as a member of a team. Usually this attribute is related to one's ability to delegate. In any discussion of management talents, delegation of responsibility is always stressed; but strangely, in discussions of a salesperson's talents, it rarely is. The ability to turn a job over to another or bring in required help can make the difference between success and failure. The ego-driven salesperson, by definition, wants the thrill of conquest, and is more often than not the ultimate individualist. Yet questions often arise to which the salesperson does not know the answer. Perhaps the most intelligent, most credible (and most honest) answer that any stumped salesperson can give is "I don't know, but I will find out." Unfortunately, some salespeople appear to be constitutionally incapable of that kind of reply. Instead, they are more inclined to blunder along, faking answers they don't have, frequently misleading the customer, and, quite likely, losing him or her forever. It follows that one of the key requisites of a successful salesperson is the ability to bring in technical help when necessary and to make use of the manager's skill and experience. In short, the salesperson must often be able to play as part of a team, not just as a wheeling-and-dealing individualist.

The sports world offers a close analogy. Many a ball team laden with superstars has stumbled and failed because each star played for himself, instead of submerging his strength into the body of the team. So it is with a salesperson.

Assertiveness

Many people may possess ego-drive (the motivation to persuade) and yet may not be assertive enough to ask for an order in spite of their intense desire to get that order. A time comes in every sales situation when, after the presentation, the gathering of customer information, and all the other elements that go into a sale, the prospect has to be told "please sign here." It is at that moment of truth when the customer gives the final yes-or-no answer, when the salesperson's assertiveness or lack of same can be the difference between success and failure.

The term "assertiveness" is frequently confused with aggressiveness. Assertiveness is not pushiness and, in fact, should never really be perceived as pushiness, aggression, attempted dominance, etc. Rather, assertiveness is the ability that enables an individual to get other people to do willingly what they might not spontaneously do on their own. Assertiveness allows an individual to have a special effect on others which commands their respect and admiration and causes them to respond in a positive way to what that individual is asking or suggesting. Assertiveness involves the ability to get a positive response from others and use that response to bring about a desired attitude or course of action. Putting it in simplest terms, the assertive salesperson is willing to ask for the order and is capable of asking for it in a sufficiently effective way to ensure that the prospect will willingly give that order.

Aggressiveness

Aggressiveness is often confused with assertiveness. The two, however, are distinctly different and, in some instances, even opposite qualities. Where assertiveness, as we just discussed, involves getting people to do what you want them to do without pushing, aggressiveness is precisely that pushing. Aggressiveness is the willingness to actively oppose someone else's position, interests, or point of view, even if it could adversely affect that other person. Unfortunately, too many salespeople, particularly those with somewhat deficient empathy, are purely aggressive, as opposed to genuinely assertive. People do not want to be pushed into making a decision, and so the psychological difference between real assertiveness and pure aggression is far more than an academic distinction. Yet there are sales situations in which aggression of a certain kind is essential. For example, there are many telephone sales situations in which the salesperson is simply blocked from talking to the potential prospect. Pounding away at the locked gates often requires simple, though polite, aggressiveness. After all, you cannot use empathy, ego-drive, and assertiveness on a prospect with whom you have no contact. This can mean multiple conversations with a secretary before finally wearing him or her down and getting through to the boss, the prospect. Interestingly, once the door is opened, the prospect often will say, "How could I say no after such persistence?" and "You really must believe in what you're doing if you were willing to work that hard to arrange a meeting." One can look at these multiple calls as simple persistence, but the reality is that while persistence was certainly involved, each conversation had to include a pushing (polite, but still a pushing) toward the goal of eventually talking to that secretary's boss. Simple persistence (the willingness to make 18 phone calls without the aggressive push) would probably not have achieved the goal.

Here again is a perfect example of why, though we talk about individual qualities, they cannot really be viewed separately. The aggressiveness we just described would have done no good without persistence and without empathy. There had to be ego-drive to persuade the secretary to let the call through, empathy so that the secretary did not become angry, and persistence to keep trying. All these qualities, not just one, had to come into play to achieve the goal. In fact, we should mention another quality used in this situation—ego-strength—because there was a great deal of rejection on the road to achieving the goal.

Shrewdness

Shrewdness is the ability to read between the lines and to further process information, rather than accept it all at face value. There is certainly a relationship between this attribute and empathy, and yet they are very different in the sense that empathy deals with the understanding of the person, while shrewdness deals more with insights into a situation. Here again, the combination of empathy and shrewdness really makes for the ideal salesperson, particularly when you are dealing with more complex conceptual sales, as opposed to the sale of a simple, tangible product. Often, a prospect will tell the salesperson what is needed on one level, but shrewdness will allow the salesperson to read between the lines and to get to the next level of real need. In fact, many salespeople will relate instances in which their insight—their shrewdness—allowed them to ascertain needs of which the customer was not even aware. Shrewdness and empathy allow the salesperson to act as a consultant, helping customers discern their real needs and meeting those needs through the product or service being sold.

Again, there are many sales situations in which shrewdness is less important because the situation is simple, and what is on the surface is all that is really there. In other situations, however, shrewdness can prove to be as important as some of the central dynamics themselves.

Sense of Inner Urgency

The individual with a great deal of inner urgency needs to get something, or everything, done "right now." This individual has a need to move quickly and finds delay extremely frustrating. Typically, he or she cannot stand long deliberation over a subject, but rather is motivated to act, and keep acting, until a successful outcome is achieved. To individuals with inner urgency, there is no waiting for a call; instead there is a move to action—to pick up the phone and make the call themselves.

Individuals with little inner urgency will be much too laid back, complacent, and even passive. Even if they possess ego-drive, they are likely to feel that closing opportunities will present themselves, and they feel little need to actively seek those opportunities. When such individuals are presented with a prospect, their ego-drive will allow them to close effectively. But if they seriously lack inner urgency, they will not be proactive but, rather, will only be reactive. On the other hand, individuals with too much inner urgency could be so bent on immediate response that they could make bad judgments. In trying to get an immediate decision, they could end up with a negative one.

In understanding inner urgency we should look at this quality in relationship to ego-drive and to impatience, with which qualities it can easily be confused. Ego-drive is the need for victory, but that does not necessarily imply that that victory has to be immediate. Ego-driven individuals with the right amount of inner urgency will not let grass grow under their feet—they will move with all deliberate speed. On the other hand, they will not act recklessly and perhaps wrongly just for the satisfaction of this need for immediacy. However, we have seen many potentially successful salespeople, even with a great deal of ego-drive, who simply do not possess enough inner urgency to impel them to actively seek ways of satisfying that drive. For example, we can recall one young man whom we tested and found to have ample amounts of empathy, ego-drive, and ego-strength. He turned out to be, in fact, a reasonably successful salesperson, though, as our client told us about a year later, he never achieved the top performance level that would be indicated by his level of ego-drive. After some investigation, we found that his conversion ratio (number of closes to number of contacts) was quite high. What we also found, however, was that his number of contacts was among the lowest on the sales force. After interviewing him, it became apparent that he made no effort to maximize the number of calls he would make in a given day. If one call was completed at 11:30, rather than try to make an additional call before lunch, he would use that time to take a somewhat longer lunch. If a call was completed at 4:30, he would not rush to get to a prospect's office by 4:55, but instead would take the opportunity to beat the traffic and go home. Individuals with inner urgency would probably have made those additional two calls, because they would have the need for immediacy that would drive them to use the time to get work done. The result, given this young man's conversion ratio, would likely have been at least one additional sale per day.

What we see here is an individual who is making full use of his ego-drive; once he was in front of a customer, he closed that customer effectively. His lack of inner urgency, however, substantially reduced the number of these closing opportunities. The result was adequate, though not outstanding, sales performance.

As we said earlier, inner urgency is also confused with impatience. The difference is that the individual with inner urgency will act to obtain immediacy, while the individual who is simply impatient may be bothered by delay, but not necessarily do anything about it. An individual, for example, may be terribly impatient while experiencing the inordinate waits typical in doctors' offices, but the individual with inner urgency is likely to walk over to the nurse, tell her it's impossible to continue waiting, and either get taken earlier or reschedule the appointment. Mere impatience does not denote action. Inner urgency, for good or ill, most often leads to action.

Self-Discipline

In Chapter 7, we dealt with conscientiousness or self-discipline as the fifth factor providing the foundation for sales success. As described in that chapter, self-discipline involves the inner motivation to do what needs to be done whether or not the task involves something that the individual really wants to do.

What we want to focus on here is the connection between urgency and self-discipline. If a salesperson has enough self-discipline, he or she might try to make that final 5:00 meeting even though the inner urgency to do so is absent. This salesperson would do so because he or she should, not because there is the inner desire to do it. On the other hand, the individual with inner urgency will make that meeting because he or she wants to—because such a person has the need to get that little extra done during that day. As you read this you might ask, what is the difference? If the salesperson in fact makes that meeting, aside from academic interest, why do we care if it is because of inner urgency or self-discipline? We do, in fact, care, because—as is the case with so many things we are discussing in this book—we do things we like and want to do much more effectively than those things we have to do or are forced to do by external pressure. Thus, if the individual makes that meeting at 5:00 because he or she is compelled to by an inner sense of urgency, he or she is likely to pursue that meeting full tilt, making every effort to make that meeting effective and successful to satisfy their need for immediate results. On the other hand, if the individual makes it to the meeting because it was the proper thing to do, but he or she is basically yearning to be home or to be playing golf, the process may be carried out in a pro forma way to satisfy the individual's self-discipline, not done with the intense enthusiasm that might result in the closed sale. Obviously, if someone possesses both the right level of inner urgency and the self-discipline to plan and organize work and time efficiently, you have the best of all worlds.

Many other qualities could be touched upon, but we hope that the foregoing discussion has essentially made the point that as important as empathy, ego-drive, service motivation, conscientiousness, and ego-strength are to sales success, one must not stop there in determining whether an individual will be successful in a specific sales job. The job match—making certain that the individual's central qualities match the functional requirements of the particular sales job—is the critical factor in that determination, and many attributes beyond the five central qualities play a key role in making that job match.

13

Job Matching: The Bottom Line

Once you have the information about the job and you have an applicant for that job, the actual job-matching process can begin. As we discussed in Chapter 10, the first step of this process is to define the job. What is needed here is an understanding of the hour-by-hour, day-by-day functional requirements of the job—competencies—which will enable the holder of that job to attain the goals and objectives set by management. In other words, what is needed here is not simply a job description, but a thorough understanding of what the jobholder needs to do to achieve success in the job.

The next step is to determine what qualities are needed by an individual to perform effectively in that job. For example, if the Midwestern auto dealer that we discussed in Chapter 10 had evaluated his job, he would have come to realize that individual initiative, persistence, and patience were three critical attributes required to do his job. Completing the kind of job analysis we discussed should permit management to determine the qualities an individual must have to excel in a particular position.

The third step of the job-matching process is to look at the individual being considered and determine whether he or she has the qualities needed for the job. The fourth step only needs to be taken if there is such a match —if the strengths of the individual match the strengths required by the job. This step involves determining whether there is a fatal flaw.

The Fatal Flaw

All human beings are made up of an enormous package of motivations, abilities, and attributes. All of us are in the top 2 or 3 percent of persons possessing some particular qualities or abilities. But then we are also in the bottom 5 or 10 percent for some other qualities, and, more likely, somewhere in the middle for other qualities. No human being is, or can be, everything. There is the great myth that is represented by the following statements: "You can be anything you want to be," "All you have to do is work hard enough and you can do it," and "There is nothing you cannot achieve." All these add up to the idea that because winners work so hard, anything they touch turns to gold. On the other hand, the losers fail at anything they attempt. At the risk of sounding irreverent, we must say that statements like those we quoted, and the entire concept of the winner-loser, are nothing but rank, destructive nonsense. We have found that the winners in this world all share one thing in common. They are lucky enough or perceptive enough to be doing a job for which they are ideally suited. Winners play to their strengths. They do not attempt to work at jobs for which they are unsuited.

On the other hand, losers are trying desperately to do something totally alien to their basic personality. In sales, losers account for 80 percent of the people scratching, clawing, and fighting over the remaining 20 percent of what is not sold by the professionals. Losers in effect are trying to be what they are not; that is why they lose. However, if those losers in sales were to become administrators, teachers, lawyers, engineers, accountants, or whatever they were ideally suited to, they might quickly become winners.

Allow us another sports analogy to make this point: How many great quarterbacks could have made their team as a defensive lineman, a flanker back, or a tight end? We are sure you will agree that if they tried, they would have been labeled "losers." How many great pitchers, with the obvious exception of Babe Ruth, could have made their team as an outfielder or a shortstop? And for that matter, would the greatest shortstop have been a winner as a pitcher?

The key is for individuals to play to their strengths, do the best they can to improve their trainable weak areas, and not be particularly concerned with the fact that they possess, as do all human beings, a number of weaknesses. The key to success in selling, as in all other professions, is playing to your strengths, being the best at what you are, and playing away from weaker areas.

We think that this is a terribly important point to understand as we look at ourselves, as we look at people we are currently supervising, and as we look at those whom we are considering to hire. No one can be everything, and so the key word, as you are dealing with people, invariably is "trade-off."

So we go back to the central job match and to the fatal flaw. One trade-off that cannot be made is the match between the functional job requirements and the key strengths possessed by the person who must fill that job. The fatal flaw comes in when we look at the weaknesses of an individual and determine whether those weaknesses would make it difficult for the person to do the job.

The word "nontrainable" is extremely important to understand as we look at this fatal flaw. There are some weaknesses, as we said, that are simply a basic part of the individual and, regardless of training or motivation, really cannot be expected to be substantially altered. For example, if people simply do not enjoy the persuasive process—if they seriously lack ego-drive—you might, through training, prop them up to some degree in terms of tools or techniques. But you will never really make them enjoy selling, and as a result, you will never really make them effective salespeople; nor should you. That lack of ego-drive is simply too basic to their personality, and the reality is that such individuals simply should not be selling. On the other hand, if someone has some weakness in time planning, that person might be helped through a good time-planning program. A bit more difficult, but still possible, is a situation where an individual is inconsistently assertive. Again, depending on degree, a good assertiveness training program might help the individual assert himself or herself with more consistency. Certainly, where the weakness involves lack of knowledge or lack of a particular skill, and the individual has enough intelligence, openness, and willingness to learn, such weakness will not constitute a fatal flaw. On the other hand, if that knowledge requires a 4-year degree to obtain, then it indeed might fall under the fatal flaw category.

Thus, if we focus on the fact that all people have strengths and weaknesses—that nobody is everything—and we look to match appropriate strengths to the real requirements of a job and make certain that there is no nontrainable fatal flaw among the individual's myriad weaknesses, then we have a job match, with the resultant likelihood that, given training and proper supervision, the individual will perform at a high level of productivity in the position.

Results of Job Matching

Earlier we said that the existence of so many inappropriate people in sales jobs is traceable, in part, to the fact that people are hired for the wrong reasons. We mentioned that, in spite of legal issues, age, sex, race, experience, and formal education are frequently used as hiring criteria, and that our studies have found that these criteria are invalid. It is appropriate here to describe the most comprehensive of these studies, not only to debunk these invalid criteria but also to show how the job-matching process, if substituted for these invalid criteria, could indeed go a long way toward solving the high turnover, overall poor productivity, and the 20-80 pattern that characterize sales across industries.

Job Matching for Better Sales Performance

The results of our comprehensive 14-industry study were published in the September/October 1980 issue of the *Harvard Business Review*. With the permission of the *Harvard Business Review*, we present excerpts from that article.* The findings we report are based on our study of more than 360,000 individuals in the United States, Canada, and Western Europe since 1961.

The study covered 14 industries:

Automobiles	Banking and Finance
Chemical Manufacture	Business Forms Manufacture
Life Insurance	Data Processing
Media and Publishing	Farm Equipment
Pharmaceutical Manufacture	Heavy Manufacturing
Real Estate	Printing
Stock Brokerage and Mutual Funds	Property and Casualty Insurance

The seven industries in the first column characteristically have a high turnover of salespeople, while those in the second column have a lower turnover.

A random sample of individuals who were hired after testing were selected from each of these industries, and performance data were gathered. The members of the sample were then compared by industry, and on the basis of age, sex, race, experience, and education. Finally, they were compared as to whether or not they had been recommended for hire on the basis of their possession of appropriate dynamics for their specific sales job. In other words, they were compared in regard to whether or not they were appropriately job-matched.

Author's note: Our consulting firm, Caliper Corporation, has currently evaluated more than one million individuals.

Age

The worship of youth has long been recognized as a feature of the American culture. The myths relating to the value and attributes of youth have done wonders for clothing designers and cosmeticians. Few others, however, have benefitted from our neurotic obsession with youth. It is not our purpose, however, to deal with the tragedy of setting aside people at the very time they can contribute most to society. Rather, let us focus on the sales talent that industry loses in the over-40 age group.

When comparing the job performance of people over-40 with that of their under-40 counterparts, we found no statistically significant difference. Nearly

*Reprinted by permission of Harvard Business Review. "Job Matching for Better Sales Performance" by Jeanne Greenberg and Herbert Greenberg, September/October 1980. Copyright 1980 by the President and Fellows of Harvard College; all rights reserved.

the same percentage of individuals in the older and the younger groups performed in the top quartile of their sales forces after 6-month and 14-month periods. The same similarity between the groups held for second-, third-, and fourth-quartile performance. Even in turnover rate, the two groups remained extremely close, although the older group did turn over at a slightly lower rate.

Gender

For a number of years, of course, it has been illegal to discriminate in employment according to sex (as well as race, age, national origin, and so on). But women continue to be substantially barred from many occupations in which they could succeed perfectly well. Real estate is one of the few industries that over the years has offered women excellent opportunities to actualize their potential in sales and management.

Can women be the same rich source of talent in other fields? How well do they perform in sales in comparison with their male counterparts? The results show, beyond statistical question, no performance difference between men and women, even in industries such as stock brokerage and auto sales, which until recently were considered exclusively male bastions. Virtually the same percentage of women and men performed in the top quartile of their sales forces after 6 months and 14 months. Moreover, the two groups had virtually the same failure rates, whether failure is described as performing in the bottom quartile after 14 months or as termination because of poor performance.

Race

The law and a sense of justice tell us we cannot discriminate against individuals because of race. The data indicate clearly that it is not good business to do so, if for no reason other than self-interest. Blacks perform on the job as well as their white associates, and turnover rates were virtually identical.

From our sales force data, we conclude that sales performance has absolutely nothing to do with race.

When placed appropriately in jobs suited to their abilities and given proper training, counseling, and supervision, blacks and whites perform equally well in sales positions.

Experience

Experience is usually a principal criterion for making hiring decisions. Someone with experience in a particular industry, in selling any product or service, or even in doing unrelated work in the same industry, enjoys a great advantage in applying for a sales or a management position in that industry. Yet we found little difference in performance between these experienced individuals and those with no experience. The person with no experience, given training and supervision, is as likely to succeed as the person with 2 or more years of experience.

As in the results previously discussed, in the high-turnover industries there were no discernible differences.

There is an old saying that 20 years' experience can reflect 1 year's bad experience repeated 20 times. Our findings confirm that this is often the case. Too many people cling tenaciously to their unsuitable jobs and do just well enough not to be fired. Thus they accumulate years of experience. It is these individuals—the 80 percent in the wrong jobs referred to earlier—who make the value of experience nil as a prime criterion for the selection of successful salespeople.

Education

During the 20 years between the publication of our *Harvard Business Review* article and the publication of this book, much has occurred pointing toward additional emphasis on education. The emphasis on more and more high-technology products and the increasing emphasis on the consultative rather than the hard sell have geared the sales profession toward the better-educated individual, especially on the highest levels. With this said, however, our more recent studies continue to show that degrees per se, or number of years of education per se, are not a good predictor of sales success. Where education really is essential, the necessary level must obviously be a requirement, but using education itself as an absolute criterion for predicting sales success continues to be a fallacy.

As a value to be cherished and encouraged in our society, education cannot be challenged. The use of formal degrees as an absolute criterion for judging someone's potential effectiveness in a sales or a sales management job, however, must be challenged.

Obviously, in certain specialized fields, complex technological knowledge is required to sell the product. The computer salesperson must know the technology necessary to deal with the specialist in the company who may purchase a new system. Of course, intimate knowledge of the product or service is necessary in all sales situations. But normally such knowledge is obtained through the company's training programs, not through a college degree. Our probing research shows that people with little education, given their basic intelligence, can be as successful in many sales jobs as those with college degrees.

Unlike the four other criteria discussed earlier, we found some industry-to-industry variations according to levels of education. The college graduate and the multidegree recipient slightly outperformed the less educated competitor in industries characterized by big-ticket, highly technical sales and by sales requiring lengthy follow-up. These differences, however, seldom reached 5 percent.

As in the examination of the other hiring criteria, virtually no differences surfaced in the proportions of salespeople who were fired or who quit during the two periods.

Job-Matching Approach

In view of these findings, an obvious question arises: If these long-used criteria are invalid, what criteria can industry use that would better predict job performance? The answer is, criteria that make a better match between the person and the job.

The experience of companies that have tried to match applicants with their sales openings shows distinct differences in performance. A final aspect of this study was a comparison of new hires in terms of whether they were job-matched.

Persons who had been job-matched in the first 6 months with appropriate sales positions outperformed, to a statistically significant degree, those who had not been job-matched. Moreover, the differences widened after 14 months. Finally, the turnover rates of job-matched individuals were much lower in all cases.

For the purposes of clarity, we reformulated the data from the study so that performance could be compared among individuals still on the job after 14 months. We compared the performance of those individuals whose personality dynamics matched the job for which they were being considered against those who were not recommended but were hired because they met the old criteria or because "they looked so good in the interview."

Tables 13-1 and 13-2 illustrate performance of job-matched individuals compared with those who were not job-matched for both high-turnover and low-turnover industries.

Performance of Those in High Turnover Industries Who Were "Job Matched" Compared to Those Who Were "Not Job Matched"	
Measurement Period after Hiring: 14 Months	*Top Half*
Job Matched	85%
Not Job Matched	17%
Note: Sample sizes - 4,362 people who were job matched and 8,740 who were not job matched.	

Table 13-1

Performance of Those in Low Turnover Industries Who Were "Job Matched" Compared to Those Who Were "Not Job Matched"	
Measurement Period after Hiring: 14 Months	*Top Half*
Job Matched	76%
Not Job Matched	21%
Note: Sample sizes ~1,800 people who were job matched and 3,961 who were not job matched.	

Table 13-2

It can be seen from these tables that in the high-turnover industries, 85 percent of the individuals recommended for hire on the basis of their appropriate personality dynamics (and still on the job) were performing in the top half of their sales force after 14 months, while only 17 percent of the individuals hired who were not job-matched were performing at that satisfactory level. In the low-turnover industries, 76 percent of those recommended were performing at that high level, while only 21 percent of those not job-matched were doing as well.

The study reveals another important difference. In the high-turnover industries, 57 percent of those individuals hired by the old criteria were no longer on the job after 14 months, while only 28 percent of those who were hired on the basis of job matching quit or were fired. The turnover difference was even more dramatic in the low-turnover industries, where only 8 percent of the recommended individuals quit or were fired, while 34 percent of the not-recommended group were no longer with their companies after 14 months.

As we wrote in the *Harvard Business Review*, "While error free personnel selection will remain an impossible dream, this study points out a direction business can take to reduce such errors." We are convinced from this study, and many other smaller studies that we have conducted within individual industries and across industry, that if job matching replaced the old invalid hiring criteria, the sales profession, because of the quality of its people, will indeed achieve the level of productivity and professionalism to which it is entitled. There is no doubt in our minds that if management moves toward job matching in its hiring of salespeople, and if many existing salespeople who have sales talent but who may be selling the wrong product or service are allowed to shift positions, the sales profession will be characterized by the quality of what is now only the top 20 percent.

PART

4

Building a Winning Sales Team

Until this point, we have spent a good amount of time dealing with the psychology involved in what it takes to succeed in sales. We have talked about sales as a profession; dealt, at least to some degree, with the problems holding the sales profession and salespeople back from achieving their full potential; and discussed the central dynamics needed by an individual if he or she is to succeed in any kind of sales. We then talked about the job-matching process, which included a review of many other qualities beyond the central dynamics needed to succeed in specific sales situations. Finally, we looked at the job-matching process and compared its results with results obtained from the use of old, traditional hiring criteria; we found that by using job-matching, a far higher level of sales productivity could be achieved.

It is now time to begin dealing with the "how-to." We will start by examining an organization's existing sales team as the first step in upgrading the productivity of that team.

Then we will explore the team through a "sports'-eye view." Many expressions commonly used in business are directly drawn from sports: "The deal was a slam dunk." "We need a good game plan." "He or she hit a home run." "We need to get into a full court press." "We better punt." These and many other expressions tell us that there are clearly lessons to be learned in business from sports. So we'll share with you some of our work assisting sports teams in the selection and development of professional athletes, and explain what it can mean for sales.

Following this, we will explore, in detail, sources of potential sales talent, recruitment of that talent, and all the steps involved in effective selection of productive salespeople.

We hope that by the end of this part you will be able to begin integrating the theory of what it takes to succeed in sales with some ideas about how to use that theory to build an effective sales team.

14

Inside the Team

How many coaches, general managers, or owners of professional sports teams spend time fantasizing how wonderful it would be if they could replace their entire team with one of the greatest teams in the league? What a wonderful fantasy to suddenly have your basketball team, which has not made the playoffs in years, replaced person for person by the roster of playoff finalists. A wonderful fantasy though this may be, such dreams really do not come true. What is true is that the only way the cellar dweller, a team perpetually at the bottom of the league, can be turned into a championship team is through painstakingly building that team into a winner. Since you cannot suddenly replace 12 basketball players, 25 baseball players, or 49 football players with an equal number of better players, the first key step is to make the best use of the talent you have on hand. There are, in fact, as all sports fans well know, many teams that perform far beyond what their individual talent level would indicate because they are able to totally maximize the talent that exists as a team. On the other side, many talented teams fall short throughout the years because they are not able to maximize the existing talent.

So the first step in building a winning team, whether in sports or in business, is to get the most out of what you have and then add to the roster. In sports this is done through trading and the draft; in business it is done through recruiting and selecting productive people.

Start with the Manager

For the purpose of this discussion, let us look at the sales team as one unit led by a sales manager. In a large organization, there may be many of these teams divided into districts and regions, but each of these teams really must be viewed separately, and worked with separately, if real progress is to be made.

A team must be viewed as a totality, and not simply as individual elements. Every team has particular strengths and weaknesses. We should start, however, with the team leader—the sales manager.

The first thing that needs to be done is to really understand the strengths and weaknesses of the individual leading the sales team. Most managers fall into one of two broad categories. The first category is typified by an outstanding salesperson replete with empathy, ego-drive, ego-strength, conscientiousness, and service motivation, but seriously lacking some key management attributes. Sales managers in this category need a group of self-reliant, well-disciplined, self-starting salespeople reporting to them. In all likelihood, such sales managers cannot be counted on to be highly effective at delegation or follow-up. They are is most likely not very strong in structuring the work and time of subordinates. On the other hand, such sales managers are likely to be extremely effective at going into the field with a salesperson and helping to close tough deals. Of course, one of the things that these highly driven sales managers might have to work on is the tendency to want to do too much themselves. Typically, they have difficulty delegating. Their motivation often is to show the salespeople how to sell by outselling every one of them. In our work with these sales managers, we have to get them to literally sit on their drive if they are to be successful in developing the potential of their sales force.

The second category of sales manager is exemplified by those who possess strong administrative skills. Managers in this category help plan and structure the work of a sales force, follow up effectively on the work of others, and are adept at analyzing data. They set goals and objectively evaluate performance. They may possess some sales instincts, but they do not intensely need the close; therefore they are effective delegators. Lacking strong sales instincts, they might not be helpful in closing deals and, in some instances, might even have some problems relating to highly driven people reporting to them.

By presenting these two broad categories of sales managers, we are trying to highlight the fact that, in order to understand the dynamics of a team, it is essential to start out by understanding the strengths, weaknesses, and motivations of the sales manager. A team's productivity can obviously be greatly affected from the top down.

One brief case history on the sales management relationship illustrates this point. We were asked by the vice president of sales for an international computer firm to conduct a team analysis of one of the firm's regional offices in a major city. The primary purpose of this study was to explore the region's strengths and weaknesses and to make suggestions for improving sales productivity. The executive also wanted us to help increase morale and enthusiasm among managers and other sales personnel.

The region had recently experienced a change in top management. The previous regional manager was held in high regard by the branch managers and sales personnel. After 12 months under a new manager, the organization continued to grow, but not nearly at a level consistent with its previous record. We conducted interviews with the regional management staff and salespeople. During those sessions, our findings for each manager and his or her sales staff were reviewed. Suggestions were provided to the managers regarding methods of supervising the people who reported to them.

On the whole there appeared to be a strong negative mindset on the part of the region's management team. Part of the problem was solved by comparing the personalities of the old manager with his replacement. The original manager was a strongly driven, dynamic individual who was a classic example of the so-called charismatic leader. On the other hand, his replacement was an individual who was superbly trained in the technical end of the business and possessed the personality dynamics typical of a technically oriented, highly capable administrator. However, the new regional manager could never have been accused of being charismatic.

Loyalty to the charismatic leader, along with the concomitant resentment of his replacement, certainly was part of the problem. More important, however, was the fact that when the old leader would set goals or demand effort, the tendency of the team was to respond positively. On the other hand, the very same demands or goals put forward by the new manager were viewed as unrealistic and were resisted. A negative mindset was established which served to erode confidence in management. If people feel that goals cannot be met, they will not, when push comes to shove, be met. Motivation in this case was a "top-down" activity. In other words, the new regional manager would have to embrace his goal with enthusiasm and project his optimism downward to his staff, which, given his personality, he was not able to do.

What the original manager was able to accomplish through sheer leadership dynamics was to drive the team toward meeting tough quotas tied to compensation. He was also able to cover up, through sheer activity, two fundamental problems that became apparent when the new manager took over: limited formal sales management training for branch managers and an inefficient developmental program for the unit sales force.

One of our first suggestions was that the new manager, with the full participation of the managers reporting to him, re-establish more realistic sales quotas that could be attained The fact that the old manager could, at least for a short term, drive the team toward the higher goals did not mean that over the long haul the team, led by the new manager, could hope to attain that consistent level of productivity. In interviews, even the strongest supporters of the old manager admitted that some of his projections were optimistic and contained certain inaccurate assumptions that, in the long run, could prevent those projections from being attained.

Establishing sales quotas that are realistic, achievable, and, at the same time, challenging is essential to creating a positive, high-energy environment. We strongly recommended that quota-setting activities be carefully reviewed and given sufficient attention so that the goals were challenging, rather than defeating. In addition, we felt that it was important for the new manager to recognize his role in creating an environment that was energizing, optimistic, and results-oriented. Moreover, he must convey these values to his organization with great concern for the welfare and success of the sales staff, his branch managers, and his own personal gain. Further, as mentioned, by and large we found that the branch managers were poorly prepared for their role as sales managers. None had direct selling experience, and formal sales management training had not been provided. It was strongly recommended that all these managers participate in a formal sales management training program. By sharing the experience together and acquiring a common language, this training would facilitate a greater team orientation.

The existing sales force was next broken down into three groups organized around individuals' specific areas in need of improvement. Once these targeted needs were established, trainers were brought in from corporate headquarters to design and implement programs geared to the special needs of each group.

In addition, we developed composite profiles of the most successful sales representatives, which were then used to assist managers in evaluating new applicants. These profiles helped managers to identify strengths and weaknesses in relation to successful employees; and improved management's ability to identify applicants with the greatest chance of success.

As can easily be seen from the foregoing, this sales team needed assistance on every level—from the regional manager, who needed specialized assistance in setting realistic goals and motivating his subordinates; to the branch managers, who needed hands-on training in the sales field; to the sales force, who broke up into three groups, with each group receiving training targeted to meet its specific needs.

What can readily be seen from this case is how differently a team will perform, depending on the nature of its leadership. At least in the short run, this particular team was producing as a result of the sheer intensity, dynamism, and leadership of the old manager. When that force was removed, however, the real quality of the group found its true level. Very different techniques had to be applied, and specific solutions to each problem had to be found in order to move productivity back up to an acceptable level.

Hiring in One's Own Image

One of the most common problems we have encountered in studying sales teams is that they reflect many of the manager's particular strengths, as well as his or her weaknesses. This is because very often people are hired in the image of the manager. The problems stemming from this kind of imbalance can be myriad.

We have seen many situations over the years in which a sales force with this kind of imbalance has literally come across to the public as "a bunch of animals." There is little or no cooperation among the salespeople themselves. Rather than viewing one another as colleagues, salespeople in such situations view each other as direct competitors. We have seen situations where a salesperson will work harder to thwart their colleagues—to grab sales out from under them—rather than to fight the company's competition. The issue of who is first in this month's sales report can become more important to the members of the sales team than the level of overall productivity for the company. The manager, in this scenario, is unable to control this jungle atmosphere because he or she is essentially cut from the same cloth, so tends to exacerbate the problem rather than cure it.

What finally happens is that people who might tend to balance the group will not come aboard because they do not like the climate, and so the people who are brought on often tend to be essentially the same personality types, thus compounding the problem.

At the other end of the spectrum are teams we have evaluated where the existing salespeople almost entirely lacked ego-drive. Typically, they survive through good service and ongoing relationship building. In most cases, such companies are well known, so the salespeople are doing adequate business in spite of a total lack of dynamism. Still, twice as much business would result if such companies had real salespeople. The problem is that strongly driven, dynamic salespeople are generally not attracted to teams with such "sleepy" atmospheres.

The majority of sales forces are not representative of either of these extremes, but consist of people with a range of abilities and personality attributes. Most, however, suffer from some imbalance, and all have to deal with the realities involved in the strengths and weaknesses, motivations, and differing personality dynamics of their team members.

Using Chemistry to Build a Championship Team

The chemistry that exists between management and salespeople, as well as among the salespeople themselves, will strongly impact whether a company's goals will be achieved.

There are indeed some companies that see each salesperson as a totally independent island who makes or breaks it for himself or herself, with no relationship to other people on the team. If their product is also a small-ticket one involving a quick, hard, one-time close, perhaps their vision would be realized by having a team of "animals." There may even be some companies that are so convinced that the salesperson's only job is that of an order taker and servicer that the "sleepy" climate we discussed would be totally congruent with their vision. Though neither of these extremes normally fits a corporate vision, our point is that the vision must define the qualities needed and the chemistry of the team. We suggest that, management meet first by themselves, and, if needed, work with an outside consultant, to determine their corporate vision and define their goals. They should ask such questions as:

How much would we like our team to sell during the next fiscal year and over the next 5 years?

Who are the targets for these sales?

Ideally, how should these sales be made?

What is the relationship between acquiring brand-new business and expanding and maintaining existing accounts?

How much of a gap are we willing to tolerate between the productivity of the top and bottom performers on the sales force?

Will we earmark funds to further develop our sales team if necessary?

What kind of climate do we want within the sales team—cooperative, competitive, etc.?

Once a corporate vision is defined, a plan can then be developed to reach the goals prescribed by that vision. The next step is to define the tasks needed to achieve these goals, communicate the goals and required tasks, and analyze members of the existing sales team to see if they have the abilities needed to get the job done. Each person must be evaluated to determine whether he or she has the ability to do the job as defined, or whether, through training or a shift in responsibilities, the ability can be developed. The relationship between the sales manager and his or her people has to be understood. Then it has to be determined how that relationship acts positively or negatively toward achieving corporate goals. And, of course, the chemistry of the team itself has to be studied to see how its dynamics affect the likelihood of reaching those goals.

There are many excellent tools available to help management move the company forward. Objective measurement of performance geared at developing people in areas of deficiency can go a long way toward increasing productivity and achieving goals. Attitude studies, valid psychological tests, employee productivity workshops, and team-building activities are just a few worth noting. Whatever tools are used, it is most critical to have a thorough understanding of both a company's sales team and the way that team meshes with the company's goals if there is to be any hope of developing a strategy to improve the productivity of that team.

A good example is a study we conducted with a mature company that found it had fallen behind in recent years in new business development and account expansion. We started out by examining management's standard job description and making a field evaluation of the sales representative position. We found the primary emphasis was on sales through the existing distribution network—not new business. Through job analysis, we discovered that, essentially, the sales force established relationships with major distributors but paid little attention to direct sales to end users. As a result, competitors were short-circuiting the sales process and thus gaining market shares.

When we analyzed the sales force, we uncovered that the vast majority of the sales representatives were, in fact, service-oriented people. Their solid service ability allowed them to retain their accounts since they were extremely good at developing long-term relationships. What they lacked as a group were the strong dynamics needed to persuasively compete for new business.

Several additional concerns were identified during the course of this project.

We interviewed a large number of individuals who expressed concern over the company's current methods of tracking and evaluating sales performance. These salespeople and managers stated that the company relied heavily upon the subjective impressions of supervisor ratings. While the company had made some attempt to base their evaluations on standardized performance factors, these factors did not actually correspond to real performance. To a great extent, the performance of the representatives was directly tied to the performance of the distributor. Once the sales representative persuaded the distributor to stock the line, the role of the representative immediately became more service-oriented. The distributor, in these cases, assumed the active sales role, while the sales representative took the role of technical expert, servicer, and factory representative. As a result, tenure was often the most significant factor utilized to differentiate sales representatives who were rated as successful from those who were rated as unsuccessful. Given the new goals and direction the company wished to pursue, a new performance appraisal system was definitely needed.

Further complicating the firm's performance tracking was the fact that although sales representatives were responsible for sales calls directly to end users, the company encouraged end users to contact and deal with any authorized distributor within the network system. Thus, despite territory assignments, it was often unclear which sales representative was responsible for making a particular sale. Clearly, this imposed a significant barrier to developing a more objective performance measurement system.

As a result of these findings, we recommended a series of structured sessions, using a focus group–task force approach to explore and make recommendations concerning performance tracking options for service and acquisition sales activities. Members of this group included sales representatives, managers, and human resource personnel.

A major problem immediately became obvious in the area of communication. Field personnel expressed feelings of isolation from the corporation and an inability to effect change. While their concerns primarily centered on the issues of performance tracking and compensation, there was a general expression of the company's lack of concern for, and recognition of, its field sales staff.

Where possible, we suggested that field sales representatives and managers should be included in forums in which goal setting, strategy development, performance tracking, and compensation systems were to be designed. By including employees in the problem-solving process, they would be more likely to own the solutions and make the systems work.

As noted earlier, this sales organization as a group was psychologically more oriented toward service and did not exhibit a strong level of ego-drive. The group members could not, therefore, derive a strong inner gratification from persuading others. While some individuals might be effective in developing new business, most focused on retaining existing accounts and providing technical support. If the company wanted to focus, as a primary goal, on the development of new business, it would require new people with different personality dynamics, along with a totally restructured performance tracking and incentive plan. While in an ideal world, there might be an abundance of candidates equally suited for both sales and service roles, reality teaches that very few people can do both well. We strongly suggested that job differentiation in this specific case would allow for greater flexibility in attaining corporate business objectives. In essence, we recommended establishing separate sales and service roles within the company's structure. Implementation would require a more strategic approach to hiring 2 different types of salespeople—one who was more driven to persuade, the other who was motivated to service the needs of clients.

Our study was effective in pointing out characteristics that differentiate a productive service-oriented staff from successful new business developers. The study also pointed out the need to develop a more strategic orientation toward using human resources to accomplish corporate objectives. Our strong bottom-line recommendations to this company were to (1) redefine sales jobs in terms of sales and service components, (2) develop a performance measurement system that related objectively and specifically to sales and service tasks, (3) define a compensation-incentive system that was tied to performance and the motivational characteristics of the sales and service people it covered, and (4) develop a strategic hiring plan that would incorporate overall corporate goals and the individual personality characteristics needed to get the job done.

Upgrade Productivity

The solutions that our own client companies have found to achieve productivity upgrades are so numerous and so varied that a full description of all of them would take us well beyond the scope of this book. Here are just a few of the things our clients have done to upgrade productivity successfully, even before embarking on the hiring of new people:

- Offer developmental programs, internal or external, in these areas: assertiveness training, time management, listening skills, closing techniques, presentation skills, approaches to prospecting, and technical training, to name just a few.

- Provide training to enrich the product knowledge (technical know-how) of salespeople.

- Conduct team-building sessions among the salespeople and between salespeople and management to increase morale and productivity.

- Develop a team selling system that allows the strengths of one salesperson to augment the weaknesses of another.

- Reorganize compensation geared to the particular dynamics of the sales team.

- Develop an incentive program built on group, in addition to individual, productivity.

- Divide sales responsibilities between those capable of new business acquisition and those more suited to maintenance and expansion of existing accounts.

- Reassign salespeople to managers with whom the chemistry would be more effective.

- Teach managers how to be more effective in working with sales teams, given the dynamics of that team.

- Counsel salespeople and managers on a one-on-one basis, making them aware of their own strengths and weaknesses and helping them more effectively play to their strengths and away from their weaknesses.

- Develop a series of one-on-one meetings between individual salespeople and their managers, with top management, or perhaps an outside consultant, as a meeting facilitator.

- Install objective performance measurement systems (or review and update old ones to be sure they reflect changes in the company's direction).

- Utilize focus groups to uncover and resolve problem issues.

The activities, or combination of activities, appropriate for a particular company again depends on that all-important understanding of the gaps that exist between the team and the company's vision of the future.

15

Sales and Sports: The Psychological Connection

In the mid-seventies, we developed the theory that the job-matching process discussed in the previous chapter could be applied in the sports arena. We had the first opportunity to test this theory for 2 years with the Rutgers University football team. But it wasn't until 1984 that we were able to test our concepts on the professional level with the then Minnesota Northstars hockey team, and the NBA's Cleveland Cavaliers. Since these initial trials, we have worked with 23 major league sports teams and 6 colleges in five sports, and have developed a substantial body of data validating the fact that job matching can be as effective in sports as in business. The tables that follow present data from studies conducted in baseball and basketball. In these studies, the performance of players recommended for drafting because of their psychological match to their sport and their position is compared with the performance of players drafted in the same rounds who were felt to be not matched. Obviously, talent played no role in these assessments. The only data we had the psychological test results.

The theory behind this study, and behind all our work in sports, is exactly the same as the theory underlying the question of what it takes to succeed in sales. In sales, we find that "experience" is not a good predictive criterion. Similarly, in sports, we postulate that virtually all the players seriously looked at by scouts, coaches, etc., have a great deal of talent. They've been noticed for their talent. Yet a vast majority don't live up to their scholarships, and don't make the major leagues. So talent alone cannot be the predictor. The fact that a player dominates in college because of talent simply does not mean that he or she could dominate on the professional level when going up against people of equal or better talent. More often than not, it comes down to the head and the heart that make the difference, and that's where the psychological job match proves to be effective: to separate the players who simply have talent from the players who have talent, and also the heart and the head to use that talent on the next level.

It can be seen from Table 15-1 that in baseball the young men who were psychologically job-matched had significantly more hits, walks, home runs, etc., than their peers who were drafted, again, in the same rounds but who were not psychologically job-matched. Similarly, Table 15-2 shows that in basketball the job-matched players outperformed their non-job-matched competitors better than 2 to 1 in most statistical areas, such as: average points scored, assists, steals, rebounds, etc. The only difference between the two groups was the job matching.

Since the data have proved to be so parallel, let's examine the psychology of sports and sales so that we can understand why these data prove to be strikingly similar.

Competitiveness

This is obviously a term that applies to sports, and that anyone who knows sports would view as a positive quality for an athlete. When looking at salespeople, aren't we also, however, looking for the individual with competitive drive? In athletes, we first look for strong competitiveness which relates to, but is not the same as, ego-drive (the need to get the yes) in salespeople. Defined briefly, competitiveness is that burning need to win with every move you make. It's not just the desire to win the game, which every athlete has; it's that instinct to compete with every move you make on the field or the court. In other words, if someone comes dribbling the ball downcourt, you may want to block him, stop him, get the ball out of his hands—whatever you need to do to win at that moment.

Now in the case of the salesperson, that desire to win is very specific: It's the desire to get the yes. It is not a matter of making a lot of money. Making money to a salesperson is like winning the game is to the athlete. Sure you want to make a lot of money, but the key to the successfully competitive salesperson is that need to get it done now. He or she wants to get the yes immediately.

Assertiveness

While competitiveness is essential to the success of all athletes, we have found that another quality, assertiveness, is only important for certain positions.

Assertiveness is the ability to lead strongly, yet without having to push or bully—in other words, the ability to lead so others believe they are important. In sports this is essential in coaching and in certain team positions requiring leadership, such as the point guard in basketball,

BASEBALL STATISTICS

Average per Player per Season Overall		
	Recommended	*Not Recommended*
Number of hits	145.78	70.96
Home runs	9.53	4.83
Total bases	208.86	102.57
Runs scored	80.1	38.48
Runs batted in	68.94	34.7
Walks	65.25	32.84
Stolen bases	23.75	9.99
Pitcher ERA	3.76	4.21

Major League Statistics - Players Who Reach Majors	
Recommended	*Not Recommended*
28%	17%

Major League Statistics - Average per Player per Season		
	Recommended	*Not Recommended*
Number of hits	125.64	51.81
Home runs	14.96	4.86
Runs scored	66.39	27.48
Runs batted in	62.75	26.86
Walks	52.29	20.29
Stolen bases	5.7	3.67
Batting average	0.24	0.2
Batting average (Pitchers omitted)	0.273	0.237

Table 15-1

BASKETBALL STATISTICS

Average per Player per Season Overall		
	Recommended	*Not Recommended*
Points per season	909	376
Rebounds	320	160
Blocked shots	51	23
Assists	207	91
Steals	77	33
Minutes played	1,919	1,004

Table 15-2

quarterback in football, or catcher in baseball. For these positions, when we help a team make a decision about drafting a player, we look to see whether that player has the necessary leadership for the position. On a number of occasions we've said to a general manager, "If you want to draft that player, fine, but not as a catcher. Never mind his talent; he just doesn't have the leadership to be a catcher."

The parallel in sales is in sales management. In straight sales, depending on what you're selling, assertiveness may not be critical, but in sales management it's absolutely essential.

Aggressiveness

As noted previously, assertiveness and aggressiveness are not the same thing. While each has its place in the athletic and sales arenas, too much aggressiveness can stand in the way of a player's success and often stands in the way of a salesperson's success.

Aggressiveness is more a physical or psychological need to just push things out of the way. It can be either a negative or, if under control, a positive attribute. Aggressiveness means creating your own opportunities, rather than waiting for opportunities to appear. Some people have described the difference this way: Say you have an assertive person and an aggressive person in a tunnel and they come upon a barrier blocking their way. The assertive person will get beyond the barrier by climbing it or going around it; the aggressive person is going to drive through it and knock it over.

In football, for example, you want a defensive end to be aggressive because his job is to knock over everything in his way to get to the quarterback. In basketball you can recognize a player who has a lot of aggressiveness because he or she probably fouls out too much of the time. In sales, however, unbridled aggressiveness is often seen as bullying. The customer says, "The salesperson just wants to make the deal and doesn't really care about me." Traditional high-pressure sales tactics that make the customer feel ill at ease often indicate too much aggressiveness.

Ego-Strength

Whether in sports or in selling, even the top performers must learn how to face rejection and failure if they want to succeed. The ability to move beyond life's inevitable rejections will determine success much better than talent alone. In baseball, a Hall of Fame hitter might bat .333 over his career. But if he bats .333, that means that for every three times he comes up to bat, two times he doesn't get a hit. He fails two out of every three attempts.

Similarly, even the best salespeople are rejected more frequently than they are accepted. With one of our stockbroker clients the hope is that out of a hundred cold calls a salesperson will get three appointments and close one sale. And that is successful. So whether it's in selling or in sports, the way someone deals with failure is as critical to their success as their talent.

An all too frequent story is the phenomenon in baseball—the hot rookie who comes to camp batting .400 or striking out everybody in sight. Everything seems golden. Then he encounters an inevitable slump—and doesn't know what to do. He starts changing his swing, holding the bat differently, but nothing works, and within a few months he's out of the game, never to be heard from again.

With two salespeople of roughly equal ability, the difference between short- and long-term success is often determined by self-esteem.

Self-esteem is one of the most critical attributes to success, but a lack of self-esteem is probably the single most common characteristic that defeats good athletes and good salespeople. As with athletes, no matter how successful salespeople are, they are going to experience slumps and rejections; and no matter how strong their ego-drive, they are not going to want to face that next rejection.

To move beyond feelings of vulnerability and rejection, you've got to have a sense of self, that self-esteem that we call ego-strength. That characteristic is what enables you to say, "OK, I know I'm going to get four turndowns before I get to a yes." It basically comes down to not taking the rejections personally, not having to disappear for a 3-hour lunch or do anything else just to avoid facing more rejections.

The athlete may manifest a lack of ego-strength or self-esteem by getting injured frequently—if you're not playing, you can't fail. Without good self-esteem, an athlete is likely to freeze in the clutch by missing that critical foul shot, or dropping that winning touchdown pass, or striking out with the bases loaded. We evaluated a player who was a brilliant wide receiver, everyone's All-American. He could catch a pass with one hand while he was surrounded by three defenders. Interestingly, however, in certain situations—crucial situations—the football could bounce off his chest with no one around him. We suggested that he be used as a decoy in those crucial situations and the ball be thrown to a less talented, but ego-strong, tight end. It worked.

How does this apply to sales? The point is that if a salesperson lacks sufficient ego-strength to take frequent rejection, that salesperson should be placed in a situation in which the sales are more automatic or at least where the prospects come to the salesperson as opposed to the salesperson's needing to aggressively pursue those prospects. There simply is no point in placing someone who cannot deal with rejection in a situation in which rejection is a given.

Self-Discipline

Along with competitiveness and self-esteem, self-discipline is critical to success in both sales and athletics. Essentially, self-discipline is that internal taskmaster that says, "I want to do things in an orderly, systematic way." Self-disciplined athletes say, "I want to practice because it will make me better; I don't need a coach to tell me to practice; I want to practice. I want to come into camp in condition because if I come into camp overweight, I'm going to be off to a late start and I'll have a lot of extra work to do." Self-discipline is that ability to plan and organize one's work and time systematically, thoroughly, and efficiently—all without that external carrot or stick.

The self-disciplined salesperson says, "OK, I am going to start on the north side of town to see Jim and Sally and that should fill my morning. Then I'm going to make an appointment midtown with Joe for lunch, so that I can see Carlos and Harriet on the south side in the afternoon. If I finish that appointment by 4:30, I should be able to squeeze in an extra meeting with Lee, whose office is near mine, and I won't have to waste a lot of time in transit."

If a salesperson lacks this quality, it might or might not prove to be a fatal flaw. In some sales situations—where people essentially come to you—self-discipline is less important. Also, if management is willing and able to provide tight, ongoing structure, perhaps a less disciplined salesperson can still be effective given that external support. Similarly, if an athlete is not sufficiently self-disciplined, coaches or managers must determine whether he or she is worth the extra attention that will be needed to provide that external structure. Is the coach willing to monitor the player practicing foul shots, or running, or using the weight room, etc.? In other words, whether in sales or in sports, there is a huge advantage to the individual possessing self-discipline. Judgments must be made where other qualities are so strong that the individual is worth the extra effort. Also, of course, the judgment must be made about whether the company or the team is in a position to provide that external structure to a sufficient degree to overcome the individual's inherent lack of that attribute.

Other Attributes for the Job Match

As we discussed previously, it is insufficient to make a judgment about the effectiveness of a salesperson simply by looking at his or her empathy, ego-drive, ego-strength, and even service motivation and self-discipline. We start there, but we then look at many other attributes in order to determine not simply if the salesperson can sell, but more importantly, can the individual sell the specific product or service for that company? In the same way, while we start looking at athletes in terms of their competitiveness, self-esteem, and self-discipline, we then must look at a number of other qualities to help determine whether they match the team, and whether they match the position for which they're being considered.

On a number of occasions, just as we've suggested shifts of salespeople to other sales roles or even to non-sales roles within the same company in order to make a better job match, we have suggested shifts in position within a team in order to effect better performance. For example, on several occasions, we have suggested that a catcher not be kept in the same position, but rather be moved to first base, third base, or left field if he's physically capable of playing those positions. We've suggested moves from point guard to shooting guard, from middle linebacker to defensive end, from offensive line to defensive line, and even in a very recent case, from running back to wide receiver. These suggestions were not based on any knowledge on our part about talent or even the physical capacity to perform in the new position. That judgment obviously had to be made by coaches, managers, etc. Our suggestions were based purely on psychological issues—matching individuals to positions based on their intrinsic abilities and motivations.

Some examples here might make this point clear, and will also demonstrate the strikingly similar issues that must be dealt with in sales and in sports. Take, for instance, a good quarterback, a good catcher, and a good point guard—all must possess several additional attributes, talent aside, if they hope to perform at the very top level of their position. They must be intelligent and so be capable of making good judgments. They must be willing to occasionally be wrong in order to get their job done. They must be a leader, and they must possess sufficient team orientation—be a team player—so they can maximize the abilities of the players around them.

The attribute of being a team player is also critical on the offensive line in football and for the second base combination in baseball. It should be noted that this quality—being a team player—is very close psychologically to service motivation, which was discussed earlier in the book.

We, of course, can go on, position by position, describing the specific qualities required for top performance, but we hope the foregoing is sufficient to make two points. First, there is a striking similarity between building a sales team and building a sports team from a psychological perspective, and, second, as a team is built, consideration must be given to the interaction of that team. The best quarterback who ever lived will fail if he does not have the offensive line to protect him and the receivers to catch the passes he throws. Many great basketball teams with five all-stars starting have not won because "there were not enough basketballs for all the players." Even in baseball, where there's more individuality than in basketball or football, great teams, loaded with great players, have failed to win the pennant because they were not a "team."

So as we look at building a sales team, we must look not simply at what each person can or can't do, but at how each person fits into the team—and fits into the game plan that the team is supposed to implement.

16

Building from Your Best

While you certainly want to start out by hiring salespeople who have innate ability—that is only the beginning. The real key is to identify those qualities that distinguish your best salespeople from the rest of your salespeople. Then, you can use them as a model for developing your mid-range performers *and* for hiring new people.

Exactly what do your best salespeople have that the rest of your team does not? Are they more conscientious? Or persuasive? Do they follow rules? Or make their own way? Are they able to juggle multiple projects? Or do they prefer completing one task before moving on to another?

Your best employees can actually provide you with a road map for your next hiring decision. By identifying the distinguishing qualities of your best salespeople, you'll know exactly what you are looking for in your next employee.

The Medium-to-Large Company

For a company with a sales force of 30 or more, we suggest developing an ideal profile of the best employees. The process is actually quite simple. The top salespeople should be assessed for their inherent strengths, limitations, and potential. This number of assessments could be as few as 10, but usually does not need to exceed 50, even for the largest of sales forces. What is important is that the group labeled "top" consist of genuinely superior performers, based on objective performance criteria. The process begins to fail if the "top" invades too much of the middle group.

The idea is to develop a composite profile of the personality strengths and motivations of this top group. In other words, the group is combined statistically as though it is one individual; thus, that top group might average, for example, in the 70th percentile of ego-drive, the 85th percentile of empathy, etc. It would also provide mean scores for between 30 and 40 other qualities beyond the central sales characteristics. Thus, for example, one company might see its top-producing salespeople being in the 83rd percentile of urgency, while another in a different sales situation might see its urgency mean score at the 50th percentile level. The differences in sales situations create the differences required for each characteristic.

At the same time that the profile of the top producers is developed, a similar number of marginal producers should be assessed. Then the two composites—the top and marginal—can be compared. The result of this comparison is usually quite telling, highlighting the key qualities that sharply distinguish one group from the other. For example, the top-producing group having a mean of 85 for urgency might be compared with the marginal group whose urgency is at the 33rd percentile level. This difference then points to one critical characteristic beyond the key five that should be looked at in making a hiring decision. The hiring manager in this case would want to think long and hard the next time an attractive candidate was interviewed who was low on urgency—if this quality is determined to be a key factor for success in this particular sales job.

This exercise allows management to do two things: First, if psychological testing, or a similar assessment technique is used, it allows management to compare an applicant's assessment with the top-group profile to determine how closely his or her profile matches the ideal. This will provide a clear picture of whether an applicant who interviews well truly matches the job. The second benefit of this approach is that it allows management to see where the deficiencies are in the marginal performers—and start to bridge those gaps with very targeted training and coaching.

A vice president of sales at a major car rental company had a composite profile developed of his most successful salespeople and discovered, as he says, that "the make-or-break quality for succeeding with us is the ability to listen closely enough." He adds, "While salespeople have been glibly described as having golden tongues, we have found that our very best salespeople have golden ears. What we need to know is whether a promising applicant is empathic enough to be able to truly listen and understand where our prospects are coming from."

And the training development coordinator for a major graphic communications company in the Chicago area, who has adopted this approach to hiring and developing employees, says, "I now look for five qualities in new employees: attitude, attitude, attitude, attitude, and then skill."

We've found that the distinguishing qualities of our best employees are centered around their personalities—who they are. We used to judge applicants primarily on their skill set. But we've found that the people who succeed for us—managers, salespeople, artists, and craftspeople—are all team players. They have to be open to one another's suggestions, to listen well and be very flexible. You can always provide technical training. But the ability to think outside the box, to handle chaos and like it, and to juggle many projects is something that is part of someone's personality. Those aren't the kinds of things we can teach. So that's the profile we look for now whenever we're hiring. It may take more patience and training to bring someone up to speed. But in the long run, we've found it's definitely worth it.

The Smaller Company

Obviously, far more companies fall into the smaller size category. It is only marginally useful for a company with six salespeople to attempt a benchmark using their top two people. The exercise could be interesting, but is likely to produce erroneous results, because two employees are simply not enough of a sample to be valuable from a statistical perspective. What then can the smaller company do?

First, it would be useful to assess the sales force both as a means of upgrading individual productivity and as a way to get a sense of the team's overall strengths and limitations.

In hiring for smaller companies, however, we feel it is most appropriate for them to use industry norms as the benchmark for judging promising applicants. Clearly this cannot be as customized and well targeted as it is when a company can use its own personnel as that benchmark. However, comparing an applicant to industry norms provides a far better and more precise criterion than simply depending on the five sales dynamics.

The following is an example of how an industry composite might look. Some actual industry composites can be found in the chapters devoted to specific industries later in this book. This composite presented here is the result of a study conducted in conjunction with *Sales and Marketing Management* in which 189 companies assessed 208 individuals whom they identified as their very best salespeople. This composite can actually be seen as an across-industry standard for top salespeople. But again, we caution the reader that there are certainly differences to be found within industries and within specific companies. More precision will be found by developing your own corporate benchmark or even utilizing a benchmark for your particular industry. Failing either of these possibilities, the benchmark shown in Figure 16-1 can provide some guidance, particularly if you are looking for more of the classic hunter-type salesperson.

Even as this benchmark approach is utilized, it must be understood that trade-offs will continue to be necessary. As a practical matter, it is often difficult to find enough candidates who match your ideal profile, who possess the highest level of every key quality you are seeking. However, the ideal profile can serve as your road map for future hiring. It will allow you to make informed decisions about which trade-offs in a particular candidate

Top Salesperson Benchmark

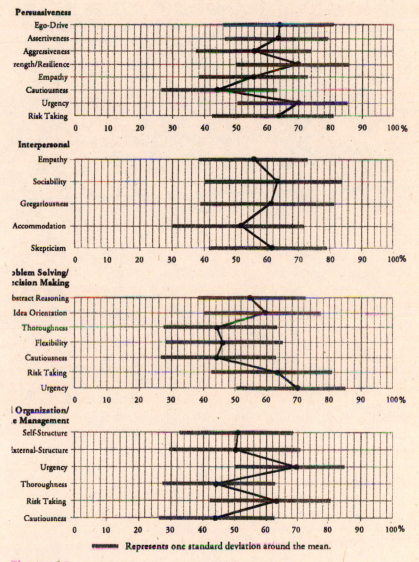

 Represents one standard deviation around the mean.

Figure 16-1

might be acceptable, and what kind of training or coaching would be appropriate to address any particular weaknesses—from the beginning.

Thus while some compromises will inevitably have to be made, the overall result of this approach is most likely to be a substantial increase in the hiring batting average, with a resulting sales force that more closely approaches the ideal—more closely represents the composite of the top producers.

17

The Marginal Producer

Salespeople, broadly speaking, fall into three categories. There are those precious few—typically the 20 percent of a firm's salespeople that are highly productive—that sell 80 percent of what is sold. These individuals have precisely what it takes to sell in their particular sales situation. They can sense the desires of a prospect, are driven by a need to persuade, and can bounce back from the rejection that is an inevitable part of their work. They have enough service motivation to meet the requirements of their job, are conscientious enough to make sure that all their clients' needs are met, and possess most of the other qualities needed in their unique situation. These top performers sell effectively and need only be managed in a manner related to their key motivations, and not managed or compensated in any way that would demotivate them. These are the superstars of whom managers will say, "I just point them in the right direction."

At the other end of the spectrum are those who fundamentally lack the dynamics to sell or the particular personality attributes required to sell their particular product or service. In all likelihood, these people derive no pleasure from closing a sale, or if they do, they lack the qualities needed in their specific sales situation. Since you cannot make someone want to sell or feel the gratification that a real salesperson would obtain from successfully closing a sale, it is very unlikely that there is much that can be done to develop this group. Our approach is to ascertain their real basic occupational motivations and, if possible, place them in more appropriate positions within the company, since, after all, they do know the company and its products. If it is at all possible, it is preferable to salvage the company's investment in them by placing them in a more productive position. In addition, it is obvious that there is a valuable morale factor if this kind of job crossover can occur.

The second action to be taken, where the above is not appropriate or possible, is to replace members of this group as quickly as possible with appropriate and productive new hires.

It is the middle group in most sales teams into which most salespeople fall. This is the most difficult group to deal with. They produce sales, but not with consistently high performance; they are simply not up to par. Management has already invested time, money, and effort in them, so it is important to try to make that investment pay off. The important issue is knowing which specific strategy might be designed for them individually to allow them to produce at a higher level, if, indeed, they possess the potential to do so.

There is obviously no single solution or formula. Analyzing each person's strengths and weaknesses within a group and separating the overall group into subgroups with similar weaknesses is the first step in determining management strategies to overcome these limitations. What we typically have found is that one group will need assistance in closing techniques; more often than not, this group can greatly benefit from formal assertiveness training. Another group that is not totally lacking in empathy, but is extremely impatient, can be greatly helped by attending a listening skills workshop. Another group may have less than average ability in the area of personal organization. Acquiring tools that will assist these individuals in time management and improve their overall self-starting ability might be all they need to function more productively.

The list could go on, but these examples should be sufficient to make the point. Often, these middling producers (people who are just good enough not to be fired, but not really productive enough to meet the needs of the company) can be helped enormously by focusing on one area of weakness and, through targeted training and supervision, helping them work through that weakness so they perform at a substantially higher level. A batter in a slump takes extra batting practice. A basketball player who does not shoot foul shots well works with coaches to improve technique and practices foul shooting. In the same way, the salesperson dragged down by one weakness can be helped by working to improve that specific area.

Let us examine why some people, given proper management and training, can succeed, while others, under the same circumstances, will turn up empty-handed. Marginal, as we will see, turns out to be a very big word.

The key factor is to determine whether an individual's marginal performance relates to his or her fundamental lack of appropriate dynamics or whether it is limited by some particular personality factor that can be corrected. We must also determine whether outside factors might be working to lower productivity in relation to his or her real potential. Let us look at three cases from our files, which exemplify this point.

We assessed the sales potential of a young man (we will call him Phillip) who was working for a large manufacturing company. He had great references, he had impressed the management of the company in the initial interview, and he had scored well on our test. Yet with all that going for him, and after a good start making three important sales in the first month, he had sunk into a 6-month slump.

The vice president of sales was perplexed. She asked us to review all the facts to see whether there was a better solution than terminating Phillip, who had seemed so ideal at first.

Psychological testing indicated that Phillip possessed very strong sales dynamics. He was empathic, enjoyed persuading, and could deal with rejection. However, he had a strong need for approval, particularly from authority figures.

Realizing that, we assessed Phillip's manager. When the personality profiles were placed side by side, the problem became apparent. The manager, who had come up from sales herself, was a hard-driving, extremely aggressive, assertive individual, with adequate empathy. She was an individualist. When dealing with salespeople, her tendency was to leave them alone unless there was an obvious problem or concern that required her attention. She was from the school that believed that performance tells the story. "When I was in sales," she told us, "the last thing I wanted was to have a manager looking over my shoulder."

The problem, as it turned out, was not with the manager, because, after all, she had sold successfully and, in fact, managed a rather productive sales force. Nor was the problem with Phillip, the salesperson, who had the ability to sell. Rather, the problem related to the chemistry between manager and salesperson.

Had the company been small, we would have suggested that the manager try to provide more approval, guidance, and ongoing support to help relate better to Phillip and improve his performance. Of course, it is difficult to reprogram one's particular management approach and technique, but when possible, behavioral modifications should be made to improve overall effectiveness.

Since the company had offices in other locations, however, a better suggestion was that Phillip be shifted to another office whose manager was the type who characteristically functioned in a more supportive, caring way. The shift resulted in an almost immediate turnaround for Phillip, and today he is functioning at the level of production that was expected of him initially. By altering the outside factor—the management approach as related to Phillip's needs—productivity was substantially improved.

The problem with Holly, a real estate salesperson, was much simpler to solve. She, like Phillip, had tremendous sales dynamics but was clearly not performing well after having been promoted to a position that called for selling commercial real estate. Interestingly, when management first reviewed her application and psychological assessment, she was not considered for that particular target market. However, after having succeeded at selling moderately priced homes, she asked to be promoted and, fearing the company might lose her to a competitor, management complied. She was promoted to a position that called for selling commercial properties.

Holly was impatient, highly driven, somewhat disorganized, and desperately in need of instant gratification. She was a classic short-term, goal-oriented individual who wanted quick and frequent closes. As a result, she simply lacked the patience for long-term follow-up and service. Obviously, with commercial properties, long-term follow-up and service are as critical to success as the ability to sell. Thus, the job that she was promoted to because of her strong sales ability was precisely the wrong job for her.

At our suggestion, the manager decided to move her into a listing responsibility. Selling listings involves the need for a strong close and the kind of immediate yes or no response that Holly's drive and impatience demanded. Listing therefore made for an ideal job match. The move was made, again with excellent results.

As a footnote, we should mention that management had been rightly concerned that Holly might consider the suggested shift a demotion since the new position did not carry the prestige of commercial sales. However, the manager had emphasized that many of the listings Holly would be securing might be highly prestigious commercial properties or estate homes. The manager explained that the only difference would be securing the listing for the company, as opposed to going through the long, agonizing process of following up. By describing the move in that way, the manager was able to tap into Holly's basic personality attributes and so was able to save an otherwise losing situation.

The final example relates to Sally, a salesperson for a printing firm, who, unlike Phillip and Holly, was performing adequately. The problem was that she was performing just adequately. Her manager felt strongly that, given her presentation, appearance, knowledge of printing, and overall manner, her performance should have been near the top of the sales force.

Her good qualities included empathy and the drive to sell effectively, as well as time management skills, excellent service motivation, and the attention to detail and sense of responsibility necessary to follow up and to provide the kind of expertise often required in printing sales. However, she needed approval and was unassertive. She would sometimes hesitate to push strongly enough for the close lest she incur disapproval. Whenever there was some resistance to a possible sale, her tendency was to back off a bit too soon.

Of course, no salesperson, particularly in the printing industry, should be overly pushy or aggressive. Yet there are times when an effective salesperson senses that the prospect is on the verge of making a decision and needs only the slightest push in the right direction. However, when such an opportunity would present itself, Sally's tendency was not to risk that slight push.

The sales she made, therefore, were the automatic ones—jobs that sold themselves or called for only the least bit of soft persuasion. Far too many sales were slipping through her fingers because of her unwillingness to be assertive at the right time.

She attended an assertiveness training program and a few counseling sessions dealing with her reluctance to risk rejection. The combination proved effective. Although she is still not selling at the very top level of the sales force, she has moved from below average to well above average, and her manager feels that growth will continue.

After gaining an understanding of the key strengths and key weaknesses of these three marginal producers, management was able to substantially upgrade their production by taking actions relating to these strengths and weaknesses. Phillip needed only to be placed under a manager whose style played more effectively to his needs. Holly's job responsibilities had to be shifted from one involving patience and follow-through (of which she was constitutionally incapable) to one playing to her specific strength: assertive, highly persuasive closings. Sally simply needed some assertiveness training and counseling to overcome a particular weakness, thus freeing her to be far more productive.

By understanding the particular qualities of marginal producers, management can frequently upgrade their performance by making modifications that are sometimes far simpler than the examples we have just presented. We have seen situations in which simply attending a one-day time planning workshop, or having a manager slightly modify his or her approach, or building in a modest incentive program can make all the difference in the world. Sometimes these small modifications can literally convert a salesperson skating on the edge of termination into a highly productive contributor.

The key in all these situations is whether the individual is marginal because of one or another correctable situation or whether the problem is that the individual is basically not suited to the position. In the former case, management will benefit by making every effort to make those corrections, as in the three cases we presented. However, in the latter case, as painful as it may be, it is better for management, and in the long run better for the employee, to make whatever changes are necessary - but not to allow that unsuitable employee to continue frustrating himself or herself and the company through unproductive performance.

18

Training and Compensating to Achieve Maximum Productivity

At a recent corporate management meeting, tension was palpable. The company's president was angry, and it was clear that someone was about to catch hell.

"The sales training program you endorsed fell flat on its face," he said to his top sales executives, "and these charts prove it."

Sales charts were flashed onto the slide screen, and the president was in no way disposed toward understatement in pointing out the source of his displeasure. Despite an extensive and costly countrywide sales training program for which salespeople had been taken out of the field for a full 3 days, the charts showed only a modest initial sales increase, which almost immediately fell to the original base figure.

While the sales vice president and the regional sales managers squirmed, the president noted the high costs, both direct and indirect, of the training program, and demanded an explanation: "It's obvious that the training failed. Now I want to know why."

As is typical in situations such as this, both the sales training team and the sales training approach were blamed, but no one doubted that the fault lay somewhere between the trainers themselves and the training curriculum they were using. The automatic assumption, however, that the fault lies with trainers and/or the training program is simplistic and, as often as not, simply wrong. In fact, in many instances, the fault lies elsewhere; it lies with the sales trainees.

Over the years, we have discussed this problem with many top professional trainers, and most agree that, all too often, valid training programs fail because they are expected to train people who are simply not capable of doing the work. Most of these pros will affirm that sales training often ignores the most basic reality not only of selling, but of human personality as well: People cannot be trained to do what they are fundamentally not suited to do. Attempting to make someone do what he or she is not capable of doing will only result in frustration and failure.

Indisputably, every salesperson can benefit from appropriate sales training. The person who is new to selling—the young man or woman in a first job or the converted schoolteacher, farmer, or mechanic—must be oriented to the business of selling and given insights into some of its techniques and requirements, regardless of the person's inherent abilities. Experienced salespeople can benefit from more advanced training in areas such as the development of proposals and presentation skills. There is a continuing need in many businesses for ongoing product training, particularly now, when rapid change is the norm, not the exception. This training can range from a basic review of product features on simple product lines to detailed scientific indoctrination in advanced technological equipment. In addition, training must precede the introduction of new products into the marketplace.

There is, then, an important place for several varieties of sales training. And with the large investments that companies make to build and maintain their sales forces, there are invariably large amounts of money riding on the outcome of sales training programs.

But when these training programs do not produce the expected results, there is a predisposition to characterize trainers and sales training programs as failures. The truth of the matter is that they are often given the impossible task of making silk purses out of sows' ears.

We are convinced that training can succeed only if selection succeeds. Good raw silk must be provided before the training department or consultants can be expected to produce a purse of the requisite quality.

Appropriate training can make the inherently successful salesperson more productive. But people devoid of sales potential—for example, rigid, opinionated, and unempathic individuals—rarely respond to training, no matter how thorough and scientifically valid the training may be. People lacking ego-drive, those individuals who gain no personal gratification from the sales process or from closing a sale, are not likely to respond to sales training because the sales process is too much of an effort and they do not enjoy the work. They may go through the motions prescribed by the trainers, but the long-term results are likely to be nil. In addition to attempting to train people who lack basic sales dynamics and so should not be trained, many otherwise excellent training programs fail because they attempt to provide exactly the same training to an entire group with little or no recognition of individual differences.

Effective training involves the recognition that no two people operate in precisely the same way. The salesperson who is extremely impulsive and ego-driven needs little urging, through training or otherwise, to push for a close. His or her training should more appropriately stress the best techniques for listening and for acquiring insights into the customer's needs and point of view.

In a training class, however, the individual seated near this impulsive, driven salesperson may very well be in need of help in closing sales. He or she may be extraordinarily empathic when relating to prospective customers but somewhat too hesitant to move toward a close. The training for these two distinct people must obviously have different emphases. The important point here is that training that does not recognize these individual differences and provide for them will fail one person or the other, or both.

A genuinely successful training program for 25 people must, in effect, be 25 separate training programs proceeding simultaneously. Only this approach can show each person how to operate to his or her fullest potential and in accordance with his or her own personality makeup. But even here each of those 25 persons had better have at least some potential to do the job for which he or she is being trained.

While, at first, this approach might appear to be an outline for chaos in the training room, the results can be dramatic. Such a program does, however, require somewhat more careful preparation than is usual and certainly precludes the purely canned training program. With knowledge of the specific makeup of the group in terms of both experiential and personality factors, trainers can design role plays and other targeted exercises.

These specific learning exercises can be configured to deal with the specific strengths, weaknesses, and motivations of the individuals within the training group. If training is to be effective, it must be geared to the individual as opposed to providing an approach that supposedly covers everyone in one fell swoop.

In addition, skilled professional trainers, whether on company staff or retained to carry out a specific training project, must acquire knowledge of the company's products, marketing approaches, and support systems. Only then can the training be geared to the individual in terms of personal qualities, as well as to the job function that person must carry out.

If an outside training firm is to be effective, it must overcome the concern that it characteristically works across a broad spectrum of business and industry. The team training mutual funds sales representatives this week may be training salespeople from a light machinery manufacturing firm next week and software salespeople the following week. There are certain similarities among selling jobs, but problems differ so vastly from one industry to another and, in fact, from one company within an industry to another that a realistic grasp of the sales situation within the specific company by the trainer is a vital prerequisite for maximally effective training. This grasp can best be attained by the trainers spending several days in the field with salespeople and their sales managers, experiencing the selling firsthand, seeing sales resistance, and developing successful responses to that resistance.

The foregoing is not to imply that in-house training programs are superior to those of outside firms, even though the former may have a better initial grasp of a company's sales situation. Very often as a practical matter, because of the size of the company or the infrequency with which training programs are needed, a full-time, in-house training staff may not be advisable or even possible. Our advice, simply, is that an outside training firm, when retained, should be as aware of the specific company's situation as would an in-house training operation. The best training firms are perfectly capable of reaching this goal.

With a prior evaluation of each person to be trained, and with a thorough, firsthand study of the field sales requirements, the training group is ready to put the program together and proceed. However, there remains the problem of personalizing the training for each salesperson. This can be handled by structuring a training format that allocates minimum time to lectures and maximum time to a combination of intensive individual counseling and group sessions, both small and large.

The individual evaluations are used to structure groups. Individuals possessing intense ego-drive may be put together in a group, while other individuals needing help with personal organization might be doing other exercises. A group might be made up of ego-driven people and individuals with less ego-drive but outstanding listening skills. In short, prior knowledge of the dynamics of the individuals in the training group allows the trainers to use the strengths and weaknesses of those individuals as a key part of the training process. It allows for the most ideal training situation, where the trainees will be working to train each other through participating in joint activities.

Admittedly, the overall approach to training we are describing is more difficult and requires some innovation on the part of the trainers. But it meets the three requirements we consider absolute:

1 It offers a thorough picture of each person's real abilities and personality dynamics.

2 It optimizes, on the basis of this picture, each person's potential.

3 It deals with a "real-world" situation; that is, it trains people to sell their particular products in their particular markets, taking into consideration their particular sales problems, in terms of their particular personalities.

There is no single best way to sell to which all can conform. There are no perfect formulas, no magic words that apply to all men and women equally, any more than there is one single way in which all pitchers should throw baseballs or all batters should hit them.

Training should be seen as an approach to help salespeople maximize their own abilities in their own way. Forcing them into another mold simply does not work, and if anything, it helps to guarantee failure for a person who may have enormous natural potential.

Compensating the Salesperson

Compensation as a sales motivator has been explored, scrutinized, pondered, and analyzed by experts countless times. No reasonably good business library fails to yield innumerable books detailing the "best methods" of sales force compensation. This embarrassment of riches turns out to be of dubious value. A sales force is composed of individual human beings with broadly varying needs, points of view, self-perceptions, and psychological characteristics who cannot be infallibly categorized, measured, and punched out according to set formula. It therefore follows that there is no one best plan for compensating all of them.

It is safe to make only one generalization about compensation: The program that motivates best, or, perhaps even better put, that does not serve to demotivate, is one that is geared to the specific needs of each person. For example, a highly ego-driven salesperson with inordinate self-confidence is likely to be most acutely motivated by a compensation system based on incentives, that is, one that offers little base in the form of draw or salary, but that has a steeply graduated top end; this individual would be demotivated and frustrated by a program limiting top-end potential even if it provided for more security. On the other hand, such a commission-oriented program can be inappropriate (and, in fact, may have a reverse motivational impact) for a person with less confidence and ego-drive. In all probability, he or she will respond more positively to the higher draw or salary base that his or her associate might find unappealing.

Obviously, one compensation plan cannot have equal motivational effects on both of these individuals. So why not introduce a flexible plan that provides both individuals with the kind of compensation to which each will respond best? Clearly, many firms, particularly smaller firms, cannot, as a practical matter, have a number of compensation plans—a different one for each salesperson. Yet even in these situations, some creativity and imagination could cause subtle differences within basically similar plans to produce a positive impact on individuals. A number of our clients, including some relatively small companies, have prepared three or four plans. They sat down and worked with individual salespeople to select the plan with which they were most comfortable. In a small company, where people tend to know each other's business, there is the danger of jealousy when an individual under one compensation plan outearns someone working under a different plan. However, if an open discussion was held and the individual voluntarily chose his or her plan with all the facts (including the earnings potential and the security) laid out, that jealousy would be less likely to occur.

What we are suggesting here, just as we did in our discussion on training, is a far more difficult approach to implement. It is certainly easier to set up one unified compensation plan that covers the entire sales force, whether a company develops a compensation program itself or brings in outside experts to help. Yet as tempting as taking this easier road may be, thought should be given to how much is invested in the sales force and how critical maximum sales productivity is to the success of the company. Thus, if, with a little more effort and a little more creativity, compensation plans can be created to help maximize the productivity of each salesperson, isn't that extra work well worth it? A compensation plan that speaks to each individual's motivations not only will enhance productivity, but can play an important role in substantially increasing the retention of the most productive salespeople.

Another aspect of compensation that should be touched on is the fact that salespeople, regardless of their personality dynamics, are not totally immune to the lure of the "golden handcuffs." An attractive pension and retirement package, profit-sharing program, and frequent bonuses help to develop an identification with the company, a feeling within the salespeople that they are in fact part of a team. We have found that the more an individual feels a sense of participation in the overall success of the firm, the more he or she will be motivated to contribute to that success. This applies to the full range of sales personalities. Security-oriented individuals like bonuses and profit-sharing potential because they can get side benefits without having to run the risks inherent in straight-commission sales. To commission-oriented salespeople, bonuses and profit sharing provide more opportunities to share in the big money and, in addition, enable them to feel that they are working for themselves, which is often the real desire of hard-driving salespeople.

Before completing our discussion of compensation, we want to stress this point: As important as money is, and as potentially valuable or inhibiting a compensation plan can be, the key to sales success still remains whether the individual possesses the basic dynamics or motivations and whether he or she has the other requirements necessary to sell successfully in a specific sales job. It is that inner motivation that drives the salesperson to the next prospect and propels him or her out the door the next morning. Money helps the successful salesperson keep score. Like a medal in the military, a trip to Hawaii, a pat on the back, or number one ranking on the sales chart—money is a symbol of success. But it is the inner motivation, the desire to get the yes and the emotional gratification that closing brings, which is the force behind the real salesperson's performance.

Obviously, no one can live on emotional gratification alone, but as we have suggested in these pages, it is critical that the financial rewards be tied closely with the kind of emotional gratification the individual requires.

In concluding this discussion of training and compensation, it is important to reemphasize the fundamental point that the key to an individual's sales success is the attributes and motivations that exist within the individual. Training will fail if it is not geared to helping a person play to his or her unique strengths and overcome specific weaknesses. In the same way, compensation will fail if it does not enhance each person's unique attributes. Only with this kind of individualized approach can training and compensation achieve what they are designed to do—enhance, not inhibit, performance.

19

Non-Traditional Sources of Sales Talent

Despite all that has been said about the importance of maximizing the productivity of a company's existing team, there is a point when hiring must be undertaken to meet corporate goals. On the negative side, if too many people are simply inappropriate to do a company's sales job and either leave on their own or are terminated, some of these people will have to be replaced. On the positive side, the company may be growing and markets may be opening to the degree that additional people are needed to get the job done. Even here, an understanding of a company's existing personnel could provide one of the best sources for new talent before going through the time, expense, and risk of hiring from the outside. Many of our insurance agency clients find their new producers from among their secretaries, underwriters, or customer service representatives. Likewise, many auto dealers we work with are able to find excellent service writers among their mechanics. Many production people in printing firms, given the opportunity, have proved to be the company's best salespeople. Some of our largest clients have been able to recruit top salespeople from their accounting departments, engineers, and even factory personnel.

One case may serve to illustrate this point. An insurance company asked us to evaluate an employee—let's call him "Fred"—who was an actuary for the company. He was a 20-year employee, but was simply not performing at a level that would allow the company to keep him on despite the fact that he was loyal, hardworking, and extremely popular. The company wanted him tested prior to terminating him essentially to be kind and so that it could make some outplacement suggestions.

When we evaluated Fred's test, we were totally amazed that he was able to survive as an actuary for as long as he did. He disliked detail and found routine difficult. On the positive side, he possessed intense ego-drive, phenomenal empathy, and solid ego-strength. While he lacked strong self-discipline, he did possess service motivation, was assertive enough to ask for an order, and possessed the sense of urgency that would drive him to get things done in a timely way. Simply put, from a psychological perspective, Fred was absolutely not an actuary. Instead, he possessed the sales potential of a member of a million-dollar round table.

When we presented this report to the management staff members, they were totally incredulous. They indicated that while he was certainly social and pleasant to be with, he never manifested the strong, outgoing nature stereotypical of the salesperson. When, however, they provided feedback to Fred, he revealed that he had wanted to sell all his life, and that he was selling a health care product on the side—a multilevel marketing situation and, in fact, was doing fairly well at it.

This story, unlike so many others, has a happy ending. Fred entered training, earned his life insurance license and within a year was, indeed, a member of the million-dollar round table. He, of course, started with an enormous knowledge of the industry, so all he had to do was learn a few sales techniques and exploit those core strengths that were buried in the actuarial role.

We could literally recite dozens of similar cases, but Fred's story should suffice to make the point. There is golden potential within a company's personnel, and much can be gained by assessing that potential and fully tapping it.

So before turning to the outside, a company should take a hard look at its existing people to see if some of its employees, who may be performing in non-sales jobs not fully suited to their abilities, might not be the best available candidates to fill any new sales job openings. Obviously, the advantage to the company of knowing the individual and his or her work habits and having the individual know the company is enormous. This does not even include the morale factor to be gained by giving people an opportunity to better themselves within the company.

Whether recruiting from within a company or turning to the outside for new salespeople, a thorough knowledge of the existing sales team is critical to the success of the recruiting and selection process. Both the way a prospective salesperson's personality fits into the climate of the existing sales force, and the chemistry between the manager and the potential salesperson are factors that are as important to effective hiring as matching the personality to the job itself. Only by knowing the manager's dynamics and taking into account the dynamics of the entire team can the right hiring decision be made.

After companies have done everything in their power to maximize the productivity of their existing sales team and to recruit sales talent from within their own company, there will invariably come a time when external recruitment of the sales talent is required. To use the sports analogy one more time, while a team can improve markedly through good coaching, practice, and team spirit, very often one or more additional players obtained through the draft or in a trade will turn an average team into a champion. The success of the team often depends a great deal on the effectiveness of draft choices. There are entire franchises that somehow avoid drafting superstars, while others have the Midas touch, selecting superstars from small schools in the tenth round.

The business of recruiting and selecting for industry is quite similar. Companies that make selections from good sources of talent will build their winning team, while the others will perpetuate their mediocrity. As a start, let us look at the sources of sales talent, and then, in later chapters, we shall discuss the process by which recruits can be selected and turned into effective producers.

It is difficult to explain why the abundance of sales potential surrounding every sales executive so often goes undetected, particularly since the sales and marketing profession is in most other ways one of the most creative, inventive, and progressive elements in today's business community; and it has the tools and methodologies available to find and cultivate the required people if it would but use them.

Sales managers and personnel directors work very hard to recruit salespeople. But rarely do they consistently find and hire genuinely successful sales personnel. Obvious sources of good people frequently are ignored, while an incredibly large proportion of recruiting energy and dollars are misguidedly spent elsewhere.

Earlier on, we said that more than half of the people now working in sales jobs should not be so employed. This incredible statistic tells us that the average company wastes well over half of the dollars it spends on recruiting, selecting, and training its sales force. This amounts to billions of dollars annually.

What makes this all the more remarkable is that while companies spend billions in vain attempts to create salespeople, they ignore an enormous, but essentially untapped, reservoir of genuine sales talent around them.

In evaluating the widest variety of population segments in this country, we have discovered that one out of every four people has more inherent ability to sell than well over one half of the people currently attempting to earn their living in sales. Statistically, what this means is that if the entire population, regardless of what they are currently doing, was used as an enormous source of sales talent, with proper selection, one out of four of these people would be found to have excellent sales potential.

So much of the failure in recruiting results from companies searching for sales talent in the wrong places. Companies continue to attempt to attract and steal salespeople from their competitors, feeling that the experience factor will place them way ahead of the game. However, when one accepts the statistical fact that 80 percent of the salespeople attempting to sell today either are in the wrong job or are attempting to sell the wrong product or service, then one quickly realizes that this attempt is doomed to fail. Companies that steal from their competitors are luring away someone who may very well not have been successful in the competing company, but will probably not be successful for them. After all, why would a successful person with seniority and experience leave the company? Of course, the individual never blames himself or herself for the lack of success; he or she uses all the old familiar excuses of failure— the manager I worked for was not a professional; the company's compensation plan was not equitable; etc.

This point was brought home to us when a large manufacturing firm retained us to evaluate its 300-plus sales force for four of its divisions. Our finding was that less than 10 percent of the salespeople we assessed had potential for selling in their current jobs. When we reported our findings to the firm's management, we were surprised that the results shocked us more than they shocked the management staff. They had known for some time that something was radically wrong, but they did not know what is was or how to cure it. They asked us to uncover the reasons for their extremely poor recruiting and selection results.

We found that their problems lay in (1) their recruiting sources, (2) their hiring criteria, and (3) their random assignment of people to sell specific products. Since then, we have found that this pattern is hardly atypical of many companies.

Salespeople recruited by this firm were primarily from closely related businesses. They had an ongoing aggressive effort to pirate salespeople from competitive firms, often through enticing them with escalated salaries. This method provided the company with a continuing flow of "experienced" salespeople. Rarely, however, did these experienced people prove to be top-level performers. Although it is true that they started out better than novices, and they certainly required less product training, more often than not, they leveled off at a mediocre plateau after a short time and remained there.

In examining this pirated group, it became quite clear that over 80 percent lacked the critical characteristics to be successful in sales. The result of recruiting "experienced" salespeople was to build failure into the recruiting process.

A second source of talent from which the company recruited was recent graduates from engineering colleges. Only individuals who placed in the top quarter of their classes were considered.

Upon interviewing the salespeople who were recruited in this manner, we discovered that, in essence, the job had been misrepresented to them. Most of them had never previously considered selling as a career, but were persuaded to join the company when told that sales was the best stepping-stone to management and that they would not be selling in any real sense, but, rather, providing technical service and consultation to customers. Thus, people who by predisposition and training were set to be engineers were almost deceived into taking sales positions. It was not surprising to find that the majority of the graduates did not like or want to sell, and that most lacked the raw ability to do so even if they wanted to. It was readily apparent to us that this recruiting procedure could hardly be expected to produce a dynamic crop of highly motivated and successful salespeople.

In analyzing this college recruitment program, we wondered why only the top quarter of the class was eligible for consideration. No executive could give us a reasoned answer. We asked whether individuals with C+ graduating averages from the same schools would not have enough engineering knowledge to sell the products, and the answer was that they would.

We then had our next reasons for recruiting failure.

Paradoxically, the individuals they were recruiting on campuses were the least likely to be top salespeople. They were literally tapping the worst possible source of sales talent. Typically, those who excel in scientific subjects—those with an unusually high degree of technical orientation—are not "people-oriented" (for lack of a better term). This type of graduate is generally more interested in pursuing research and development activities than in dealing with people. Scientists are inclined to regard sales as an activity somewhat beneath their dignity. The engineer or scientist who does slip into sales usually becomes dissatisfied and is an early candidate for resignation or dismissal.

We are certainly not saying that among these top-grade recipients there are no individuals who have sales ability or who indeed should be selling. Those individuals certainly do exist, and we have evaluated and met a number of them. We are emphasizing, however, the fact that, from a statistical point of view, limiting a company's recruitment to this source of sales talent unnecessarily reduces that source and actually focuses on a pool of talent that is more likely to produce lower numbers of successful sales candidates.

A company selling technical products should, by all means, seek technically educated people to represent it. However, logic and experience dictate seeking those performing in the middle of the graduating class. The reason: A person's grades below the first quartile may not reflect less intelligence or understanding of engineering, but it may reflect the kind of personality that goes toward making an excellent salesperson. Such students may have lower grades because they diverted their attention from books to a wide range of extracurricular activities, often at the expense of the top scholastic rating they might otherwise have easily earned.

Technical expertise and understanding are highly desirable in certain kinds of selling. However, sales ability is still more important, and this cannot be taught, whereas product knowledge can. A more valid approach in this type of recruiting is to ask not how much the potential salesperson knows, but how much he or she really has to know in order to sell the product.

The third problem this company had in its overall selection and recruiting process proved more difficult to pinpoint. But finally, after considerable digging, we found that the problem was a failure to "job-match."

In the past, little thought had been given to which individual, once recruited, should be placed in which sales situation. It was usually assumed that a salesperson should start with the smaller products division and work his or her way up to selling in the large-contract division. In looking at the salespeople in the two divisions, we found that at least half of each group would be more effective selling in the other. For example, many possessing the strong ego-drive needed for fast, frequent closes were trapped in selling large-contract orders to the government, where the most sales they could hope to close would be a few each year. Others possessing the patience to handle and enjoy the long-term sales situation were trying without success to compete in the hard-closing, highly competitive small-products field. Once we uncovered this problem, we recommended (1) massive switching of job assignments and (2) careful matching of people to jobs in the future.

That was our final major recommendation. Quite naturally, the firm's management required some convincing when we pointed out the three principal error factors we had uncovered, particularly since the first two had always appeared to be real virtues in recruiting and, in addition, were long-standing and well-accepted practices in the field. However, after we had documented our conclusions, the company's recruiting procedures began to change. Over the next several years, the firm assembled one of the finest and most effective sales organization of any its size in the industry.

It should be emphasized that the error factors in recruiting stemming from tapping the wrong source of talent are in no way an isolated phenomenon. Actually, the mistakes the firm had been making were much less obvious than in many other firms. In fact, by seeking talent in very limited areas, a great many business executives with hiring responsibilities appear to turn their backs on the very people they are seeking.

Our experience indicates that the universe of potential salespeople is much greater than most managers realize. An excellent source, for example, is individuals who might now be working in administrative jobs, who may be frustrated and would welcome the opportunity of being in sales. Other hidden talent can be found among the misemployed and the underemployed. For example, capable women returning to work after raising families constitute a huge resource that is all too often overlooked due to industrial reluctance to put women into certain selling jobs. Keep in mind, however, that those industries that have pioneered in hiring female sales talent, such as real estate and insurance, have experienced enormously successful results.

In short, people with sales potential are there, waiting for an opportunity to be productive. What is needed is for recruiting and personnel managers to relax outworn notions about where to find them, how to identify them, and where to mobilize them.

The range of "knockout" factors—that is, the automatic disqualifiers many managers apply to job applicants—never ceases to amaze us. A recruiting manager who laughs at the absurdities of another recruiter's insistence on job experience may automatically eliminate from consideration everyone over 50 and not even bother to see anyone who does not fit his or her preconceived notions about sex, marital status, race, job stability, and education.

What does this cost? It may add up to the difference between success and failure. Our experience shows that a man of 50 may have more open-mindedness and youthful vigor than a man half his age; that women have the same ranges of business talent as men; that race has absolutely nothing to do with ability to sell; that being divorced or single, experienced or inexperienced, or stable or a "job-hopper" are never by themselves reasons for rejecting an applicant.

Printing companies have discovered outstanding salespeople among their factory employees. Dozens of realtors have discovered that file clerks or secretaries in their offices possessed the ability to outsell their salespeople. Machine repairmen have turned out to be top-notch salespeople of the products they repair. Of course, the mere fact that someone repairs a product, or that he or she works in the factory where it is manufactured, does not automatically mean that the person can sell that product. But it is logical to look at talent close to home first, since (1) almost invariably some of this talent exists there, and (2) when you find it, you have the important advantages of product and company familiarity and the morale boost that accompanies promoting from within the organization.

Another source of talent is the tremendous number of underemployed people in business. We had the opportunity to demonstrate this point dramatically in a program we conducted in Canada. We were asked to administer our battery of tests to a wide range of clerical workers and others in non-sales positions. By typical standards, this should be an unlikely population to produce sales talent. Yet afer testing 450 of these people, we found that 187 had real sales ability. Interestingly, this proportion is higher than is typical for the general population.

Of the 187 with sales ability, 175 entered a 4-week sales training program we conducted, covering eight 3-hour sessions and emphasizing personal counseling. At the end of the 4 weeks, we were able to place 152 of the 175 in good sales jobs; and in following up 1 year later, we found that the great majority were still on their jobs and performing well.

All our experience in this area tends to document our contention that recruiting problems diminish or even disappear when recruiters discard false preconceptions about recruiting sources and hiring criteria, substituting instead the only really relevant question: Does he or she have the raw ability to sell?

Postings for sales jobs can be easily found in our local newspapers and on the Internet. There are many, many companies in desperate need of sales talent. Why? One of the major reasons is because they limit their search. There are many people who can excel at sales if only given the chance. It's just a matter of opening our eyes and our minds.

To consider the problem in human terms, we have only to reflect upon the impact on the lives of thousands of people without hope, without dignity, without future, and without sense of fulfillment in normal societal terms. From a thoroughly selfish perspective, as a society we pay a large price, both financially and personally, by perpetuating this unfortunate situation. We cannot emphasize enough that in all our studies over the last three decades, we have found that there are thousands of unemployed people who possess the personality dynamics necessary for successfully filling many sales jobs. Although in the past there have been scattered programs designed to bring this unemployed group into jobs, most programs fail to provide an effective mechanism for real and lasting results. Even to this day, many managers negatively label unemployed people as unmotivated, unskilled, irresponsible, and lazy. The result is that, while hundreds of thousands of sales jobs go unfulfilled, seven times that number of people who could fill them are arbitrarily excluded from consideration.

Meanwhile, because business has failed in so many instances to persuade the unemployed that there are job opportunities for them, fear, lack of confidence, and lack of external qualifications effectively bar many of these individuals from applying for most of these jobs. This unfortunate societal condition is made more painful by the fact that, recognized or not, the same range of abilities exists among the underemployed or unemployed as among any other segment of the population. Among this group one out of every four persons possesses the ability to sell successfully, given the requisite training and product knowledge. However, cultural factors and the communication gap between business and the unemployed keep these potentially successful salespeople out of the sales profession. Most programs established to bridge the gap between those needing jobs filled and those in dire need of jobs have failed, mainly because there was a tendency to place people in jobs without regard to their basic inner motivations. The failure to consider the individual differences in this group stems back to the labeling we discussed earlier and the assumption that this entire group shares an identical personality.

It is small wonder then that the unemployed have been haphazardly placed in programs with resulting turnover rates in excess of 60 percent. Another paradox exists, however, when one considers that the turnover rate that has been accepted for decades by insurance, real estate, and automobile industries is just as high. Yet when the turnover rate occurs in people who were previously unemployed, it is seen as conclusive evidence of a fundamental lack within the group.

In the late 1960s we undertook two major programs, one in Puerto Rico and one in New York City, which provided conclusive evidence that the unemployed and underemployed are an untapped and exceptionally rich source of talent. Suffice it to say that in these two programs, when people's personalities were job-matched to a specific job, people succeeded. Not only did people become highly productive and remain in their jobs, but many were promoted and moved on to managerial positions.

In all, more than 3,000 were placed with some 70 companies; nearly half of them filled sales positions, and the remainder were placed in more than 50 other job categories. And in follow-up after 2 years, it was found that less than 3 percent had been terminated because of the inability to do the job. To reemphasize the importance of this figure, few, if any, of these individuals had sold before or had filled jobs similar to the ones in which they were placed. What they had was the basic ability to do the job in which they were placed, and, of course, they were also given the necessary training in technique and product to do the job.

These programs put our hypothesis "that sales ability exists across the population regardless of what individuals have or have not done in the past" to the test. These programs demonstrated that if the broadest possible source of sales talent is tapped, and effective training techniques are used, highly productive people can be brought into the sales profession in sufficient numbers to fill most, if not all, of the sales openings.

Literally, hundreds of cases could be presented in which individuals totally lacked any of the typical criteria that would encourage management to hire them, and yet given their inherent core strengths, they were able to perform brilliantly. Let us cite just a few in order to hammer home this important point.

In the Puerto Rican project, anyone earning more than $1,800 a year was not eligible. This project was funded by the then existing Office of Economic Opportunity, and was cosponsored by Sales and Marketing International of San Juan.

Maria was a 42-year-old woman whose earnings were well under the required $1,800-a year-figure. Testing indicated that she had sales and even sales management ability, and so she went through 2 weeks of job-readiness training and then entered a sales training program that was conducted by a large mutual fund sales organization. She became the first woman to be licensed to sell mutual funds in Puerto Rico, and 6 months after her initial training, she came back to the program to hire five people to work for her.

The New York program was under the auspices of the National Alliance of Business and was funded by the U.S. Department of Labor. Participating in the program were 52 New York area companies that offered 55 job categories to the so-called hard-core unemployed.

One of these "hard-core unemployed" was a 22-year-old young man from Harlem. The only work he had ever done was some deliveries and other scattered odd jobs. When he was tested, it was discovered, as his counselor put it, "Georgie could sell sand in the Sahara Desert."

The plan was to refer Georgie to a life insurance company that was participating in the program. When he was approached with this idea, he literally laughed and asked, "What's life insurance?" He totally ridiculed the idea of being a salesperson, and particularly of attempting to learn a profession of which he had absolutely no knowledge. It took five counseling sessions to finally get Georgie to laughingly admit that maybe he did have some sales ability. "I guess I do. I guess I can sell."

Georgie went for the interview and was given the job. Now to understand what followed, two premises of life insurance sales must be stated. First, you need a market—Georgie obviously had no market. Second, you cannot sell ordinary life insurance door-to-door. However, Georgie had no other way to do it. The result? Georgie was a member of the million-dollar round table within a year and a half of acquiring his license.

A third example is perhaps closest to Herb Greenberg's heart. A young man—let's call him "Ralph"—fell asleep while taking the test early one morning. There was a fear that drugs were involved, but as it turned out, Ralph had tended bar till 2:00 a.m. that morning and was simply exhausted at 7:30. In any case, his test indicated that he not only had enormous sales potential, but also possessed even better management ability. There was one problem, however. He had a rap sheet, and it was a rather extensive one. There were no violent crimes, but there were enough arrests and even convictions to block him from consideration by most companies. Gimbel's, however, had had some very good experiences with a number of people that we placed with them and took the chance on Ralph. He received 5 promotions in 2 years; like Maria, he hired some people from within the program; and when Herb Greenberg's daughter was born, he received a dozen roses from Ralph with a note saying, "To a new life from a life you saved."

As one other example, let us describe the program conducted for Oppenheimer Management which had nothing to do with sales. Oppenheimer, a financial services organization, was looking for 15 "back-office personnel." It had advertised extensively in Spanish papers, papers aimed at the black community, etc., and found that Wall Street figuratively presented a wall, preventing most inexperienced people from applying for those jobs. We contacted the Department of Welfare, had 68 people referred to us, were able to match 15 of them to Oppenheimer's jobs, and were able to successfully place 30 others in other New York area companies. Recently, the former senior partner of Oppenheimer called and told us that two of the people placed years ago from the Department of Welfare were given a retirement dinner, and were now worth many millions of dollars. Under normal conditions, and using normal criteria, these brilliantly successful people would never have been hired.

Since the welfare reform bill was passed in 1996, we have again become active in the effort to move welfare recipients into the work force. Currently, we're involved in four projects in New Jersey, as well as projects in Los Angeles, and Tacoma (Washington), and several other programs are under consideration. These programs, like the earlier ones, involve a range of jobs offered by employers, the assessment of core strengths of individuals, and the matching of those core strengths to appropriate jobs. As in the earlier programs, it remains clear that when appropriate job matching is done, success on the job is likely regardless of the individual's past experience and regardless of whether or not the individual meets the other stereotypical criteria.

What, then, are the sources of sales talent to which management can turn in its effort to recruit productive people? First, as we emphasized earlier, perhaps the best source of talent (certainly the easiest) is a company's existing personnel. Companies of any size are most likely to have people doing non-sales jobs; and some of them could potentially be highly productive salespeople. Some of them may, in fact, be individuals who are not doing particularly good work in their current position. Their below-par performance may result simply from the fact that they are not currently doing what they are best suited for; if they were in sales, they could be outstanding. Management should look at home first, before expending the time, money, and effort involved in external recruiting.

Another source of talent can involve people working for competitors, but not necessarily in sales roles. Competitors' secretaries, technical people, and production people know the industry and may have sales potential. Thus, while stealing from one's competitor by hiring away salespeople is likely to result in recirculating mediocrity, finding sales potential from another company's mechanics, technicians, or secretaries might indeed prove to be an excellent source of talent.

Women in transition provide another source of untapped talent. Thousands of women may have been secretaries, nurses, or teachers, or may have been doing other work stereotypically assigned to women. They may have married and taken time out to raise families over the past 10 or 20 years and now are ready to return to the work force. Must they return precisely to the jobs they filled earlier? Again, what a woman may have done in the past may or may not be relevant to what she is able to do today. So a woman returning to the work force, whatever her past experience, should be looked at as a source of talent because at least one in four of them will have excellent sales ability.

Another important source of talent is the displaced worker. Thousands of workers are "downsized" or "automated" out of jobs. A man may have been on the General Motors assembly line for 20 years and is now out of work. How do we know that the assembly line was the right job for him? All we do know is that he stayed with it and that he had a sufficiently good work ethic to keep the job for 20 years. Again, there is a one in four chance that this assembly line worker was not well matched to the assembly line job and actually should have been a salesperson all that time. So let's look at the thousands of displaced workers and recruit that one in four to fill some of our sales jobs. The concept here is that regardless of what they've done before, today is the first day of the rest of their lives, and you as a manager may have the opportunity to receive great sales productivity from them for the next 20 years of their lives.

Still another source is older citizens. As we indicated earlier, age is not relevant as a predictor of sales success. Thus, why do we feel a 50- or even 60-year-old person is too old to hire? Isn't there a tremendous advantage in many sales situations of the salesperson presenting a more mature, more dignified image to the prospect? This is only an advantage, of course, if the individual has sales ability. However, wouldn't we rather hire someone at 55 who may give us 10 or 15 years of top productivity as opposed to hiring the 25-year-old who might give us 40 years of mediocrity? There are thousands of older people who would welcome the challenge of a new career, and this is, again, a largely untapped source of talent.

We can go on in this vein citing physically handicapped groups and others, but we'll conclude here by mentioning again welfare recipients. Studies conducted by the President's Welfare to Work Partnership, and very much confirmed by our work, have proved beyond statistical question that welfare recipients properly placed have a lower turnover rate than exists for those persons hired in more traditional ways. Again, we have found beyond question that people with sales ability exist among the welfare population, and looking at that group as a source of talent can only benefit the companies and, of course, our society.

We primarily suggest that the entire population be thought of as a virtually limitless source of productive talent. Rather than arbitrarily establishing knockout procedures or barriers to limit such sources, management should focus on those few qualities that are really and objectively necessary as limiters. If there is a certain level of prior technical knowledge or special education necessary to do a job, then, certainly that factor should be used as an initial screen. In other words, if there is prior knowledge or background necessary that management really cannot provide to an inexperienced applicant, that obviously reduces a company's sources of talent. But only those truly objective requirements should be utilized.

In short, management should try to minimize the reasons for screening out people and emphasize the fact that if an individual has the basic ability, he or she is worth providing all the training necessary to actualize their ability.

20

Recruiting Productive Talent

In Part 3, we described the job-matching approach as an effective alternative to the traditional, tried and untrue selection techniques and criteria that have contributed significantly to high sales turnover and the dreadful fact that only 20 percent of all salespeople are responsible for 80 percent of what is sold. To facilitate successful hiring decisions, it is essential that each step of this job-matching process be completed in a thorough, comprehensive manner. Failure to appropriately address any one step could have a serious negative impact on the quality of the final hiring decision.

These essential steps are the base from which the entire selection process is conducted. Their importance cannot be overemphasized. In order to select the candidate with the greatest likelihood of success in a particular position, the hiring manager must be clear about the specific responsibilities that constitute that job. This sounds simple, but it is often the biggest stumbling block in the entire hiring process.

Job Description

A critical part of analyzing and understanding the job for which people are being recruited is the development of an objective, detailed job description. The job description should avoid statements that are too general and do not relate specifically to a performance outcome. If, for example, an insurance agency is hiring a salesperson, it is not enough to say, "Sales for a property and casualty insurance agency." Rather, the job description should include management's specific expectations. It would be important to indicate that the acquisition of new business is a critical expectation of the job over and above simply retaining and expanding an existing book of business. Some element of performance appraisal—how the new employee will be judged—should also be part of the job description.

If developed correctly, the job description can serve both as a tool allowing management to view applicants more objectively and as an excellent self-screener allowing potential applicants to screen themselves in or out. If applicants have no desire to do what is objectively described in the job description, it is far better that they know this early on rather than go through the long, time-consuming, and expensive selection process only to make that discovery in the end, or worse, to make the discovery after they are on the job.

Profiling Required Competencies

Each task in the job description must be considered in terms of the qualifications and skills objectively required to do the job. It is here that a profile of the individual to be hired should be developed. As with the definition of the job itself, the profile should be both comprehensive and realistic with regard to a company's specific expectations. While it is likely that few, if any, candidates will match the profile in every way, it will serve as a yardstick by which "goodness of fit" or job match can be measured and evaluated. What management should try to do here is to judge the kind of motivations, skills, and personality strengths that are required to do the job as it is understood and described. If, for example, the insurance agency wants an individual who will produce a good deal of new business, accomplishing some of this through outside cold calling, the agency would certainly want to include ego-drive and ego-strength as part of the required profile. If, on the other hand, the agency emphasized internal retention and expansion of business, it might want to deemphasize the level of ego-drive, perhaps not emphasize ego-strength at all, but definitely stress service motivation, detail ability, and sense of responsibility. What we are suggesting is that management should go as far as it can to spell out and describe the kind of individual capable of filling that job.

Other Factors

In addition to profiling the factors objectively required to do the job, other personal factors relating to an individual applicant's suitability to the specific job need to be outlined in order for the most effective job match to occur. A number of these factors can be classified under "chemistry." How the individual's personal chemistry meshes with the chemistry of the team can play as important a role in determining success or failure as the basic match of personality attributes to the job.

One more personal factor should be touched on here—an applicant's career aspirations. Candidates who indicate a strong desire to move up in the organization will not be well suited for a role from which there is little or no upward mobility. There are many jobs that need to be done with great skill and professionalism that simply do not lead to higher positions. If that is the case, such should be stated to the applicant. A classic example is the situation in which an individual is applying for a sales job, but clearly wants to use sales as a vehicle toward rapid advancement to management. If such rapid advancement is not realistically possible, or if it is determined that the individual has a lack of management talent, that individual should probably not be hired. At the very least, an objective, frank discussion should be held where the individual is presented with the realities of the situation. If the individual continues to express an interest in the job, management has to decide whether the individual is just saying this as a short-term expedient or whether he or she has really come to terms with the fact that upward mobility, at least into a management role, is not a short-term reality.

Be realistic about the career opportunities you have to offer. Honesty will help you avoid hiring a frustrated employee who quits within a year of employment.

Recruiting Viable Candidates

We have spent a great deal of time bemoaning the fact that less than one in four people currently selling is properly placed in a sales role.

What is just as true is that one in four people in the general population also has good sales ability. Though it may be a radical thing to say, the truth is that there is just as high a proportion of potentially talented salespeople who are not in sales as there is in the sales profession itself. This negative fact provides management with an exciting recruiting opportunity—if management has the courage to take advantage of it.

If management is willing to scrap the old criteria—age, sex, experience, etc.—and is willing to open up its recruiting efforts to the entire population, providing only realistically necessary knockout requirements, the potential resource from which sales talent can be tapped is literally limitless. Thus, the first step in recruiting salespeople should involve putting out the broadest possible net, designed not to arbitrarily limit applicants, but to attract as many applicants as possible who might possess the potential to do the job. Of course, the use of such a broad net has to include management's willingness to provide product knowledge and sales training since many of the applicants willing to enter the company lack these tools. As we have said, you can teach product and you can teach sales technique, but you cannot teach the raw, basic ability—the motivation to sell.

To risk stating the obvious, if there are objective requirements without which an individual cannot be considered, those requirements should certainly be included. But one should always ask, "Is this really a requirement, or if we find the person with the right ability, can we teach it?"

The key to utilizing this broad net is a comprehensive recruiting plan. A multifaceted approach to attracting applicants is ideal, particularly if there is any urgency and if a number of positions are in need of filling.

Newspaper ads are the first and most obvious means of recruiting candidates, but radio, cable television, high school and college placement offices, and employment agencies all could play an important role in an integrated, effective recruitment effort. Of course, the Internet can also serve as an important tool in recruitment. There are services that match job openings with applicants. Whatever the recruitment source, it is critical that the ad sell the company. Include whatever limiting requirements realistically exist. But if management really wants to tap the available talent pool, it must stress that "we care far more about what you are than what you might happen to be doing or what you might have done in the past." This sentiment should only be expressed if it is truly meant, because it will create substantial numbers of applicants. People are afraid to apply for jobs for which, on the surface, they are not qualified, but these may include some of the very best applicants, and a company's advertising approach must invite these people to step forward and apply. Some of our clients have placed recruitment ads outside of the ads category. They have been concerned that some of those people without sales experience would not look under the sales category for a job. They placed their ads under "new opportunities" and had very good results. It is not sufficient to use terms like "equal opportunity employer," or even "no experience necessary." If management really wants people with potential but without the obvious qualifications to apply, it must ask such people to do so in a very aggressive, direct, unambiguous way.

Proactively inviting people to apply through contacting social services agencies can also prove to be a further invaluable, cost-free means of tapping outstanding talent. Programs designed to help older citizens, women, physically handicapped people, displaced workers, and even welfare recipients, as we discussed earlier, could provide screened candidates and provide them quickly. Some proactive contacts here could, in the long run, grease the wheels of the recruiting process to a large degree.

Referrals

Beyond the broad brush approach to recruiting, which involves newspapers, radio, employment agencies, and schools, there is an additional, and exceptionally effective, approach. Just as job seekers must network to identify leads, hiring managers must communicate their staffing needs and objectives to as broad a range of contacts as possible. Employees, fellow members of the chamber of commerce or professional and trade associations, and even friends, neighbors, and country club members all possess the potential to know just that individual who is right for the job. Companies have offered employees bonuses for recommending individuals who are hired, and this is certainly a positive way of involving the company's employees in the process of improving that team.

Career Night Programs

We have worked with a number of our client companies in helping them to develop what we have termed a "career night program." This approach works with a company seeking to fill multiple openings for a specific job, and also can work where a group of companies can get together in a joint hiring effort. For example, city auto dealer groups, insurance agencies in a particular area, or members of a real estate board can pool their efforts to put together a career night program that might not be appropriate for any one of them but, when combined, might work extremely well.

Whether a career night is sponsored by one company or by a group, the aim is to get a maximum number of candidates into a room at the same time. A representative of the company or the group can tell the company or the industry story and describe the job, including details about requirements, performance expectations, difficulties, and opportunities. If numbers permit, the first step in the screening process could start by having the individual candidates speak for 30 to 60 seconds, during which time some judgments could be made about their ability to articulate, their appearance, and the like. During the same evening, people could be asked to fill out application forms if they still want to be considered after the job has been described, to hand in a résumé, and to complete psychological tests if these are involved in the screening process. What the career night accomplishes, simply, is to do with several dozen people at the same time what management might have to painstakingly do with one applicant at a time—describe the job, answer questions, hand out application forms, administer tests, and so on. There are obviously many variations on the career night theme. But the concept of this kind of group screening has worked well for many of our clients and, where applicable, can be an efficient and rapid means of filling multiple positions.

Bank of Applicants

Each company should establish its own "applicant bank" in which are filed résumés and applications that companies invariably receive throughout the year. To make this applicant bank most effective, the applicants should receive a letter indicating that the company has sufficient interest in them to bank their resumés for future consideration.

This contact can make an applicant's response to a future offer of an interview a far more positive one.

When developing an applicant bank, it is important to remember the one or two excellent candidates for a past opening who were simply beaten out by somebody just a bit better. Also, there may be many applicants for non-sales positions who might be suited to a company's next sales opening. Thus, their applications should be immediately available for review at the start of the recruiting process.

In conclusion, effective recruitment should begin by tapping into the enormous pool of talent that exists across the population. Knockout requirements should be kept to an objective, realistic minimum, and recruitment should be aimed at finding individuals with the raw ability to do the job, regardless of what they may or may not have done in the past. Such a broad brush approach using all the techniques we discussed will produce large numbers of applicants, many of whom obviously will not be suited to the job, but there will also be many who are well suited, many of whom would be screened out by old approaches. If proper screening is conducted and proper selection techniques are employed, substantial progress will be made in finding and hiring salespeople who will be productive and who will remain with the company because they are simply too successful not to do so.

21

Screening Out
the Inappropriate

If the recruiting process discussed in the last chapter is as successful as it should be, there will be large numbers of applicants expressing interest in a position, about 25 percent of whom are likely to have good sales ability. If the recruiting approach was appropriate, some of these will be well suited to the specific sales position for which the recruiting program was undertaken. Although every recruiting program aims to recruit large numbers of applicants from which to choose, the existence of those large numbers creates certain problems. Thus, what we suggest is a pyramid approach to the selection process, starting with the broadest base of applicants that can be created by good recruiting, and then narrowing, step by step, to the peak of the pyramid from which the finalists are studied and from which the individual or individuals are selected to fill the position.

Broadly speaking, this pyramid process is divided into the screening-out segment narrowing the base to manageable numbers, and then a final screening-in process designed to make the best possible selection from among those under consideration. In this chapter, we will look at the process by which inappropriate people are screened out, while the next chapters will deal in depth with each component by which the screening in takes place and the final hiring decision is made.

Review of Résumé

The first step in screening out the obviously inappropriate is the résumé review. This typically can be done quickly and yet can accomplish a great deal toward reducing the sheer numbers of applicants with whom time must be taken. We should insert a word of warning here which applies to any step in the screening-out process. In order to deal with the practical necessity of screening out large numbers of people, a few diamonds in the rough could be screened out from the group. This should be kept in mind as the résumés are reviewed so that where there is some doubt, if numbers permit, the benefit of that doubt should go to the applicant, at least carrying him or her to the next step. This is particularly true if the employer is looking at nontraditional sources of talent. The complete résumé of a woman in transition or of a displaced worker might not appear to be directly relevant, but elements of it might indicate that a further look is warranted.

Résumés should be reviewed in order to ascertain the degree to which applicants possess the essential job requirements. To this end, applicants who have submitted résumés can be separated into three distinct groups: those having most of the requirements; those possessing some of the important requirements; and those clearly not qualified to assume the job responsibilities.

The third group will obviously be screened out immediately. In doing this, management should be certain that it is not screening out on the basis of invalid criteria, but that it really is screening out on the basis of clear, objective facts that would preclude the individual from being effective on the job. In this connection, judgment should not be swayed by the writing style or appearance of the résumé. Content should be the main concern. Professional résumé writers can enhance the appearance and style of a résumé and even, without specifically lying, doctor its contents. On the other side of the coin, individuals who do not have the money or the sophistication to use the professionals may not sell themselves nearly as well in the résumé but, of course, still may possess excellent potential to do the job. So while it is absolutely necessary as a practical matter to screen out people on the basis of their résumés, some care should be taken to avoid being trapped in superficials. In reviewing the résumé, it is important to get an overview to ascertain an applicant's complete job history. Then read between the lines to assess not only the information stated on the résumé, but the story behind job changes, periods of unemployment, seeming inconsistencies in dates or other information, etc.

On the positive side, above and beyond sales experiences, which, as we have repeatedly emphasized, may be totally irrelevant, management should look for job and life experiences that indicate specific accomplishments and the overcoming of obstacles. Ideally, these accomplishments should be measurable and should involve clear, hands-on experience. In other words, since sales is so much an individual activity, some evidence that the applicant has accomplished something individually, whether in sales or not, is certainly a positive.

Another obvious positive is a pattern of job changes, all of which move in the direction of enhancing the individual career. On the negative side of that coin is the job-hopper who explains each change by indicating poor environment, little opportunity, etc. Also, the job-hopper who appears to be at most running parallel, or, at worst, cycling down from job to job, could present an important red flag. Job-hopping per se should not be a knockout, as it all too often is, but the reasons for those changes and the kind of changes might be. What always should be borne in mind is the enormous number of people in the wrong jobs. Individuals with the kind of strong personality a company might wish to hire might be just the people who will not tolerate boredom or a job that obviously does not meet their needs. So, in some instances, and we have seen many examples of this, the very people who are automatically eliminated because they are job-hoppers can be the very people that the company might really want. Again, knock people out if the job-hopping is evaluated as an obvious negative, but do not let job-hopping itself be the knockout factor.

Another positive element relates to an individual's community involvement—memberships in community organizations, volunteer work, etc. This may be particularly pertinent where experience is lacking. Many women, for example, who have been out of the work force for 10 or 15 years raising a family may not bring pertinent evidence of their effective work in the community. However, successful volunteer work for, say, the American Cancer Society may be as indicative of sales potential as many paid positions.

Additional red flags might include unexplained gaps in the chronology of the résumé; focusing on the myriad trivial details, which often can be a means of taking up space to cover up the lack of real substance in the résumé; and the overuse of phrases such as "familiarity with," "knowledge of," or "participated in the development of." Equivocal words such as these are often set up to vaguely qualify an applicant for a particular position. Use of these words is certainly not a knockout but should be viewed with at least some suspicion. If people have strong knowledge of a product or service, or have really developed a program or product, they will say so and in fact emphasize it in their résumé.

The review of the résumé, then, permits management to eliminate obviously inappropriate people from further consideration, but in no sense allows management to make a positive hiring decision. All that a review of a résumé can be expected to do is to narrow the pyramid, and to point to those individuals who are worth further exploration in the next step.

The Telephone Screen

While there can be no doubt that an in-person interview will yield more data than a telephone conversation, again, as a practical matter, if the number of applicants demands it, the telephone screen becomes as valuable a tool as a less time-consuming next step in the screening-out process. What we are suggesting is that those individuals grouped in the first category of résumé review—those having most of the requirements—should be telephoned. Most often, this telephone call can be limited to between 5 and 10 minutes, because its purpose is not to make a positive hiring decision, but simply to screen out clearly inappropriate people. If, for example, someone's voice is absolutely atrocious and the manager who telephones knows perfectly well that this person could not be exposed to customers, that knowledge becomes available in 30 seconds to 1 minute; a polite 2- to 3-minute conversation can serve to screen out that applicant.

What the telephone interview is designed to do is simply to determine whether or not the applicant is worth pursuing further. To accomplish this, the interview should serve to straighten out any discrepancies in the résumé; briefly explain the job, including its negatives; answer the applicant's questions; and permit that applicant to briefly sell management on himself or herself as a viable candidate. So while this method is not foolproof, if an individual fails to sell the hiring manager on the telephone, this could be a good indication that the screening process for that individual should stop right there, for telephone sales are accelerating rapidly and will continue to do so over the next decades.

If the decision is made that an applicant should be brought to the next step, a brief initial interview should be scheduled. If the manager is not certain (perhaps he or she wants to screen other applicants before deciding whom to bring in) or has definitely decided not to pursue the particular applicant, the statement can simply be made that the applicant will be contacted shortly about the next step. We do suggest that in situations where there is not a next step, a polite letter be sent indicating that there are simply too many highly qualified applicants at this time, but that the person's résumé will be kept on file should future opportunities occur. This is simply good personnel policy and good public relations for the company.

The Brief Initial Interview

This initial in-person interview should, again, be brief, no more than 10 to 15 minutes. It is terribly important that the brevity of the interview is spelled out on the telephone when that interview is being scheduled, so the applicants do not feel they are being pushed out in too short a time.

Just as in the telephone interview, the in-person interview is not designed to produce a positive hiring decision. In our view, management simply does not have enough information, nor can it at this stage, make a good judgment. What happens all too often is that the initial interview becomes the hiring interview, and the only way it can is if management uses the superficials—experience, appearance, markets, age, etc.—as the criteria for hiring or not hiring the applicant. What this brief interview is designed to do, then, is simply to examine additional factors in a little more depth to permit screening out still more people.

The interview should also be used to review the application form, which the applicant should have been asked to fill out before the interview, and to review the résumé together with the applicant to clarify definitions, resolve discrepancies, explain gaps, etc., and to briefly permit the applicant to again sell himself or herself to the manager. As we will discuss in far more depth in a later chapter, the interview is severely limited as a means of gaining objective information, but much of what the interview can provide to management can be obtained in those first 10 or 15 minutes as readily as in a prolonged, 1-hour "dance." A screen-out can be as simple as "I do not think I would enjoy working with that person." Here, as in any other screening-out process, a manager might not enjoy working with an individual who has great potential to do the job, so someone valuable might be lost. However, since the manager is the fixture, that risk sometimes must be taken, because if the manager does not want to work with the person, that individual's objective potential might not be realized.

So like the initial review of résumés and the telephone screen, the initial interview should serve to screen out still more individuals who, in the manager's judgment, are not likely to be appropriate for the position. Individuals who are screened out should simply be told that they will be contacted; and, of course, they should receive the same letter explaining that there were simply too many better-qualified applicants for the position. On the other hand, those individuals management wishes to pursue further should be asked to provide a minimum of two business references before they leave the interview. Also, while the individual is there, it might be wise to schedule him or her for psychological testing even, if convenient, immediately following the interview. We will discuss the role of psychological testing later, but suffice it to say here that if an individual takes the test the same day and is then screened out in the next step (the reference check), that test need not be evaluated and so will not cost the company any money or any time.

Reference Checks

Many managers downplay the value of reference checking for many good reasons, but this step nevertheless should be taken as the final part of the screening-out process. Though there are some obvious weaknesses, and though the feedback received from the reference checks has to be viewed with some cynicism, if done correctly, reference checking can provide enough value to be well worth the effort.

While we strongly suggest that reference checks be done, it is still important to review their weaknesses in order to suggest how these weaknesses can be overcome and how the most possible value can be derived from the exercise.

First, the applicant is certainly going to provide references with which he or she is totally comfortable. No one is going to knowingly give a potential employer names of people who will say negative things about them. That is why it is important to ask for two references beyond the initial two so that, it is hoped, the applicant can be pushed into providing names with which he or she is at least one degree less happy.

The second problem relates to a pervasive guilt that exists among managers who have fired people. If the references are from a company from which the applicant was fired, that manager is very likely to give the most glowing reference possible as a means of alleviating his or her own guilt. A manager recently told us, "Yes, I gave that idiot a terrific reference, because I sure did not want his starving family on my conscience." Though rarely will managers express such thoughts that directly, the sentiment exists. Therefore, references must be viewed with some suspicion.

The third major problem relates to people's fear of litigation. No one wants to be accused of unfairly damaging someone; and as we are all aware, fighting a lawsuit, even one we win, is extremely costly. Thus, people are going to tend to say noncommittal, nonthreatening, nondamaging things, even about employees who they felt did harm to their company.

Finally, without knowing precisely what the applicant did in his or her previous job, it could be very difficult to get the reference to really relate the applicant's performance to the hiring company's position.

After all this, why bother with the process at all? How can any value be derived from a process so replete with problems? The answer is that if done correctly, some important value can still be derived from reference checking; it could help eliminate some people and move other people into the final screening-in process with more confidence.

The first important thing to remember is to have the hiring manager make the reference calls himself or herself. We emphasize here "make the call." When silly form letters are sent to references, we can guarantee that silly form letters will be sent back in reply, stating the dates of employment, but providing zero in terms of valuable information. Letters may be acceptable for employment verification, but they certainly are not acceptable as a valid means of checking references.

When a hiring manager makes the call, it is important to tune in carefully to the tone of the person called as well as the content of what is said. If the hiring manager uses his or her empathy, then the pauses, inflections, and things that are not said can often provide more valuable information than the glib words that might be expected. If a company cares about who is hired, the responsible manager should make the call and should use all his or her listening skills in doing so.

In this connection, who is accepted as a reference and who is telephoned is also important. A former supervisor is obviously ideal, and former peers or even subordinates could be acceptable. In any event, wherever possible, the references should be related to a job or jobs that the applicant has done; and again where possible, these jobs should be as close to the prospective job as possible. This does not necessarily mean that the former job had to be one in sales, but if there is a reference where the individual worked in community relations, in advertising, in public relations, or even in providing a key service, these would obviously be better references and more related to the job for which the applicant is being considered than, say, a foreman on a construction site. Yet that foreman, if he or she supervised the applicant for a period of time and knows something of his or her work habits and attitudes, could be a much better reference than someone who says, "Yes, so and so sold me my house, and she was very good."

There may be a time when business references are not available. We are thinking particularly of the woman who is returning to the work force after a period of years, or the college student seeking his or her first job, or an individual who has been ill for a long period of time. Judgment calls have to be made here, and references providing as much information as possible might have to be accepted, even though they are not specifically job-related.

The key to the actual discussion with the reference is to find ways to give that reference "permission" to say negative things. Ways must be found to alleviate the fear of litigation and to allow the reference to indicate negatives without feeling that he or she is hurting the applicant. One of the first things that can be done is to preface your questions with a compliment, or to reflect something complimentary said by the reference. For example, "I found Joe to be extremely personable, but have you noticed that he is somewhat impatient?" Or "That is great that he is such a terrific closer, but are there any areas in his sales approach with which he might need close supervision or some additional training?" Or "From our interviews, and from other references, we certainly agree with you about his presentation skills, but this job involves a minimum of four solid hours on the phone every day. If he is uncomfortable with that, he will fail in a week. How do you feel he will react to that, and what do you think we can do to help him?"

A summary kind of probing question could be something like this: "I am really pleased to hear all these things, and frankly I am not surprised because she comes across as a very impressive person. Now that I have told you something about the job, can you suggest ways that we can help her? Do you think she needs any kind of training, supervision, or whatever? What I am asking is, how can we help her achieve to her top potential?"

What you are doing here in asking for these suggestions is allowing the former manager to at least touch on some possible weaknesses that the reference would never state as such if asked directly, "What are her weaknesses?" We might add, incidentally, that at the very end of an interview, it might not be the worst idea to ask just that. "That is great. Now can you tell me what her weaknesses are, so that we can do our best to help her work through them?" This is not likely to get you as far as the more indirect kinds of questions, but at the very end of the interview, there is little to lose and perhaps some information to be gained.

The reference check should also, of course, include a review of the job functions performed by the applicant. Before even discussing the strengths and weaknesses of the applicant, it is important to know exactly what he or she did on the job. In this area, the hiring manager is likely to get some fairly objective information because the former employer can describe the job and the requirements for doing the job well, without getting into the individual's performance on that job. What is interesting here is that often in talking about the reference's company, and the job that the applicant held, subtle information can emerge relating very specifically to the applicant. Here again, careful listening and subtle, probing questions are important.

With all its weaknesses, careful, well-executed reference checks can provide enough information to help screen out additional people, which is important because it is in the screening-in process that a company must properly invest time, money, and effort. Thus, the more inappropriate people that can be screened out, the more effective will be the screening-in process, and so the more effective can be the final hiring decision. What is being sought in the reference checks is just a few additional facts, some confirmations of résumé and interview data, and some overall feel, subjective though it may be, about whether the candidate continues to be a valid applicant.

At the end of the reference check, management will have screened out, in all probability, a substantial majority of the broad base of applicants that their recruiting process had brought in. True, as we have said before, a few potentially good people might be screened out, but as a practical matter, this narrowing pyramid process has to minimize management's time spent screening in applicants. Although this is not a perfect process, it is hoped, at least in the vast majority of cases, that inappropriate people have been eliminated and now those who have a legitimate chance to be selected remain. They will be put through the screening-in process, leading to the final hiring decision.

22

Psychological Testing: Gaining Objective Insights

In the last chapter, we dealt with means by which individuals can be screened out. We stressed, and this is worth repeating, that neither the résumé review, the telephone interview, the short, initial in-person interview, nor the reference checks can or should serve to make a positive hiring decision. Each of these steps is designed to trigger red flags that allow management to narrow the applicant pool to a manageable degree. In other words, by the time we have reached the screening-in process, we should be dealing with candidates who are worthy of in-depth consideration, and so few of them as to make that in-depth evaluation both possible and economically feasible.

The reason that a positive hiring decision cannot be made on the basis of the earlier steps is simple. All these steps involve subjective, not objective, feedback. The résumé, as we discussed, may be professionally prepared and may or may not really reflect what the applicant has done, and rarely, even at best, will it involve an objective presentation of how well the applicant performed in the past. The telephone interview can at most provide management with a subjective impression, which may be good enough to screen out people but is certainly not sufficient to make the enormous commitment involved in offering someone a job. Similarly, the in-person interview can create impressions that, if sufficiently negative, could knock out someone, but still does not provide objective input into the dynamics of the individual. And finally, reference checking has so many built-in flaws. Even when properly conducted it is still so subjective, that only negative factors might be usable, but certainly all the praise in the world should not convince management to make a job offer. After all these subjective knockouts have reduced the applicant pyramid to a manageable size, what is needed is objective information about the individual obtained through use of a valid psychological test and the confirmatory input of an in-depth interview.

The need for this objective input has, in a large sense, been recognized by the industry at least since the end of World War II. By the late 1950s, when our work really began, tests, structured interview guides, and demographic scales had proliferated. As we mentioned earlier, this proliferation actually began our involvement in the business of testing and evaluating personnel. We were asked to review many of these then-available assessment instruments to help a company decide the most effective way to reduce its sales turnover. Even back in the 1950s, companies would state emphatically how capable they were of hiring "eyeball to eyeball," while groping for some objectivity to help them make a more balanced, sound, and correct hiring decision. In their attempt to reach objectivity, they would set up arbitrary cutoff scores on invalid tests, use tests developed for one purpose for a totally unrelated purpose, and, in short, flounder through the jungle of available instruments and procedures, often making matters worse instead of really infusing the objectivity they sought into their hiring.

While we emphatically state that the use of valid psychological testing is critical to effective hiring, we should begin our discussion of testing by examining why, despite millions of dollars, and more than half a century of work involving thousands of Ph.Ds, so many of the tests offered are totally invalid, inappropriate, and ineffective as an aid in making objective hiring decisions by management. It was our in-depth 4-year study of why so many tests misfired which led us to the development of our own testing instruments.

Why Tests Misfire

There are an unlucky seven basic reasons that most tests fail to produce the accurate results that industry seeks.

1. Tests have been looking for interest, not ability.

The concept that a person's interest can be equated with the person's ability is an important cause of test failure. Tests have been developed by asking questions of applicants, with the assumption that if an applicant expresses the same kind of interest pattern as a successful performer, he or she too would be a successful performer.

This assumption is wrong. Psychologically, interest does not equal aptitude, and this is quite simple to illustrate. Someone may have exactly the same interests as Michael Jordan, or Wayne Gretzky, but may be entirely lacking in athletic skills. By the same token, an individual might have the same interest pattern as a successful salesperson or manager, but have little talent for selling or managing. Even if the person wanted to sell or manage, it does not mean that he or she could.

2. Tests have been eminently "fakable."

Anyone applying for a job will attempt to give answers he or she thinks the potential employer wants to hear. An intelligent applicant knows enough to say that he or she would "rather be a manager of people than a librarian," "rather be with people than at home reading a book," "rather lead a group discussion than be a forest ranger," or "prefer talking at a public meeting to listening to good music.

Much has been written on how to beat aptitude tests, but even without such help, a person of average intelligence can quickly see what is being sought and then give the tester what the tester wants. Thus, the tests may simply succeed in screening out the notably unintelligent or the notably naive. The perceptive interviewer, however, is likely to notice blatant stupidity more quickly than tests do, and the individual who may be too naive to fabricate answers could conceivably be the applicant with the best real potential.

Perhaps an example of two test formats might serve to illustrate this point of fakability. Figure 22-1 demonstrates an easily fakable test.

Obviously, the test taker wanting to get the job will know how to answer the questions in this test. He or she will undoubtedly answer "true" for all the items.

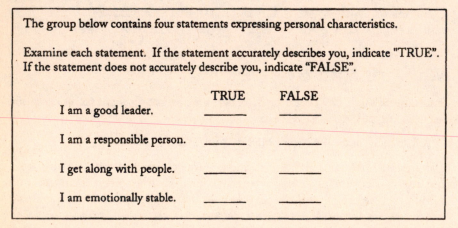

Figure 22-1

The second example, shown in Figure 22-2, illustrates a more sophisticated, valid test design, which is much more difficult to fake. Applicants who look at the four items, shown in the figure realize that there is simply no way to claim everything good or reject everything bad. They may try to convey a more positive image of themselves, but in the end, what they leave out can be just as important as what they select to say.

The group below contains four statements expressing personal characteristics.

Select the one statement that is most like you and fill in the "MOST" circle on your answer sheet. From the remaining choices, select the one statement that is least like you and fill in the "LEAST" circle on your answer sheet. Be sure that for each set of four statements, you fill in only one "MOST" circle and one "LEAST" circle on your answer sheet.

	MOST	LEAST
I am a good leader.	O	O
I am a responsible person.	O	O
I get along with people.	O	O
I am emotionally stable.	O	O

Figure 22-2

3. Tests have favored group conformity, not individual creativity.

Recent critics of psychological testing decry tests that seek conformist and standardized approaches of judging salespeople, managers, and other applicants. This criticism is all too valid. The creative thinker, the impulsive free spirit, the original, imaginative, hard-driving individual is often screened out by tests that demand rigid adherence to convention—an adherence, in fact, that borders on passive acceptance of authority and a fear of anything that might upset the bureaucratic apple cart. Paradoxically, while this fearful, cautious, authoritarian conformist might make a good civil servant, a reasonably effective controller, or a rule book executive, he or she would never be a successful salesperson, a dynamic sales manager, or an assertive administrator.

Many of these tests not only fail to select good salespeople or managers, but possibly screen out top producers because of their creativity, impulsiveness, or originality—characteristics that most tests downgrade as evidence of weakness, or even instability.

4. Tests have tried to isolate fractional traits rather than reveal the whole dynamics of the person.

Most personality and aptitude tests, in their construction and approach, see personality as a series or bundle of piecemeal traits. Thus, someone might be high in sociability, while being low in self-sufficiency and dominance. Someone else might be high in personal relations, but low in cooperativeness. Somehow, the whole (or the Gestalt) gets lost. The dynamic interaction that is personality, as viewed by most modern-day psychologists, is buried in a series of fractionalized, separable traits.

It is said that the salesperson, like the Boy Scout, should be very sociable, dominant, friendly, responsible, honest, and loyal. The totality—the dynamics within the person that will permit him or her to sell successfully— is lost sight of. Clearly, someone might be sociable, responsible, and so on, but still be a poor salesperson or manager.

5. Tests have depended heavily on past experience as a prime qualification.

We have emphasized that four out of five people currently earning their living in sales should not be—or, at least, certainly should not be in their specific sales job. We also mentioned that it is these inappropriately placed salespeople who constitute the 80 percent who sell only 20 percent of what is sold. Given this fact, any test that favors persons already holding sales jobs can only serve to perpetuate inappropriate typecasting.

Some sales aptitude tests use vocabulary and/or the understanding of sales or management situations to measure an applicant's potential sales or management ability. These techniques seek to ascertain experience rather than real ability. Anyone who has even sold or who has been exposed to selling, even academically, may do well in most tests, whether or not he or she has any inherent sales ability. Terms such as "close," "cold canvass," and "prospecting" will be familiar. The test taker will be able to rattle off appropriate responses, even if this person's dynamics guarantees him or her far better prospects as an engineer or manager than as a salesperson. On the other hand, the inexperienced, but potentially strong, salesperson is not likely to know these terms. If judged by experience-oriented techniques, his or her appraisal will be unfavorable. By the same token, an individual who has served as a manager for a number of years would be extremely familiar with terms such as "line versus staff," "management by objectives," and "goal setting," and, as a result, would have an unfair advantage over an inexperienced person applying for a managerial position.

6. Many tests are used for purposes for which they were not originally designed.

A very well-known test that dates back to the late 1930s in its original form was designed to study the psychotic behavior of patients at mental hospitals. The test was developed using the patients of hospitals as the study group and people visiting them as the control group against which the study group could be compared, item by item. This test, like a number of others in this category, has value in clinical use, but goes completely astray when it is inappropriately used for personnel evaluation and selection.

We like to cite the example of an individual applying for a large life insurance policy. Can one imagine the applicant, while being examined by the life insurance company's physician, pointing to a place on her chest and saying, "Doc, can you tell me if this lump might be a problem?" Or can one imagine a 50-year-old man saying to the insurance physician, "I have these pains in my chest, do you think they are a problem?" Obviously, the applicant will not do anything of the sort but, rather, will hope that the insurance physician discovers nothing and clears him or her for the policy. Perhaps the very next day those individuals might go to their own physician; at the time they certainly will point out the lump or talk about the chest pain. The difference here is exactly what the difference is when a test designed for purely clinical purposes is used for sales or management selection. When people are in psychological pain or looking for vocational guidance, they will answer a test truthfully, or reveal themselves as fully as they can within their own personal limitations in an interview, in order to get the help they seek. On the other hand, when those same people are applying for a job, looking for a promotion, or in any way taking a test for their company, they are going to cover up their weaknesses and work to sell their strengths just as surely as the two-pack-a day smoker will present himself or herself to the life insurance company as a nonsmoker, or the woman with the lump or the man with the pain will reveal nothing of the sort to the company's physician. Thus, a test may be perfectly useful when a fundamental assumption can be made that people will, at least as far as they can, attempt to tell the truth, and yet be totally invalid as an instrument designed to really uncover an individual's sales potential. However, since many of those tests have famous names, have been around for a long time, and were studied by psychologists in school, they continue to be used as part of a company's selection procedures, with the negative results that we have discussed throughout this book.

7. Many tests produce general results without relating to the specific job match.

Some tests may, with some validity, describe the personality of an individual. These are among the relatively few that have avoided all the pitfalls we have just discussed. Yet even some of these fail to provide management with the in-depth information it needs to make the correct hiring decisions. The key to this problem is the job match. Even if a test accurately describes the level of assertiveness, dominance, or sociability possessed by an individual, the question still remains of how those levels relate to the specific requirements of the job in question. It is certainly easy to say that management wants the most assertive person possible, or the most social, but as we have seen, there definitely can be too much of a quality—even ego-drive—for a specific job, and balances of many qualities are required for other jobs. These tests, which are often spit out by computers, with the results presented in a neat graph, fail in any sense to relate their results to the functional requirements of the specific company's job. It is really left to the manager to decide if the particular applicant is assertive enough, energetic enough, or driven enough to do the job; and although these tests can be useful, they often fall short in providing the precise information the manager really needs to make the best hiring decision.

If tests in this category are indeed accurate in their description of an individual's traits, this provides an important plus in that it offers management input that it can get in no other way. However, the potential misuse, misunderstanding, and failure to job-match the data can lead to incorrect and costly hiring decisions.

Choosing the Right Tests

Over the years, companies have used tests that were invalid for one or more of the reasons we discussed and have often been badly burned by such tests. When we speak to potential clients, we experience the most difficulty with those who have attempted to use psychological testing, because while they recognize the need for such testing, they have found the results to be less than satisfactory. Our sales job, then, is not only to persuade them that psychological testing is important, but also to persuade them that there are indeed tests, including our own testing instrument, that avoid the seven pitfalls and can really provide the accurate information they need.

Despite all the failures of psychological testing, it is clear that valid, job-related psychological testing must be a critical part of any effective hiring program. What is clearly needed is an objective method of penetrating the superficial facade presented in the résumé, in the interview, and even through the references. Given today's technology, the best means of doing this is through a valid, in-depth psychological test.

Such a test, if constructed to avoid the seven unlucky pitfalls, can penetrate the facade that individuals work hard to build. Such a valid test can assess the basic strengths, weaknesses, and motivations of an individual, even if that individual worked very hard to use the test as another way of constructing the facade. An effective test can literally use the means by which an individual fakes as a means of understanding who that individual really is. An effective test, in the hands of business-oriented individuals capable of proper evaluation not only can help management directly determine the strengths, weaknesses, and motivations of an individual on staff, or an applicant, but also can relate the test data to the specific functional requirements of the job; management can use the test to help determine whether or not there is a job match. The test can help determine whether the central qualities and motivations of the individual match the functional requirements of the job, while also helping to determine whether the individual has a fatal flaw that might preclude him or her from doing the job. If properly used, the same test results can help guide management about the best ways to manage and motivate promising applicants to maximize their productivity should they be hired.

But how can management select a valid test? Literally thousands of test are on the market, ranging from score-it-yourself versions for a few dollars to batteries of tests in assessment centers costing thousands of dollars. As we have said, a vast majority of these tests, regardless of price, are not job-related, valid predictors of success. Thus, as important as the use of a psychological test is to the selection process, it is even more important for management to be certain that the test is valid and effectively assesses the particular qualities needed to succeed on the job.

With thousand of tests available, many looking quite similar, how can a test be selected that is legal and will help predict whether an applicant can really do a specific job? Without extensive research into each test, it is extremely difficult to make this choice. Yet this choice is of critical importance.

Making the right hiring decision is too vital not to use the best input available. That input definitely includes the data that can be provided by a valid psychological test. Using the wrong test, however, can be costly.

First, there can be serious legal implications if a test is discriminatory and not provably predictive in relation to a job. To be provably nondiscriminatory, women, minorities, and older people have to "pass" in the same proportion as men, majorities, and younger people. This also means that the test must be provably predictive for the job for which the test is used.

In other words, if the test is used to select a salesperson, that test should predict sales success with good statistical accuracy. The operative legal language is that the test should have "no adverse impact on protected groups" and that it should have "job-related validity."

Using the wrong test could be even more costly if it is inaccurate. It could influence management to hire the wrong person and perhaps prevent the hiring of potentially productive people. The cost of such a mistake is enormous.

Therefore, in order to reduce the problem of test selection to a manageable level, we have developed a series of questions that management should ask about any test before deciding to use it. If the answer provided by the test publisher to any of these questions is no or noncommittal, that test should not be used under any circumstances.

1. Is the test specifically job-related? Does it measure qualities required for your particular job?

2. Does the publisher of the test provide published proof that the test does not discriminate against individuals by sex, age, race, color, religion, or national origin?

3. Does the publisher provide published proof that the test has a high level of predictive validity across the industry and specifically in a situation at least closely related to the position for which the test is being given? Is there proof that people actually do perform as the test predicts they will?

4. Is the database from which the test is developed, and on which the test's reliability and validity are measured, large enough and compiled over enough years to provide dependable evidence of its reliability and validity? In other words, has the test publisher tested enough people and followed actual performance over enough years to prove that the test works?

5. Does the publisher provide you with a list of customers you can contact who have used the test long enough to judge the results?

6. Are the test results related specifically to a company, or are they generalized results? The key here is whether the test is evaluated against a company's particular requirements, i.e., job description.

7. Are results of the test provided promptly so that management will not lose good applicants as a result of waiting?

8. Does the company provide a trained test evaluator who is a specialist in your field? Will the evaluator discuss the test results with you and provide assistance in relating those results to the other steps of the assessment process?

9. Will the testing company provide ongoing help if problems or questions arise relating to poor initial performance, slumps, future promotions, training, and management issues?

10. Are the qualities measured by the test those that are essential to performance in the job for which the test is to be used? If, for example, the test does not measure ego-drive (persuasive motivation), it probably would not be appropriate for use in sales selection. It is important that the test clearly measures exactly those qualities that management wants to assess in its developmental, promotion, or hiring decisions.

Even when using the best psychological tests, there are admonitions to keep in mind. The test should be simple enough to administer in a company's office. As a practical matter, except in the selection of the highest-level executive, it is not effective to have potential candidates travel great distances to a testing office, or to have test administrators travel the country to visit the company.

Under no circumstances should an individual be allowed to take a test at home. Even the best test will be distorted and become invalid if the responses are a group collaboration or the product of someone other than the individual who is supposed to be taking the test. A couple of years ago we spoke rhapsodically about the virtues of an applicant we evaluated, including making such statements as, "This is one of the most assertive, driven, and yet empathic people we have ever evaluated, and we certainly feel that he can make a real contribution to your sales force." All of us have had the experience of having said something and knowing, with certainty, that we have somehow made a colossal blunder. The silence on the other end of the phone after our comment conveyed precisely that message. When the client was able to speak, he said that we had described an individual who was exactly the opposite of his applicant.

Though we readily admit that no method, including our own testing , is 100 percent accurate, rarely do we make a mistake as colossal as this one. Thus, purely out of self-defense, we probed the situation and found out that indeed the applicant had taken the test home. It took only a bit more exploration, and our client's questioning of his applicant, to discover that his wife had actually "helped" her husband. She, of course, was the assertive, driven, empathic individual we described.

Naturally, most situations are not quite this dramatic, but the danger of invalidating even the best test by having someone take it home and allowing one or more persons to contribute to it is a serious one and should be avoided whenever humanly possible.

What Can a Valid Test Do?

A valid psychological test that uncovers an individual's basic occupational motivations can go a long way toward reducing costly mistakes. It is capable of accurately assessing dozens of attributes and integrating those attributes to describe a human being's strengths, weaknesses, and key motivations. It should also be capable of integrating these qualities with the job requirements to make the job match.

A valid test should be able to penetrate an individual's facade and provide management with objective insights into his or her basic personality and motivations. By way of example, our psychological test can provide answers to such questions as:

- Does the individual have persuasive motivation?
- Can he or she listen effectively?

- Can he or she take rejection?

- Does the individual have service motivation?

- Is the individual assertive enough to ask for an order and tenacious enough to follow through?

- Is the individual a good self-starter?

- Can the individual organize his or her work and time and follow up on the work of others?

- Can he or she make decisions?

- Does the individual have the potential to grow on the job, or can he or she only be expected to perform at the entry level?

- Is he or she intensely competitive or laid back?

- Can the individual cope with detail sufficiently?

- Is the individual shrewd in judging situations, as well as people?

- Is the individual an original, innovative, creative thinker, or is he or she tradition-bound?

There are, of course, many more questions. But whether we talk about our test or any other valid test that is used for the evaluation of sales and sales management personnel, these questions and many others related to the sales job should be answered reliably. The right test can provide data that in no way can be objectively provided by the earlier steps in the screening process. The data can only be provided by penetrating the individual's facade and getting at the reality of who the individual is; which is best done by a test that meets all the criteria we have discussed.

In addition to being a vital part of the decision-making process, the test results can also play an important role in structuring the final step of the process—the in-depth interview. By integrating the data provided by all the earlier steps with the insights provided by the test, the interviewer can structure the interview in such a way as to probe discrepancies and apparent weaknesses, and to move the interview away from the superficial and toward specifics. For example, if the test shows the applicant to be rigid and opinionated, this fact might be presented in the interview and the applicant's reaction studied carefully. In short, the test results, as well as all of the previous data, form the basis for a more effective interview with the potential to produce more valid results.

In addition to its use in the selection process, an in-depth psychological test can be used to develop appropriate prescriptive training programs designed to strengthen an individual in areas where he or she is weak. Rather than waste valuable training dollars, management can use the test results to pinpoint specific areas in which training is most needed and gear supervision toward providing the specific support the salesperson requires.

Similarly, a test should provide important insights on how to effectively manage each person currently on staff. It can point to who might be promotable and into what positions.

A valid test, in short, is vital as part of an effective selection process, and can be equally important as a tool in upgrading the productivity of an entire organization.

23

The In-Depth Interview

After receiving the evaluations of the psychological test, management will probably have eliminated some additional candidates, now narrowing the pyramid to those very few who should be brought to the last stage of the selection process—the in-depth interview. It is at this point that an interview should be as long as necessary to help make that all-important final hiring decision. All that could have been done has been done to eliminate people who are clearly inappropriate for the investment of this kind of time. The use of a valid psychological test should give some clear indications that the remaining people have some of the important attributes for a potentially good job match; there should be no indication that they have a nontrainable fatal flaw that would preclude them from doing the job effectively. What remains now is to bring together all the data that have been gathered by all the steps in the screening process, to use the in-depth interview or interviews to integrate the data, and to use every technique available to confirm, in as absolute a way as possible, the efficacy of the hiring decision.

A further purpose of this in-depth interview is to make certain not only that management wants to hire the candidate, but that the candidate fully knows and understands the opportunities that the job offers and also is aware of all its negatives. This way both parties enter the relationship with all the facts in hand and all the potential problems presented up front so that any concerns can be worked out jointly. To state the obvious, it is far better, for example, to know that the amount of travel involved would create an impossible burden on a salesperson's family life before making the hiring decision than to find this out a month or two later after time, money, and effort have been invested in the individual. It is not management's job to sell the position to the applicant. Rather, management should arrive, with the applicant, at the best joint decision—whether negative or positive. If the proper screening has been carried through, by the time you reach the stage of the final in-depth interview, you are dealing with people who clearly possess the potential to do the job; and now it is everyone's responsibility to see if that potential is a practical, on-the-job reality. That is why an oversell, or a lack of honesty in presenting all aspects of the job, can serve to defeat all the work that has gone before and ultimately contribute to an inappropriate decision.

Like every other stage of the selection process, the in-depth interview, while of great importance as the final step in making the hiring decision, is still flawed; its flaws must be thoroughly understood and worked through in order to get the most out of this step. Just as a review of résumés leaves much to be desired, a telephone screen can easily fool the interviewer, reference checks have serious problems, and even the best psychological tests are not perfect, similarly, the in-depth interview has many built-in problems.

As we have indicated, the final in-depth interview is critical: despite all the flaws we will be discussing, it can provide valuable input into the hiring process. If not dealt with carefully, however, this input could confuse as much as it clarifies. How often after hiring someone who does not work out has a manager thought, "But he looked so good in the interview"?

Part of the problem is the inherent limitation of the interviewing process. Very few of us can conduct an interview with the skill, depth, and finesse of a Dan Rather. And even if we could, that would not completely solve the problem.

More often than not, instead of lending insight, interviews become a form of theater in which all of the actors are tripping over one another, trying to put their best foot forward. The employers are busy trying to create a favorable impression of themselves and their company, while the applicants are trying to mold themselves into whatever they perceive is desired.

Meanwhile, it must be kept in mind that any bookstore worth its salt has a shelf full of guides for playing this game to the hilt. Anyone serious about applying for a job has read at least one of these guides.

So, job interviews are replete with people trying to leave the best first impression. The result, all too often, is what we call "interview stars," those individuals whose best performance occurs during the interview.

These stars are able to convey a favorable first impression, but that impression bears no relationship to their eventual performance. Even for a sales position it must be kept in mind that although some applicants can sell themselves in an interview, it does not necessarily imply an ability to sell a product or a service.

One of our senior consultants relates an incident that illustrates the situation well.

Some time ago I recommended that a client not hire an applicant. There was a moment of dead silence, and after experiencing thousands of these situations, I was not at all surprised at what came next. The client, as I expected, said, "But that's impossible. This person came across so strong, and was such a pleasure to talk to." I replied that I was not at all surprised by his comment because the applicant was extremely intelligent, had good empathy, and was strongly motivated to make people like him. In fact, his strongest single motivation was to be liked—to receive approval from anyone with whom he comes in contact. I added that in addition to the overall good conversation, I would guess that the applicant told the manager how impressed he was with the company, how much he would enjoy the job, and that if I did not miss my guess, the manager probably had received or would receive a letter thanking him for his courtesy and for the time he took in the interview. The manager hesitated briefly and said, "You hit it right on the head, including the letter, which I received this morning. So what's wrong?" I explained that what was wrong was exactly what the manager liked so much in the applicant. I went on to explain that the applicant made his impression because of his intensely strong motivation to please, to be liked, but, given his lack of assertiveness, and lack of strong persuasive motivation, ego-drive, this desire to be liked could act as an important negative in relation to his ability to do the sales job. I explained that once the individual got past making the impression, he would find it extremely difficult to risk that impression—to risk the disapproval of the prospect—by pushing strongly for the order. Our consultant concluded his comment by telling us that he finally convinced the client by asking him if at any time the applicant really pushed him toward a decision. Yes, he thanked him for the interview; yes, he spoke interestingly; and yes, he wrote that very nice thank-you letter, but did he ask for the job?

The interview star is overly concerned with making a favorable impression. It is fundamental to such an individual's sense of well-being to be liked, appreciated, and perceived in favorable terms. An individual with this motivation will work very hard to make a good impression in an interview and, with the help of a few guides, will probably succeed. Yet while this motivation to be well liked is important for many jobs and can be helpful in many sales jobs, it will not, in and of itself, ensure success in sales. Sometimes, in fact, too much of a need to be liked can work against an individual's ability to make difficult decisions, let alone to risk rejection when the situation calls for it.

A tip-off provided by this case can also be helpful. The applicant did not try to get the employer to move a little closer toward offering him the job. One can suspect a definite lack of assertiveness and view the existence of ego-drive with suspicion if an applicant does not say something toward the end of the interview such as, "I like what I have heard. I am extremely interested in the being part of your organization. Will you give me an opportunity?" Even if these or similar words are said, this is by no means proof that the individual is really assertive and/or ego-driven, but certainly the absence of these words provides a warning light. Here is a good example of how test results and this kind of interview feedback can be integrated. If the test, for example, indicated borderline ego-drive and gave some cause for concern about the applicant's assertiveness, the failure to make this minimum move toward closing the sale (or getting the job) would confirm any doubts. On the other hand, given this same marginal test result, a strong push on the part of the applicant might tip the balance toward the applicant. In any event, there cannot be a simple assumption that because the right words are said in this context, the individual is going to be effective. Keep in mind that there are many instruction manuals on how to interview. You have to keep your antenna up, so as not to be taken in by an interview star.

It is in the process of penetrating the facade created by the interviewee that the data produced by the psychological test are of maximum value. The data provided by the test can be used to confirm impressions, explain them, or deny them; whatever the case, the interview can be carried forward more effectively with this information. Later, we will discuss some specifics about how the information provided by the test can be utilized to more effectively structure the interview, but suffice it to say here that every impression gained in the interview should be evaluated against not only the data provided by the test, but also the information provided by all other steps in the screening process. The interviewer, in short, is the sifter, the final arbiter of what data is real, doubtful, or totally incorrect.

Before turning to a few specific how-tos, it might be useful to look at how not to. The following interview is admittedly extreme. We strongly suspect that few interviewers will really conduct such a totally incorrect interview, but we equally strongly suspect that many interviewers make at least some of these mistakes. By being extreme, we are able to make a number of points that more moderate words or admonitions might not achieve as well.

The Interview

"Good morning, Ms. Moore," you say. "It's a pleasure to meet you."

She says the pleasure is all hers, then comments on the attractive view from your window. While you settle behind your desk, the applicant sits across from you. A friendly smile offsets her intense eyes.

"First off," you say, scanning some papers on your desk, "I was very impressed with your résumé. It was clear and concise. And your background is particularly well suited to this new opening we have in our sales department. In fact, this is an exciting time to be coming on board with us, because things are really booming. But more on that later." You quickly add, "I took the liberty of checking some of the references you provided me with, and they were all glowing," Actually, some digging revealed that she was dismissed from one position under curious circumstances, but you decide to wait until later to delve into that.

"Enough of me talking about you," you say. "Why don't you tell me about yourself? Let's see, how long ago did you start your current position?"

"The exact date is on my résumé, but it has been over 2 years." Ms. Moore goes on to say that she's been selling advertising space for a local newspaper, which she likes, but finds limiting. Though the job has enabled her to meet various clients in numerous settings, she would like to find a job that would allow her to be on the road more, with one-on-one contact.

"I'm sorry. I didn't realize you had somebody in your office," one of your salespeople says, sticking his head inside the door you left slightly ajar. "I'll check back later. Please excuse the interruption."

"That's all right," you say. "Now, where were we? Oh, yes. Well, I'm sure you have a lot of questions about the company and the job. Let me try to anticipate some of them for you. Since the company was founded a little over a decade ago, we've been on the right path, and that road is now smoother than ever. Of course, the owners keep their hands in things, which can get a little sticky at times. As a matter of fact—well, let me just tell you this one quick story to illustrate what I mean," you say, leaning across your desk, lowering your voice in confidence. "It happened just the other day, so it's still fresh in my mind, but it's a classic example of what I go through. I had been after the three owners to get an estimate out to a prospective client for the last 2 weeks. Because they must have their imprint on everything that goes out of here, the estimate was getting delayed for this reason, then for that reason. Yesterday, when I asked about it, I was told it was being reviewed. So I had to do handsprings to get all three of the owners to drop everything else they were doing and concentrate on this proposal. Not only was it aggravating, but it cost us a bundle to get it to its destination on time. But that wouldn't be a concern of yours should you come on board," you quickly insert. "But enough of me talking; you must have some questions."

"As a matter of fact, I was wondering if you could describe this sales position to me in more detail. If I accept this position, what would I be doing on a day-to-day basis?"

Pausing, you say, "As far as your job is concerned, you'll be constantly selling. Our product is known in the marketplace and highly regarded. So you'll have a solid base upon which to approach prospects. It depends upon how adept you are at persuading. But then, I wouldn't be overly concerned about that if I were you. I've always believed that if you can sell, you can sell. Excuse me," you apologize, as the phone rings. "No. I'm in the midst of an interview now. Tell her I'll get back in touch with her as soon as I can."

You continue, "One thing I wanted to ask you about was Harlequin. I see from your résumé you used to work there. Do you remember a guy named Johnson, Robert Johnson?"

"Yes, he used to work in accounting, I believe. I didn't get a chance to know him well," she says.

"Oh, Bob and I go way back. We graduated together from Pitt. Those were some times. The things I could tell you about him back then. He was wild on the football field and even wilder off," you say, laughing at the memory. Realizing that Ms. Moore isn't laughing with you, you quickly change the subject.

"One thing you'll realize if you come on board with us, Ms. Moore, and all our salespeople will confirm this, is that as far as money is concerned, the sky is the limit. Since we work on a commission basis, after your brief training period, your income is only limited by your ability."

"That was something I was meaning to ask you. Just to give me an idea of where I might stand, what is the average take-home pay for a salesperson on your force?"

"Oh, the average is nothing you should concern yourself with, Ms. Moore, since I'm sure you'll do much better than average." Smiling, you remember another question you wanted to ask. "One thing I always like to ask is what is the one thing you like least about your current job."

"That's a tough question," she says. "I mean, I don't want to incriminate myself. But let's see. I'd have to say that the job is needlessly bogged down in detail. I understand the importance of detail, but there is a tendency to waste salespeople's time with paperwork that could be completed more efficiently by someone in a clerical position."

"I'm sorry to hear you say that," you respond, "Too many salespeople think of detail as something that simply slows them down in the achievement of their goals. That impatience can be fatal when it comes to satisfying customers. That's the very attitude that can erode the success we've worked so long to build here." Leaning back in your chair, you stare at the applicant, searching for her response to one of you steadfast beliefs.

Recoiling slightly, she says, "I don't believe I have any problems handling detail. It's just that I think the operation where I'm currently working could be run more smoothly if salespeople could concentrate more on meeting clients, following up on prospects, and the other more essential parts of selling."

You could pursue this train of thought, but glancing at your watch, you realize you're already late for an important strategy session with the owners of the company. "I'm sorry. The time has just shot right by. I wish we could talk longer, but I'm already late for a meeting, and the owners will probably have my head." Rising from your seat and gathering a few papers from your desk, you add, "Listen, it was really a pleasure. I'm not sure how long it will take us to come to a final decision on this hire, but it shouldn't be more than a few weeks or so. If you have any questions concerning anything we didn't cover, please don't hesitate to call." Opening the door to your office, you add, "My secretary will be glad to direct you to the parking lot. Thanks again."

The 10 Errors

The 10 basic interviewing errors are:

1. Don't be afraid to ask tough questions.

The first mistake occurs almost immediately, when the interviewer does not pursue why the applicant was dismissed from a previous job. If you uncover anything during the reference checking or employment history review process that warrants tough questioning, do not be afraid to ask about it during the interview. It is important that you begin your relationship with a new hire on a frank basis.

2. Don't oversell your company.

The interviewer makes his second mistake by bragging about how things are booming, while not giving specifics to back up his claim. He follows this up with pat statements like, "since the company was founded a little over a decade ago, we've been on the right path and that road is now smoother than ever." An adept interviewer will lay out the strengths and weaknesses of the firm, putting them in perspective. Do not paint an unrealistic picture of your company in order to lure an applicant on board.

3. Don't ask for information you already have.

The interviewer asks, "Why don't you tell me about yourself? Let's see, how long ago did you start your current position?" This shows a lack of interest in the candidate since this information was obtained earlier. The interview should be used to obtain new information or to confirm or reject tentative information already acquired.

4. Don't allow yourself to be interrupted unless there is an emergency.

The interview is interrupted twice, first by a salesperson sticking his head in the door and then by a telephone call. Too many interviewers allow the interview to become disjointed by not taking steps to prevent interruptions. Your office door should be closed. Put calls and messages on hold.

5. Don't talk too much.

The interviewer tells the applicant, "Well, I'm sure you have a lot of questions about the company and the job. Let me try to anticipate some of them for you." This is a classic case of an interviewer who loves to hear his own voice. At the most, an interviewer should say one word for every four spoken by the person being interviewed.

6. Don't use the interview as your therapy.

As part of his need to hear himself talk, the interviewer told a confidential story about some of the problems he encounters in his position. Too many interviewers use their sessions to spout out their concerns about the company. When an interviewer vents emotions in an interview, he or she may feel better, but may lose a prospective employee in the bargain.

7. Don't be afraid to spell out in detail the requirements of the position.

When the applicant got a word in edgewise and asked about the specific requirements of the job, she was brushed off with the pat answer, "But then, I wouldn't be concerned about that if I were you. I've always believed that if you can sell, you can sell." It is imperative that people know what is required of them before beginning a job. The interview is the time to outline the job's requirements, as well as your criteria for evaluating success in the role.

8. Don't gossip or swap war stories.

Many interviewers try to find familiar ground they can tread over with the applicant. Though this might seem like a comfortable way to get an interview under way, inquiring about friends and relatives can get things sidetracked, wasting a huge amount of time. The interview should be devoted to obtaining as much information as possible in order to make a sound hiring decision.

9. Don't put the applicant on the defensive.

There is no point in creating unnecessary tension during the interview. Knowing an applicant's personality strengths and weaknesses is vital to making the best hiring decision. Openly discussing Ms. Moore's statement about detail on her former job might provide valuable insight, particularly if the test results provided evidence that there was indeed a sufficiently strong dislike of detail to create concern. A speech embodying a long-held philosophy is inappropriate, but a frank discussion of the importance of detail in the job, and how Ms. Moore might deal with the detail aspect of the job, would be constructive and would allow both people to make a more reasoned decision.

10. Don't be afraid to make the interview as long, or as short, as you deem necessary.

The final mistake was that the interview was concluded in an unnecessary rush. As the interviewer noticed the time, he realized he was late for another appointment and excused himself hurriedly. To be effective, the interview should make the fullest use of everyone's valuable time. There are no set guidelines on length, so long as you clearly spell out the anticipated length of the interview and so long as the time is spent wisely.

Additional Mistakes to Avoid

It may be difficult after reviewing this atrocious interview to imagine that there are other common mistakes that somehow were not included in this example—but there are. They include the following.

Don't ask questions that can be only answered by a simple yes or no. Instead try to ask questions that must be answered at some length and with some explanation. The key to a good question is not only to get a specific answer but to get that answer by listening to the interviewee's response.

Don't simply indulge in generalized conversation as though nothing had occurred prior to the interview. Though this was done to some degree in the interview of Ms. Moore, the point should be further elaborated here. The interviewer should have a great deal of information in hand relating to the applicant's past experience, feedback from references, early impressions from the telephone and in-person interview, and, of course, the data provided by the psychological test. All these impressions should be checked throughout the interview, and conflicts should be resolved. If, for example, the résumé speaks about a previous position as "a division manager" and the reference checks reveal that the applicant managed no one and the title was simply another name for a salesperson with a territory, that apparent discrepancy should be discussed. "Tell me specifically what you did on the job. Do the best you can to tell me how you functioned literally hour by hour and day by day." If after this explanation the discrepancy is still not resolved, the manager should not hesitate to confront the applicant with the evident discrepancy and ask the applicant to discuss it. Obviously, this discrepancy might be more or less important, depending on the nature of the job for which the applicant is being considered.

Similarly, if the applicant described his or her previous job as involving hard, frequent closes, and the test indicates some doubt about the applicant's level of ego-drive, questions could be raised about the discrepancy, giving the applicant plenty of opportunity to sell the interviewer on the fact that he or she was able to close despite what the test says—and getting the applicant to explain precisely how he or she accomplished this. What we are saying here simply is to try to avoid general conversations, and home in as precisely as possible on specifics.

Don't ramble. Although there is no precise ideal length of an interview, it is important to show the interviewee that there is a respect for time, not only the time of the manager, but the time of the interviewee as well. While being friendly, stay on course and keep the interview moving in a clearly defined direction. Finally, unless by the end of the interview you have ruled out the individual, don't leave him or her with a generalized "we will be in touch." Rather, spell out what the next steps will be, even if those steps simply involve a management decision and notification to the applicant. If future interviews are going to be requested, say so; and if group interviews, spouse interviews, and the like are to be part of the process, spell out these as well. In other words, the applicant should leave the interview knowing, with relative precision, when a decision is going to be made, on what basis it might be made, and what other steps, if any, may be required in the decision-making process.

Structuring the Interview: The Interview Strategy

As we said earlier, all too often the interview is, by its very nature, a form of theater, with the participants performing an adversarial dance. The applicant is trying to make the best impression, and in that effort is working to psyche out the interviewer, looking to say precisely what the interviewer wants to hear. Similarly, the interviewer is trying to penetrate the facade of the applicant to ascertain what is really there, what are his or her real motives, and the like.

In this ritual, the interviewer does begin with some important advantages, which all too often are not utilized. First, and of most importance, the interviewer enters the situation armed with a good deal of knowledge about the applicant. As subjective as some of this knowledge is, it still provides a body of data upon which a strategy for the interview can be laid out. Add to this the more objective input of the test and potential discrepancies between various elements of information produced prior to the interview, and the interviewer really has tools with which to probe the facade with good effectiveness.

Using these tools, however, does require planning. Before the interview begins, the interviewer should have firmly in mind, or even in writing, a series of answers that are being sought. The final interview should not simply be another place in which to gain an impression, but should be the mechanism by which everything else in the process is confirmed, denied, or left ambiguous. Thus, any discrepancies, problems, and/or doubts created in prior parts of the process must be probed in the interview, along the lines we discussed. Such probing must be well planned, and the strategy for such probing developed. If the applicant has survived through all the steps in the screening process, the odds are that there are not too many weaknesses or discrepancies, but those that exist must be dealt with if the proper decision is to be made.

Apropos of this point, and also to be fair to both the applicant and the company, it is important in this interview to fully describe the job in terms of its functional requirements, performance expectations, and potential upward mobility. If elements of the job expectations happen to fly in the face of certain motivations or weaknesses of the applicant, being aware of them could lead the applicant toward making a negative decision, which, in the long run, would be positive for the company. It is better for everyone concerned that the job be presented honestly, with its opportunities and problems, so that the interviewer and the applicant can face the issues, discuss the problems, and together arrive at the most informed and mutually beneficial employment decision.

In short, if most of the pitfalls we have outlined can be avoided, and if you are certain and clear about the information you want to obtain, the interview can be extremely important in the final hiring decision.

24

The Final Decision

We have been focusing on how a company should best go about building a winning sales team. It is our purpose in this chapter to wrap up and summarize our suggested pyramid process of recruiting, screening, and selecting productive salespeople. We will also deal to some degree with the other side of the decision-making process—the applicant, who has to make his or her decision.

As we look at the final decision and attempt to summarize how it is made, let us understand that the decision is not, or certainly should not be, a unidirectional one. The right decision must be a joint decision by the company and the applicant. There cannot be a winner and loser in the hiring decision. If the hiring decision is a correct one, it must be a positive one for both the applicant and the employer.

The Company's Decision

Let us bring together all the various facets of the hiring process. To quickly review, the recruiting and screening processes have now been completed. The company has conducted an effective search among its existing employees to determine whether some of its salespeople could be made more productive, and to see whether there may be hidden sales talent among individuals doing other, non-sales jobs for the company. After completing this at-home talent search, the company has put out the broadest possible net, attracting every potential available source of talent. It has screened out only those people who clearly lack educational or background factors which are absolutely and objectively essential to selling the company's product or service, and which realistically could not be provided through a company training program. This broad-net approach should have brought in a large number of applicants, establishing a large base to begin the pyramid approach to hiring. This base is then narrowed, first through a

169

review of résumés, which eliminates some obviously inappropriate people, and then through a brief telephone interview, which can reduce the number of applicants to be considered still further. A brief, in-person interview reduces the valid applicant pool still further; and finally, a reference check completes the screening-out process.

It is at this point that the remaining candidates should be few enough in number to permit the company to focus a great deal of attention on them in order to make that final, all-important hiring decision. The first step in the screening-in process is the use of a valid psychological test to uncover an individual's real potential—his or her strengths, weaknesses, and motivations—and to provide further insights into the final job match. In all probability, some additional individuals will be screened out after the test results are reviewed. The test should serve to help determine not only whether the individual can do the job, but also whether his or her personality integrates properly with the manager's and with the overall chemistry of the sales team. The test should also be used to help plan training and supervisory approaches, should the individual be hired, and the data provided by the test should also play an important part in structuring the in-depth interview to follow.

With all the weaknesses of the interview process, the final interview is still the step that integrates all the other steps, paving the way for the most effective final decision. It is during the final interview that discrepancies in data provided by all the other steps can be reconciled, final impressions confirmed, and doubts alleviated. It is here that no effort is too great, no interview is too long, and no further checks are too detailed, given the importance of the final hiring decision.

We are certainly not saying that even with all these admonitions and even if this pyramid approach is followed meticulously, there will not be hiring mistakes. The process of recruitment and selection still remains as much an art as a science; and when it comes down to it, it still depends a good deal on the skill of the individual doing the recruitment and selection. A good, skilled interviewer, no matter how scientific the approach, and no matter how good the test, will still produce a better hiring batting average than a less skilled individual. However, even the most skilled interviewer, using the finest, most valid, most reliable, most job-related psychological test and checking references in the most meticulous way, will still make hiring mistakes. This being said, however, it should be emphasized that there is as enormous a difference between the batting average of hiring decisions made in the way we suggest and those made in the old, haphazard way as there is between the batting average of a league leader's .373 and a journeyman's .220. Neither is perfect, but if you were a manager of a baseball team, which would you prefer?

The Candidate's Decision

Most managers tend to forget that the candidate is involved in an equally difficult decision-making process. It is as critical for the individual as it is for the company to make a valid, objective decision.

We have not offered a cute "20 questions that candidates can ask themselves to decide whether or not to be in sales." We don't have to since this pyramid recruitment and selection process, which we recommend companies use, also provides the potential salesperson with help to make a decision.

We hope that, after reading this book, many people who are not in sales, or have never even considered being in sales, might look toward the profession as an important opportunity. As people explore the various personality attributes that it takes to succeed in sales, they can look at themselves and at least begin the process of self-appraisal. They, at least initially, could ask themselves if they would be happy in an occupation in which persuasion is central to success.

A yes obviously does not mean the individual really has sales potential, but at least a yes might provide a signal that sales might be an opportunity worth further exploration. If the individual chooses to explore sales, the pyramid selection process used by the company affords that individual a step-by-step opportunity not only to persuade the company to continue considering him or her, but to decide whether he or she wants to continue to be considered.

Each step, then, in the pyramid process can be thought of by the candidate as part of his or her own information-gathering process. The telephone is a two-way device. The short telephone interview should be viewed not just as the company's opportunity to ask questions and draw out data from the applicant, but also as the applicant's opportunity to find out more about the company. A few probing questions can help the individual determine whether he or she would want to sell that product or service. Parenthetically, if that phone interview, and, for that matter, the follow-up in-person interview is viewed by the interviewee as a process for mutual data gathering, that very projection lends weight and credibility to the individual's application. The individual (while, of course, trying to sell himself or herself to the company) should be gathering enough information to decide whether the job would be "fun," because if a sales job is not fun to an individual, he or she does not have what it takes to succeed in selling.

If the process has gone that far, the final interview should also be used by the applicant to help make the final decision. There is nothing wrong with asking the employer to reveal something about the test results and to talk openly with the employer about how the weaknesses revealed by the test, or in other steps of the process, might be overcome on the job. There is nothing wrong, for example, for an individual who has poor time-planning skills, a weakness which has been revealed by the test and of which the individual is fully aware, to find out whether the company offers any help in overcoming this problem through either management support, training, or both. If not, maybe that sales job is not for the particular applicant, and even if the job is offered, it might be better to say no.

The Critical Decision

What we are saying, in short, is that the hiring decision is an extremely critical one. Suffice it say here that the costs to industry are far too great to permit anything but the best techniques to be utilized in making the hiring decision. At the same time, applicants not only must sell themselves, but must also use every bit of knowledge they can mobilize to help them determine whether or not the opportunity is really for them. As we have said in the first chapter of this book, sales provides a brilliant, unique opportunity to the right person, but the high rate of turnover and the very fact that only 20 percent of people sell 80 percent of what is sold prove beyond question that that opportunity is only a good one for the right person.

We are convinced, and we have seen in our work with thousands of clients, that when a company and an individual together make an effort to determine whether a match exists between the individual and the job, both profit enormously. Sometimes the best thing that can happen to an individual is to be turned down for a sales job for which he or she is not appropriate; conversely, some of the greatest sales success stories we have come across are people who never dreamed of sales, but who are now numbered among the sales millionaires. The opportunities are exciting; the final decision critical. If done systematically, the final decision can be the right one for the company *and* the individual.

5

The Sales Manager

Making sure that goals are met, salespeople stay motivated, talents are developed, the best applicants are hired, and the future is prepared for is quite a juggling act. It takes a special mix of talents and personal qualities.

You might think that the best salespeople would automatically make the best managers. But often this is not the case. All too often, the very qualities that enable someone to excel as a salesperson can cause him or her to be an ineffective manager.

In this section, we'll explore the underlying differences between what drives someone to be effective in sales and what motivates someone else to manage effectively. We'll also explore the difference between managing and leading, which can mean the difference between winning and losing in cutthroat markets. Pure managers make the system work. Leaders make things happen. And in the process, leaders make the people around them better.

25

Why the Best Salespeople Often Don't Become Great Managers

To promote the star salesperson to a managerial position often induces a classic application of the "Peter Principle." This practice seems, on reflection, to be almost purposefully self-defeating, since it removes that rare breed, the top sales producer, from the opportunity to produce sales and places this person in a job for which his or her competence may be, at best, questionable. Yet this practice would appear to be the rule rather than the exception. In fact, it is almost institutionalized by some company recruiters, who promise young people that a beginning in sales is the sure, and usually the straightest, road to a managerial career.

The philosophy underlying this strange practice is that if a person can sell successfully, he or she can manage salespeople with equal success. This is like saying that since cabbages and strawberries grow close to the ground, they taste equally good boiled and served with corned beef.

On its face, the assumption can be recognized as fallacious. Certainly, some salespeople can manage, and some managers can sell. But the psychological realities strongly favor less than desirable results when the roles are indiscriminately interchanged.

Most frequently, executives live to regret the promotion of their strong sales personnel into management jobs. The first and most obvious result is the loss of an outstanding salesperson and the gain of a mediocre, or worse, manager. The misfortune is compounded by a secondary consequence: The former salesperson who fails as a manager often will not, indeed cannot, go back to the sales force of the same company, since this is a tacit admission to his or her associates of failure. This person will be more inclined to leave the company, sometimes taking a sales job with a competitor, on whose behalf he or she begins to exercise the sales abilities that take business from the former employer.

This problem will come as no surprise to many experienced managers. In fact, when discussing it, they almost invariably tell us that they know the automatic promotion of top salespeople to managerial responsibilities is an unwise policy. But more often than not, they follow this acknowledgment with a shrug and an admission of bafflement: "Where else can we find sales managers?" or "Our people want to be promoted or rewarded, in some way, for good and faithful performance. What else can we give them?"

No matter how genuine their frustrations, their solutions are short-lived. But there is a rational approach that can lead to a permanent solution: Reward your good salespeople in the most imaginative and suitable ways, but promote to management only those individuals who have the ability to manage.

While most everyone strives for growth and development rewards, not all salespeople are cut out to be sales managers. In fact, the characteristics of the best salespeople are often in conflict with the tasks required of sales and operational management. Salespeople like to sell and win and derive great satisfaction from being the "one who makes it happen."

The act of persuading and the recognition of the salesperson's role in engineering that magical transformation of getting another person to say yes are the very stuff that drives the salesperson to succeed. However, once a successful salesperson beats out the competition and persuades the organization that he or she is the best candidate to become sales manager, this person often finds out that the nature of the sales management role is not what he or she thought it would be. In fact, the nature of most sales management roles requires highly successful, independent contributors to subordinate the very characteristics that make them feel good about who they are and engage in tasks that emphasize traits contrary to their very nature.

It's like our parents have told us so many times: Be careful what you wish for—you may get it!

A Balancing Act

Leader, mentor, trainer, taskmaster, coach, monitor, liaison, administrator, baby-sitter, disciplinarian, organizer, herder of cats. When performed well, the sales manager's role is the glue that keeps salespeople on course with the goals of the organization. It is the sales manager who cultivates, monitors, and protects the precious revenue streams on which every business is dependent. Often the key communication pipeline between field operations and internal operations, the sales manager plays a critical role in the selection, development, coordination, and productivity of the people who, in turn, generate the revenue lifeblood of the business. Clearly the sales manager's role is critical. However, as noted earlier, while the sales manager's role is the obvious next step up the proverbial corporate ladder, not every successful salesperson is cut out to climb the rung.

It would be a significant understatement to say that salespeople can be difficult to manage. Just ask any person who has held the role. By their very nature, salespeople tend to be demanding and impatient and have little tolerance for routine details. "Expense report? Sure, I'll get it to you next Tuesday!" " Lead documentation? No problem. I'll do it over the weekend." "New-product training? I've got this great appointment . . . maybe next week." "You want my calendar and call plan for the next month? Are you kidding?"

The sales manager's role requires organization and discipline, a high level of patience, the ability and willingness to delegate, and the capability of deriving satisfaction from seeing someone else win. When you say it out loud, it becomes obvious that these qualities are actually the opposite of an ideal salesperson's qualities.

Consider this: Very few star athletes are able to become coaches or general managers. While some are able to develop the technical skills, few have the temperament to subordinate their own desire to "make the shot" or "score the point." Some do succeed in making the transition. However, the star performer who can't give up the satisfaction that comes from scoring the winning point runs the risk of being in competition with the very people he or she must coach, mentor, monitor, discipline, and develop. It is this conflict of motivational interests that potentially inhibits the very successful salesperson from becoming a star at the management level.

The Differences

There is considerable evidence that argues that sales and managerial abilities *are not* necessarily correlated. The jobs are actually quite different. Moreover, the personality dynamics that make a top salesperson successful and those that make an excellent manager are frequently, if not mutually, exclusive, and are at the least in unremitting conflict.

Over the years, we have had the opportunity to study and evaluate the underlying personality characteristics of thousands of salespeople and managers. In looking at traditional "hunter" salesperson dynamics compared with those of top-rated managers, a number of key differences come to the surface in study after study.

Most recently, we completed a cross-industry study that contrasted the personality profiles of 629 top producing sales "hunters" with the profiles of 1,470 top-performing managers who were working for 267 companies located throughout the United States, Great Britain, Canada, Brazil, Mexico, and Japan. In general, our findings clearly confirm that successful salespeople exhibit fundamentally different personality profiles and characteristics than successful managers.

More specifically, as can be seen from the graph in Figure 25-1, the successful sales "hunters" we profiled scored significantly higher on measures of:

- Ego-drive, the motivation to persuade
- Assertiveness, the inclination to be proactive and forceful in expressing ideas
- Urgency, the need to get things done
- Risk taking, the willingness to consider and take chances
- Sociability, the desire to be around and work with other people
- Gregariousness, the inclination and confidence to network and proactively establish new relationships

By and large, the salespeople in our study are likely to derive considerably more gratification from the act of persuading others than are the managers. In addition, the salespeople will tend to be naturals in meeting and developing relationships with new people. The top-performing managers, on the other hand, while having more moderate profiles on the characteristics noted above, exhibited significantly higher scores on:

- Cautiousness, an inclination toward due diligence and "looking before you leap"
- Thoroughness, an orientation toward working with and managing details
- Self-structure, a tendency to define priorities and exercise self-discipline
- External structure, an orientation toward working within and maintaining established rules

Quite simply, the managers are built differently from the top-performing salespeople. They are more likely to have a natural orientation toward structure and details and do not have as strong a need to score every point themselves. As a result, they are more able to work through others and more comfortable with the delegating, coordinating, organizing, coaching, and monitoring aspects of the role.

To Promote or Not to Promote?

On many occasions, exasperated managers have told us that a sales management spot has just become open in the company and that several top salespeople are not very bashfully lusting after it. Our advice is unvarying: Give your best salesperson anything that is feasible—a big private office with a thick rug and a huge desk, medals with oak-leaf clusters, increased commissions, dinners in their honor—anything to show the degree to which their performance is valued and appreciated. But under no circumstances make them managers without being certain they have the proper dynamics to manage.

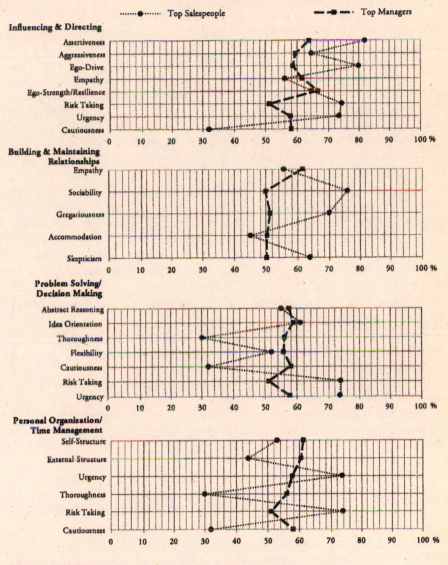

Top Salespeople vs. Top Managers

Figure 25-1

It may be difficult to make them understand that, in the long run, neither they nor you will benefit by the wrong promotional move. Though difficult, the attempt must be made.

The underlying problems seem to be rooted in salespeople's perception of the managerial role. First, they frequently feel that greater status is attached to managing than to selling. The salesperson in the field often perceives the manager as the person who "has it made"; the manager has his or her name and title on the door to the big office, is under less pressure to produce, and is judged only on the basis of others' performance.

It is in response to just such perceptions that many efforts have been made over the past four decades to professionalize sales. What generally is meant by this is the upgrading of the image of selling, not only in terms of the public's view of the salesperson, but also in terms of the salesperson's view of himself or herself.

However well intentioned, many of these efforts have been simplistic and shallow, suggesting, for example, that associations of salespeople or substitute terms to describe the job of selling might make the salesperson happier. What has not been done adequately to reach the professionalizers' goals is to convey certain facts to the public and to the trade about the salesperson, including facts about the special abilities salespeople need, industry's dependence upon salespeople, their rarity, and the prodigious amounts of energy and money spent to train them. Further, it is necessary to communicate the fact that compensation for the successful salesperson is high—so high that of all people in business earning over $100,000, more than half are salespeople. Finally, there is a need to communicate the most important fact of all: that sales offers rich opportunity for fulfillment and nonmaterial personal gain, including maximum opportunity for freedom to do a job in one's own way.

Therefore, salespeople should be careful to avoid managerial jobs unless they are convinced that their best talents and greatest opportunities for gratification lie in managing.

Admittedly, these are not easy points to sell a salesperson who hungers after the prestige and ease that he or she thinks are concomitant with a managerial position. We were recently importuned by a client in Texas to speak with his top salesperson, who he feared would resign if not moved into management. The manager, a friend of long-standing, foresaw the consequences of that step, and he valued the man too much to lose him, either before or after a promotion. So he gave the man and his wife an all-expense-paid vacation to New York with a room at the Plaza Hotel, theater tickets, a driver and a limousine, and luxury restaurant reservations. His only official business was to come to our offices in Princeton for a chat.

The dialogue was remarkable. Frank told us that his boss might just as well have saved his money, because although he appreciated the gesture, he was leaving the company. Why? He had been refused a sales management spot which, by seniority and performance, he should have been offered.

Frank said of his boss, "He promoted a guy—put him over me—who could not sell his way out of a wet paper sack. Now he can go to hell!"

We sympathized and then got on to other subjects, primarily selling. Since we had tested him previously, we knew more about him than he could ever have suspected. We knew he loved to sell, that he was tremendously driven, that he had absolutely no tolerance for detail, that activities such as planning territories and sitting in marketing meetings would bore him intolerably.

"I love selling. It's my whole life," he told us, and then launched into story after story of his sales triumphs, which still brought him a noticeable glow of pleasure.

The situation was clear. His feelings were hurt. He felt that he was not appreciated and that his honor had been impugned when a promotion went to someone seemingly less deserving. He rejected the unconscious suspicion that he would dislike the management job and kept insisting that he should have it.

Our job was cut out for us. Our first strategic move was to point out many of the things he already knew about the management spot, with emphasis on those of its features likely to be least attractive to him. Secondly, we reassured him that his boss "loved" him and valued his services and their relationship so highly he would not abet any plan, no matter how innocent, that would make him unhappy, even at the risk of losing a top salesperson and a friend. Finally, we stressed a fact he may not have known: Ultimately, he probably would earn about $20,000 less in the managerial spot. There was a ceiling on the earnings of managers, but none on those of salespeople, many of whom build excellent incomes on the basis of accumulated sales. The talk about money and unpleasant managerial responsibilities no doubt had its effect, but what turned the trick was the assurance that his boss valued him so highly.

Frank went home to Dallas the next weekend, and a call the following Monday morning from his boss verified our private prophecies. Frank was back on the job and raring to go.

Here are some of the things we told Frank that might be repeated almost verbatim to the salesperson determined to inherit the title, if not the responsibilities, of a manager. Be prepared to:

■ Sublimate your own ego; let the people under you get the glory.

■ Learn how to handle detail, for there will be lots of it, including, in addition to your own reports and administrative record keeping, all the sales reports and expense vouchers of every salesperson in your territory.

- Organize your own activities and those of your sales staff.
- Induce your staff to act without forcing compliance, an exercise that requires infinite quantities of patience (a characteristic not notably abundant in top salespeople).
- Make decisions of a more far-reaching nature than those that affect a single sale; this requires that you gather and evaluate all pertinent information and consider the consequences of your decisions.
- Plan and analyze—for countless hours—prospect lists, advertising programs, and marketing plans, instead of dealing with people.
- Figure on attending frequent meetings, listening to the problems and complaints of your salespeople, and justifying their performance—and your own—to your supervisors.
- Handle such personnel chores as firing people you like or recommending that they be fired.
- Function as a liaison between the needs of each salesperson and the company.

Those are only a few in a long catalogue of sales manager responsibilities and tasks that can be anathema to the good salesperson.

Those Who Can

There is, of course, another dimension to the matter of the salesperson turning manager. There are thousands of potentially excellent managers who are now engaged in selling. So executives looking for a sales manager would be foolish to overlook the possibility that the right person for the job is already on the sales force.

Every salesperson should be studied as a potential manager, virtually from the day the person is hired. The reasons are obvious: If the manager is promoted from the sales ranks, that person will begin his or her first managerial day with an infinite knowledge of the company's products, clientele, sales force, sales problems, and policies. The benefits of promoting qualified people to managerial responsibilities are so clear, in fact, that we have for many years evaluated and reported the managerial potential of all salespeople we have assessed.

The fact that there are so many salespeople who cannot manage does not invalidate the fact that there are many who can. Danger lies only in the belief that competence displayed in one area can be assumed to indicate competence in all other areas; or, for that matter, that demonstrated incompetence in a single activity is a guarantee of general incompetence.

The fact is that we have found far more people in the middle of a sales force who have turned out to be well-qualified managers than we have found at the very top. Again, as we noted in our research, those in the middle have tended to have somewhat less ego-drive and so are able to tolerate delegation better than their more strongly driven, perhaps more productive, sales colleagues. Also, a person with less ego-drive tends to have better tolerance of detail and a more balanced ability to make decisions and to handle work in a more organized way. Again, this should not be thought of as an absolute since certainly there are those few top people in sales forces who have become outstanding managers. The point, again, is that when you are looking for a salesperson, you are looking for sales dynamics (empathy, ego-drive, ego-strength, service motivation, conscientiousness, etc.), while when you are looking for a manager, you are searching for leadership ability, including the abilities to delegate, to make good management decisions, to handle detail, to coordinate and follow up on the work of others, etc. If all these qualities happen to be combined in the same individual, that makes for the best of all worlds due to the benefits inherent in promoting one of your own salespeople to manager. But if such a combination does not exist, be certain that the management dynamics are present regardless of outstanding sales performance.

As in so much that we have written in this book, the critical element here is matching the dynamics of a particular individual to the dynamics required by a particular job. It is only through matching relevant dynamics that you are likely to fill the job successfully.

So before concluding this chapter, let's explore in more depth the qualities an individual needs to succeed in the sales management role. A number of these qualities overlap attributes that are required to succeed in certain sales situations. To succeed as a sales manager, the possession of most of these qualities is essential.

Among extremely effective executives we have worked with, there are flamboyant extroverts as well as those who are painfully shy. While some stick to the straight and narrow, others give eccentricity a new meaning. Some are self-centered, while others are generous to a fault. For every manager who suffers over decisions, there is one who seems to make decisions with great ease and aplomb. Some have broad interests, while others know nothing except their own area of expertise.

Defining the Management Role

To be effective, managers have to sense opportunities, formulate new possibilities, build coalitions with peers, and convince those in positions of higher authority that their proposed innovations will help achieve corporate goals.

Using interviews and reviews of various task and competency surveys, 360 tools, our in-depth personality assessments, and reviews of the general literature, we have concluded that leadership and management tasks can be divided into four dominant themes:

Influencing and Directing

Building and Maintaining Relationships

Problem Solving and Decision Making

Personal Organization and Time Management

Influencing and Directing

In order for any manager to be successful, he or she must be adept at influencing and directing the actions of others. Walt Disney's CEO, Michael Eisner, believes that having a strong point of view is one of the most critical elements needed to be successful in management. He says, "Around here, a strong point of view is worth at least 80 IQ points."

Effective managers or leaders must be capable of assertively presenting their goals and ideas in a confident and straightforward manner without damaging the confidence or self-esteem of their audience. They must have the drive and empathy to be persuasive when necessary and able to provide clear direction in order to convey expectations and provide feedback. The management role requires the ability to delegate and follow through without taking over or abdicating—a tough trick for a highly ego-driven salesperson who is addicted to closing and has limited patience for people who might inhibit movement toward a sought-after goal or objective. Top managers need to be effective in negotiating "win-win" outcomes. And most important, they need to be capable of subordinating their own ego-gratification to become masters at playing the role of the coach and mentor. More simply put, they must change their frame of reference from "I" to "we" and derive satisfaction from a broader victory attained through others.

Building and Maintaining Relationships

At the end of the day, this is the one area in which salespeople and managers have the most in common. Sales and management roles are all people jobs. They require well-honed interpersonal skills, as well as the ability to maintain credibility and engender trust. The very best salespeople, managers, and leaders have the empathy necessary to relate to others. They are naturals at listening and understanding subtle cues and responses that other people provide. Effective communicators, these managers, salespeople, and leaders are able to adjust or modify their messages and styles of presentation to meet the needs and expectations of their audience, while at the same time accomplishing their own mission. In addition, top-level managers, like top-level salespeople, have the confidence and assertiveness to express themselves and sufficient outgoingness and sociability to network and initiate relationships. They generally like being around people. They don't wait for people to come to them. Rather, they are proactive in establishing rapport and in providing the warmth necessary to initiate and maintain ongoing working relationships. The best managers and leaders also have the capability of establishing and coordinating team efforts and building consensus, thus creating cooperative working environments in which everyone has the opportunity to be successful.

In general, the best managers, like the best salespeople, enjoy working with people and are very good at it.

Problem Solving and Decision Making

All management and leadership roles begin with the recognition of a need, opportunity, or problem. The most effective managers are able to spot trends, evaluate alternatives, and make decisions. They are able to synthesize and analyze vast amounts of information about performance, the competition, the marketplace, and company resources in a manner that balances the business's immediate needs with those of the future. They recognize problems and issues; analyze root causes; evaluate and consider alternatives; develop goals, strategies, and tactics; and most important, make decisions.

Top-performing managers and leaders have a high level of abstract problem-solving capability. They are open-minded and flexible in their thinking, and they balance the need to be careful and thorough with the ability to "pull the trigger." They are not afraid of risking the occasional wrong decision, as they are confident in their ability to recover and move forward. The best managers and leaders have the courage to take action and the ability to learn from their mistakes.

The effective sales manager, in particular, is likely to be a careful diagnostician who has the ability to monitor and evaluate performance trends and define tactics for engineering-improved results for both the individual and the business. Such analysis requires the patience and thoroughness to sift through data and the conscientiousness to plan a strategy, while at the same time maintaining a sense of urgency about moving forward. Most salespeople are great on the urgency but fall short on the due diligence. Both are necessary!

Personal Organization and Time Management

Organization and time management constitute *the* critical task of management. The best managers are adept at setting and juggling goals, objectives, and priorities. Working within established rules, systems, and procedures, top managers must define key tasks, establish and/or implement measurement criteria for tracking results, assign priorities and resources, and follow through to ensure timely and accurate completion of assignments. It is the consistency of sticking to a defined set of tasks and a well-managed agenda that results in expectations attained.

Staying focused, managing interruptions and distractions, persisting, making adjustments to an established plan in a timely manner, and using time efficiently—these are the hallmarks of managerial performance. The most effective managers have a high level of discipline, a thorough style of working with details, and, as well, a strong sense of urgency. They do not focus on details for details' sake. Rather, they are achievement-minded and have the flexibility and confidence to make decisions or shift the agenda to respond to developing needs. Moreover, they have the focus necessary to balance near-term objectives with long-term goals.

Unique Combination

In essence, while managers approach their work with varying styles and approaches, we have found that there are basic characteristics needed to effectively manage, regardless of the situation.

To be effective, a manager must be able to analyze situations, be willing to make decisions and take risks, be able to communicate effectively, be capable of commanding respect from others, be able to delegate and motivate, be consistent and fair, and be willing to encourage growth in others as well as oneself.

Rather than trying to fit into a prescribed mold, the best managers with whom we have worked are those who thoroughly understand their inherent strengths and limitations. Then they build a team by doing what they do best and hiring others whose strengths complement their limitations.

Allow us to close with an analogy. In sports, we have known that the moment a new record is set, every athlete throughout the world acquires a new dimension of accomplishment. For years, no one could run the mile in less than 4 minutes. Then, Roger Bannister broke through the old record, and soon runners from every neighborhood athletic club were approaching the mark, while another generation of leaders began to break new barriers.

In human affairs, the distance between the leaders and the average remains constant. If leadership performance is high, the average will increase. Thus, the easiest way to raise the performance of an entire company is to raise the effectiveness of its management.

26

Managers or Leaders

As was suggested in the prior chapter about sales management, salespeople, like many other employees, naturally look to the next step on the corporate ladder as a way to satisfy their motivation for growth, status, and development. Most all of us want and need to keep moving forward with our careers. So, what are the very best salespeople supposed to do if they want to climb the corporate ladder? For many of them, it would be like defying gravity. As our studies have shown, the characteristics of the best salespeople are often in conflict with some of the key tasks required of managers.

Yet many topflight salespeople have, in fact, gone on to become superb leaders. They bring vision, momentum, and energy to an enterprise that are contagious. Being in a "power position" plays to their strengths. They know how to recognize talents in others, energize them, and make things happen.

But the question begs: If so many top-performing salespeople go on to become ineffective managers, why do some succeed in key leadership roles? How do they overcome the odds? Part of the answer has to do with the difference between managing and leading.

We have just completed a study (spanning the past decade) in which we evaluated the qualities that distinguish the best leaders, managers, and salespeople. We evaluated and compared the characteristics of 293 presidents and CEOs with the profiles of 1,470 superior managers and 629 top salespeople. What we found was a much closer relationship between top leaders and salespeople than between top leaders and managers.

The best leaders and salespeople seem to be cut from the same cloth. Interestingly, during interviews, we found that most of the leaders actually came up through the sales ranks. That is good news for some top salespeople who aspire to new challenges. But it does not leave the doors of leadership wide open to all top salespeople.

The Essence of Leadership

Leadership is the ability that enables an individual to get other people to do willingly what they have the ability to do, but might not ordinarily do on their own.

The entrepreneurial leader is truly a salesperson on a broader scale. Whether pitching an idea to an important client, negotiating a strategic relationship, persuading a key employee to take on a new challenge, or doing a pre-IPO dot-com road show, the CEOs and other top leaders we studied embody many of the characteristics of top-level salespeople. And they too seem somewhat "challenged" when it comes to tasks requiring discipline, structure, and a conscientious focus on details and due diligence.

For most organizations, it is the leader's voice that sets the tone, defines the vision, and manages the agenda. Moreover, our research indicates that just like many salespeople are not likely to be well matched to a management role, most managers are not likely to be well suited to top-level leadership positions. They're just not built the same way.

Given these findings, organizations would do well to look within their sales ranks for future leadership candidates. For it is among these highly driven, but sometimes detail-challenged, individuals that the soul of the leader is incubated.

Like sales roles, the ability to assume leadership is, first and foremost, a function of who we are. Henato Munyoz Da Hosha, president of Inepar, one of our clients in Brazil, says, "If you put leaders in a group, within a very short period of time they will stand out—either because of their conversation and the ideas they express or simply because of the way they present themselves."

How do you identify leadership potential? Leadership is difficult to express by someone who is not in a leadership position. At best, leadership can be sporadic or situational. And when the potential is identified, it requires nurturing, mentoring, and coaching and may not be sustainable across time. But organizations have a tendency to suffocate future leaders by allowing only those at the top to have a chance to play the role. This is often the reason why salespeople who have a focus on moving forward are attracted to entrepreneurial opportunities where they can be in charge.

Warren Bennis, a distinguished professor and well-known author, describes leaders another way. He says that a leader is "a pragmatic dreamer, a person with an original but attainable vision." He further posits that "managers do things right, while leaders do the right things." (In other words, leaders may have a tendency to leave the details for others.)

From our perspective:

■ Managers focus on results. Leaders know that results are achieved through people.

- Managers are implementers. Leaders are initiators.

- Managers command through their position. Leaders inspire following because they can make great ideas come alive.

- Managers have their opinions. Leaders help form opinions.

- Managers are followed because they are bosses. Leaders are followed because we believe in them.

What we are certain about is that leaders are different from managers—and more like salespeople—in the underlying personality characteristics that define who they are. At their best, leaders are inspiring. So are salespeople. They do not merely provide direction and ideas, but create the music, orchestrate the resources, and create environments where new achievements are realized.

The Most Important Aspect of Leadership

In 1998 we completed a survey of 300 presidents and chief executive officers within our database. All these people were with companies that we have worked with over the past 10-year period. We asked them what they considered to be the most important aspects and the worst aspects of being a leader. Among the choices we asked them to rank were:

- Creating the right vision

- Getting people to embrace that vision

- Maintaining momentum (motivating, influencing, and persuading others)

- Managing change (strategic planning, problem solving, etc.)

- Surrounding yourself with the right people

- Developing staff (coaching individuals, managing performance, facilitating teams)

- Delegating authority

- Orchestrating priorities

- Making tough decisions about capital, financial, and human resources

- Staying the course

- Keeping self-confidence

These leaders told us that surrounding themselves with the right people was among the best *and* worst aspects of leading a company. "Surrounding yourself with the right people" was selected 42 percent of the time, second only to "creating the right vision," as one of the best parts of being a leader.

Interestingly, it was also selected as one of the three most difficult aspects of being an effective leader, just behind "maintaining momentum" and "developing staff."

When you are leading an organization, surrounding yourself with the right people becomes an either-or situation. Either you hire and develop people whom you thoroughly enjoy working with, people who are bright, engaging, conscientious, and adept at solving problems—or the chemistry is not there and leading becomes a constant battle.

In general, the leadership group we surveyed recognized the critical importance of first having the " right idea" and then getting other people (who embrace that idea) on board and engaged in the tasks of implementing that idea and effecting change.

Salespeople Are More Like Leaders Than Managers

In the prior chapter on sales management we compared the qualities of top-performing salespeople with the underlying personality characteristics of top-performing managers. We concluded that there were considerable differences between the two groups. However, as can be seen from Figures 26-1 to 26-4, the characteristics of top salespeople are quite similar to those of top executive leaders.

Influencing and Directing

Compared with the profile of top managers, both the salespeople we evaluated and the top executives who participated in our study scored significantly higher on measures of assertiveness, aggressiveness, and ego-drive (see Figure 26-1). In general, the executives and salespeople are far more likely to be dominant, proactive, and persuasive in expressing their ideas. More to the point, the executives and salespeople we assessed will generally be more competitively motivated and will derive gratification when their point of view is adopted. They not only like winning; they like being the one who scores the point. In addition, the executives and salespeople who participated in our studies are far more likely to exhibit impatience and take risks and are much less cautious in moving forward than are the top-performing managers. In general, both salespeople and executives are likely to present themselves in a directive, highly compelling, though somewhat intense and impatient, manner.

The top managers, on the other hand, present a more "balanced" profile of characteristics. Compared with the salespeople and executives, they are likely

Influencing and Directing

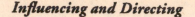

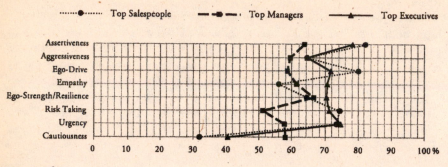

Figure 26-1

to be more willing to subordinate their own ego-gratification in favor of an individual contributor or a team win. In addition, they are far less likely to take risks and will generally be more cautious and less impulsive in their interactions with others. While they are capable of directing and influencing others, the top-performing managers are more likely to take a facilitative role rather than a dominant role. As a result, they may be more effective in supporting, coaching, and mentoring others, including the leaders they report to, than in taking the dominant leadership position. They are just built that way.

For salespeople who are "leaders in waiting," here's one important point to consider: From an influencing and directing perspective, the executives we profiled differed from salespeople in at least one important quality. Top executives are likely to exhibit a higher level of empathy than salespeople, in general. This suggests that in order for top salespeople to ascend the leadership ladder, they must be capable of guiding their vision and presenting their persuasive message with great sensitivity to the needs of their audience. Clearly not all the salespeople who participated in our study, despite their top-level status, are as empathic as might be optimal.

Building and Maintaining Relationships

When it comes to working with and interacting with others, there are some key differences between the salespeople, leaders, and managers we profiled (see Figure 26-2). The salespeople, as noted, generally scored somewhat lower on empathy than did the leaders. In this regard, they were more similar to the top-management group: able to identify with another point of view, but a bit inflexible on occasion. The most significant differences between the leaders and salespeople centered on sociability and gregariousness.

Building and Maintaining Relationships

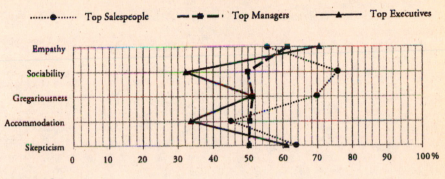

Figure 26-2

In general, salespeople are strongly outgoing. Likely to be proactive in networking and establishing new contacts, they will be comfortable in putting themselves into situations where there is an opportunity to interact with other people. In fact, they are likely to enjoy doing so. Top executives, on the other hand, while having great empathy and the ability to relate to others, are, for the most part, likely to be somewhat private. They have sufficient gregariousness to "play the game" but will be highly selective in terms of whom they choose to spend their time with. Top-rated managers are empathic in their ability to relate but generally moderate in their outgoingness, accommodation, and skepticism—not nearly as extreme as the other two groups.

Given the above differences, it is clear that not all salespeople will be entirely comfortable in the highly isolated role of the leader. We are reminded of the old saw, "It's lonely at the top." Leaders play the game but are quite comfortable going it alone. Most salespeople need and want to be around people.

Problem Solving and Decision Making

As problem solvers, salespeople are, again, much more like the top executive group than the management group (see Figure 26-3). While the top leaders generally score significantly higher than both salespeople and other managers on abstract reasoning ability and idea orientation, their style of problem solving and decision making is similar to that of salespeople.

Leaders tend to be somewhat more creative and bring tremendous problem-solving ability and flexibility to the core leadership tasks of recognizing issues

Problem Solving/Decision Making

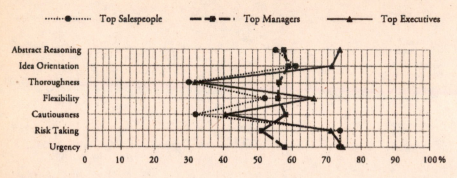

Figure 26-3

and opportunities, developing strategies, and working through barriers that impede progress toward important goals. However, like salespeople, they tend to be impatient to reach conclusions and take action, and have limited tolerance for minutia and aspects of detail. Again, the managers tend to be more balanced and moderate in their approach to problem solving—more comfortable with details and likely to be less impatient with the process of getting to the right conclusion.

Leaders and salespeople are less concerned with issues of due diligence and are, thus, much more likely to take actions based upon instincts. Here is one more important caveat for those salespeople who see themselves as leaders and want to move forward—given their superior problem-solving capabilities, top executives are far more likely to survive on their instincts, and thus their decisions usually will be more accurate. For those salespeople who have a more moderate abstract reasoning capability (as most of us do), there is no substitute for exercising a small degree of restraint.

Personal Organization and Time Management

Neither leaders nor salespeople are likely to be highly organized or disciplined in their focus (see Figure 26-4). While top-level managers are generally oriented toward defining and setting goals, establishing and budgeting priorities, implementing tactics, tracking performance and other details, and managing following through, salespeople and top executives share a tendency to be spontaneous, easily distractible, opportunistic, and impatient.

Personal Organization/Time Management

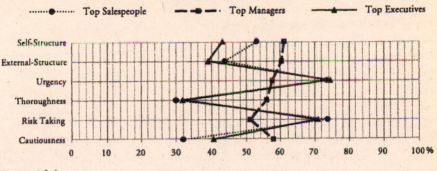

Figure 26-4

These groups thrive on chaos and are oftentimes responsible for creating it.

Exemplary managers, the people whom leaders surround themselves with and who are responsible for directing the efforts of salespeople, "do things right." Salespeople and top executive leaders frequently leave the mess for others to clean up.

From a career development perspective, the strong persuasive orientation, problem-solving style, and limited tolerance for routine all point in the direction of taking on an influencing role rather than a control role.

Knowing Who You Are

Given our overall findings, there are many similarities between the characteristics of top executives and those of salespeople—more, in fact, than between salespeople and sales managers. This poses a dilemma, both for the salesperson who wants upward mobility and a chance at the "golden ring", and for the organization that has a need not only to retain its sales force but to safeguard its future talent pool of potential managers and leaders.

You have to start out by being true to yourself. Self-awareness is one of the most fundamental concepts of getting on in the world. People who are highly self-aware know where they are headed. And perhaps more importantly, they know how to play to their strengths.

From our perspective, it is vital in managing your future career growth and development opportunities to know "who you are." Taking the wrong job even for the right reasons can have a catastrophic effect if not managed with a high degree of self-awareness. Are you someone who likes working through others? Do you enjoy the challenge of creating and managing systems? Do you get a kick out of seeing a plan come together? Are you patient? Do you like implementing and tracking plans and seeing them through to the end? Or do you like "taking the shot" and being the "star"? Do you thrive on being around people, or are you as comfortable being alone as with others? Or, in the final analysis, do you get the biggest kick out of selling?

These are important questions to ask yourself and quite relevant in thinking through how and if you should push forward. For some salespeople, the best answer may be to keep doing what you do (and like doing) best: sell. For others, sales management may be a perfect fit. And for those of you who are "leaders in waiting," there are three alternatives: First, you can define a well-thought-through strategy (not an easy task for some of us) for leapfrogging past the sales management role; second, you can go for that management role and "grit through it," with a clear knowledge of your ultimate goal of becoming a leader; or third, you can create a unique path either within your organization or elsewhere.

In the end, we are all responsible for managing our own destinies. Knowing who you are is the basis for engineering a future that "fits."

The Corporate Challenge

While individuals have a need to manage their future career growth and opportunities, organizations have an equally strong need to retain their talent.

As we have pointed out, not every employee has the underlying characteristics that will result in a successful move into a sales management or leadership role. Yet this is almost universally viewed by salespeople as a coveted goal. Organizations must, therefore, be strategic in identifying and targeting future talent. The earlier that talent and potential are recognized, the sooner the development process can begin and the more likely that talent will be retained.

By their very nature, both salespeople and an organization's future managers and leaders need to be recognized. Without that powerful social incentive, these individuals will fail to reach their full potential. The managers and leaders of the future are extremely valuable, and the sales organization is a good breeding ground for their development, provided management is aware of the potential that resides within its ranks.

In order for sales managers and future leaders to be developed, they must be:

Identified

Mentored and coached

Brought to the attention of the organization

Given responsibilities

Nurtured and developed

At the same time, organizations must be creative in professionalizing and improving the status of the sales role so that remaining in that occupation does not carry with it a diminution of material rewards, status, social rewards, and future growth opportunities.

6

Matching Sales Dynamics to Specific Industries

When sales professionals discuss what it takes to succeed in sales, they invariably fall into one of two camps. One group asserts that individuals who have what it takes to sell can sell virtually anything. Provide the members of this group with someone who can sell, and they will gladly teach the person the technical aspects of their product or service. The members of the other group insist that a set of totally unique qualities is needed to sell in their industry and very definitely in their company.

Actually, both groups are right—or, at least, partially. People who possess the basic central dynamics of empathy, ego-drive, ego-strength, conscientiousness, and service motivation will be able to succeed in some kind of sales. The question is, what kind? To a certain degree, the people in the first camp are right: An individual must begin by having the five essential qualities in order to sell. The second camp is correct, however, in that the varying degrees of these central dynamics, plus the possession of numerous other motivational factors, determine an individual's likelihood to succeed in a specific sales job.

While we have provided a fundamental overview of sales in general up to this point, we are now going to focus on specific industries in depth to demonstrate the nuances of the job-matching approach. In reading the following chapters, it will become readily apparent that there are many differences and many similarities among each of these industries. Keep in mind that sometimes the subtlest difference can account for success in a particular situation.

Since it is obviously impossible to give this kind of in-depth examination to dozens of industries, it is our hope that the six cases presented here will cover the spectrum sufficiently to allow managers to better understand some of the unique factors that distinguish their industry, and to allow individuals to look at industries to see if their own personality attributes match the requirements being sought.

27

An Agency's People:
The Bottom-Line Advantage

The independent property and casualty agency, and, in fact, the entire independent insurance agency system, offers an excellent example of the value of capitalism in its purest sense. We say this for a number of reasons, which we will discuss below.

First of all, the independent agency, unlike so many mammoth companies, remains, in most instances, a pure example of entrepreneurism. Typically, an agency is started by one or two individuals who have come up through the independent agency system and often passed down through generations. Even where mergers or acquisitions have occurred, these are often mergers of two or more entrepreneurial enterprises or acquisitions of an entrepreneurial agency by a larger group that started out as, and perhaps continues today, as an essentially entrepreneurial operation. While notice must be taken of the increasingly large role of national and regional conglomerate agencies, the small entrepreneurial agency is still very present in the independent agency system and can still be profitable in today's marketplace.

The second reason we see the independent agency system as so representative of capitalism at its best relates to the very nature of the system itself. Unlike the direct writers, the independent agency represents many companies, which must compete for that agency's placement of business. Similarly, the agency is competing—both with other agencies and with direct writers and today with banks of life insurance companies, for the consumer's property and casualty dollar. The agency must compete by offering the consumer the best value, which means meeting the consumer's needs through products offered by one or a combination of the companies it represents. Also, it must compete by providing the insurance customer with the kind of support and active representation that is unique to the independent agent. No matter how good the salesperson and how honest the claims department of a direct writer may be, they still represent that direct writer, and only that direct writer. The independent agency, however, while it must represent the companies effectively, must also, equally effectively, represent the insurance customer. In a claim situation, that agency had better support the customer, or the customer will cease to be one rather quickly. A good agency will effectively do so without offending or misrepresenting the companies.

As strong as the argument may be that only the independent agency continues to represent the insurance buyer, that argument often fails to sell the customer. A few dollars in premium savings and/or heavy advertising programs very often lead the customer to the direct writer. The reason is simple. Consumers may be exposed to the name and advertising power of the direct writer, but no one may have ever told them persuasively about the advantages of working with an independent agent. If consumers know that they can save a few dollars through a direct writer and do not know any counterarguments, their choice is obvious.

We should hasten to add here that we are not in any way attributing negative characteristics to the direct writing companies. Many of them are fine, have excellent and fair claims departments, and indeed do an outstanding job for their insurance customers. What we are saying, however, is that if the independent agent fails to sell its advantages, the direct writer increasingly becomes the only one to which the consumer is exposed. The fair competition as to their mutual advantages fails to occur, and the direct writer wins by default.

To return to the independent agent and capitalism, it should be clear that to really compete effectively the independent agent *must*, more than many companies, have people within the agency capable of competing. The independent agency, moreover, must have people all through it, regardless of definition of responsibilities, that are capable of dealing with people on a competitive sales level. Often, how the receptionist answers the phone can make as much difference about whether or not a prospect becomes a customer as the producer and the customer service representative themselves. The agency, certainly more than any large company, is thought of by the consumer as being that individual within the agency with whom the customer has come in contact— whether the receptionist, a customer service representative, or a salesperson; often that first impression remains with the prospect, for good or ill. To succeed, therefore, the independent agent must look not only at its sales force—its producers—but at all its agency staff—from underwriters, to claims people, to producers, and even to the agency head— as critical parts of the agency's ability to compete for the insurance dollar.

There was a time not that long ago when an agency, particularly in a small town, could survive by reminding people that its car insurance or home owners renewal premiums were due by simply taking orders. If you needed insurance, everybody knew to call Charlie or Joe, and he would write it up for you. Today, even in the smallest areas, and even where Charlie or Joe may have written up insurance for 40 years, that approach is most likely to lead to disaster, because Harry or Jill may write it up cheaper, and with broader coverage.

Because the total agency must be thought of as a salesperson, we want to make a slight departure from our discussion of what is takes to succeed in sales in its purest sense. What it takes to succeed in sales in the independent agency system is a good agency head, effective producers, strong customer service representatives, underwriters, and claims people. In order to fully understand what it takes to succeed in sales in the independent agency system, we must really understand what it takes to succeed in each of these roles, because it is only through an integration of effectiveness within these roles that success can be achieved. Let us then take a brief look at each of these critical agency roles and see how they tie into the overall agency productivity.

The Agency Head

There is no neat way to define the personality of the effective agency head. What is important to point out, however, is that no agency head, no matter how talented, can or should attempt to do all the jobs of the agency. Of course, in a one-person agency, the case is different. But wherever possible, the agency head should not attempt to be all things to all people. Simply put, people who try to do everything end up doing very little well.

Even in the smallest agency, we suggest that the office manager or secretary possess personality attributes that complement those of the agency head. Only in this way can a proper team be formed, one in which the agent can concentrate on those things for which he or she is best suited.

This being said, there is, nevertheless, the key need, whatever the agent's particular strengths and weaknesses, for the head of an agency to be a leader. It is the agency head who sets the tone, and, of course, it is the agency head who is the primary determinant of the quality of the people in the agency.

Thus, while we reemphasize that no one can or should be everything, there are at least three qualities that the head of an agency should possess if he or she hopes to run an effective organization: decisiveness, the ability to delegate, and leadership.

Decisiveness

In an average workday, the agency head must be a willing, effective decision maker. By this we mean that she or he must be willing to make quick decisions, even at the risk of making an occasional error. But this decisiveness must be balanced with responsibility and intelligence in order to make these decisions with judgment and thought. An effective agency head can neither be too impulsive—too precipitous—nor so overcautious that he or she would fail to act. Balance is the key here.

Delegation

If agency heads are not to do everything themselves, they obviously must delegate responsibilities to others. Effective delegating takes both a willingness to delegate and judgment about which duties to delegate to whom.

The ability to delegate starts off with not needing to do everything themselves, the patience to take the time to explain the job being delegated, and the empathy and intelligence to determine to whom to delegate what—to accurately judge the abilities and motivations of subordinates. How these factors are handled can make or break an agency.

Leadership

Leadership, of course, is really the all-encompassing term embodying effective management. Good leadership certainly includes the ability to make decisions and the ability to delegate.

But by defining it a bit more narrowly as a separate attribute, we look at leadership as the ability that enables an individual to get other people to do willingly what they have the ability to do but might not spontaneously do on their own.

Leadership involves the assertiveness to lead strongly with the empathy to be sensitive to the needs and abilities of those being led. It is the overall ability to get the job done through maximizing the abilities and work of the entire team.

And More

Even if the agency principal possesses all the foregoing attributes in abundance, human nature being what it is, he or she will have particular strengths and weaknesses that point to the need to emphasize particular functions in the agency. For instance, some agents have come up through the sales route. Having formerly been effective salespeople, this means they possess three essential personality attributes: ego-drive (persuasive motivation), empathy (ability to get feedback from a customer or prospect), and ego-strength (ability to take the rejection inevitably involved in sales).

What often happens in such cases is that the agency loses its exceptional sales productivity, only to gain a mediocre, or worse, administrator. To avoid this, such an agent, even in his or her executive position, should continue to be involved in the sales and marketing aspects of the agency. It does not make sense for someone with sales talent not to be out there selling, but to be wasting time handling administrative detail, which may be the weakest aspect of his or her personality.

On the other hand, individuals who have come up through the underwriting or administrative route, and whose abilities are primarily administrative, should not attempt to force themselves into a sales role. Rather, such individuals should make their maximum contribution to the agency through administering and running that agency. What we are suggesting is that, instead of attempting to do everything, agency heads should focus on the things they do best—the functions that are most in tune with their personality—and hire a number two person whose strengths lie in the agency head's weaker areas. The powerful salesperson must have a strong administrator as number two, while the administrator needs a driven, empathic vice president of sales and marketing.

The agent who tries to do everything himself or herself probably will do nothing very well. The best agents we have worked with know themselves very well. Rather than trying to fit into a prescribed mold, they are keenly aware of their unique strengths and limitations. They structure their agency in a way that allows their strengths to thrive.

Producer

The term "producer" is one of the more confusing titles in the agency lexicon of positions. One agency head will tell us that he or she wants the producer to do one thing: close sales, bring in new business. "Once a salesperson brings an account in, our CSRs take good care of it," the agency head will say, adding, "We don't want a producer to touch customers once they are brought on board."

Other agency heads will define the position entirely differently. The producer they are looking for will inherit a large book of business, and his or her primary job will be to service and expand that business, while, it is hoped, getting some referrals out of that business. Rather than cold calling, they expect their producers to build ongoing relationships with large accounts.

Yet another agent may describe producers as doing primarily cold calling. "Selling is still selling," as one told us. "Still, our producers are also responsible for maintaining the accounts once they are on board. We insist that our salespeople follow up x-dating and continue to work on the growth and maintenance of the accounts they bring in."

So when helping an agency select producers, what do we do?

Best's Study

We conducted an exclusive study of the top-selling property and casualty agents for *Best's Review*, which was published in the magazine's August 1996 issue. The study's underlying premise was that a simple job title is not enough to match people to jobs. The fact that two people sell personal lines does not necessarily mean that their jobs are the same. One obvious difference might be whether an individual's job is primarily focused on bringing in new business—with the necessary cold-call component—or whether the job is primarily centered on maintaining and expanding existing books of business. Therefore, we asked the agencies participating in this study to allow us to evaluate their best personal lines producer whose focus is primarily on outside sales (what we term "hunters") and, where appropriate, their best producer whose primary responsibility is the retention and expansion of existing business (what we call "farmers"). This produced 165 producers from these 101 agencies. Of those producers, 118 were identified as hunters, primarily responsible for and adept at bringing in new business, and 47 were classified as farmers, primarily responsible for retaining and expanding existing books of business.

Bringing in New Business

If the 118 top-performing hunters were merged into one person—with one collective personality—that individual would be extremely persuasive, be able to bounce back from rejection, be incredibly sociable and outgoing, be willing to take risks, have very high energy, and have a strong need to get things done immediately. On the downside, such an individual would tend to be a bit too impatient, may not be well organized, and would have a tendency to get bored when work becomes too repetitious.

In effect, if closing new business is the job, the agent must seek the classic hunter to succeed. Lack of intense persuasive ability will make it very difficult for someone to succeed in this position.

For instance, when new-business production is the prime responsibility, we can forgive impulsiveness or impatience, even lack of fine detail ability. In some cases, we can even forgive lack of good time-planning skills if the agency is structured in such a way that management can help salespeople with coordinating their work. In other situations, however, where people are out on their own without the opportunity to be closely managed, the lack of time-planning skills could be a serious drawback. Again, the situation defines the proper person.

The agent must not make the mistake, however, of looking for a good, purely new business producer and still demand certain service skills. These are unnecessary, and often this demand may deny the agent the benefit of a tremendous salesperson.

Servicing a Book of Accounts

On the opposite extreme is the so-called producer whose job really is to service a book of accounts. Such an individual should not be called upon to possess a particularly strong degree of ego-drive. This person is not asked to close new business, so why demand the ability to do so?

What this producer, who really is a senior customer service representative, must possess is the fine empathy needed by all salespeople, plus the exceptional personal organizational skills and the service motivation needed to retain and expand ongoing relationships. Certainly a little bit of persuasive motivation cannot hurt when this producer is suggesting an expansion of business at a point of x-dating or asking for a referral and the like. But basically what is needed is the ability to relate effectively to customers, to meet their needs through providing information and effective service. As a matter of fact, where maintenance is the primary responsibility, too much ego-drive can actually get in the way, because individuals with enormous ego-drive want the thrill of the close, which they will not experience in a maintenance situation. With too much ego-drive, the person whose basic responsibility is maintenance is going to become restless and will probably, in the long run, leave the agency either on his or her own or at the agent's request. The conscientious, service-oriented role is that of the classic farmer.

New Business and Maintenance

Probably the most difficult person to find is the producer whose responsibilities include both the aggressive seeking of new business and the maintenance of existing accounts. What is needed here is an individual who has sufficient persuasive motivation—ego-drive—to close sales. Yet that ego-drive cannot be so strong that the producer loses patience with the maintenance aspect of the role. The right balance of enough drive to close sales, and yet not too much, must be found. Of course, this producer must have excellent empathy and requires the same degree of ego-strength as does the pure new-business producer. Yet he or she also requires many of the attributes of the pure maintenance person. This combination producer must have enough service motivation, personal organization, detail ability, and patience to produce the steady, ongoing work involved in maintaining accounts.

Though this combination of attributes is hard to find in one person, people with these attributes do exist and, in fact, provide an excellent source of future management talent. It is really many of these same attributes that make for the effective sales manager.

From the foregoing, it should be clear that it is terribly important that the agent determine precisely what responsibilities he or she wishes the producer to undertake. In other words, only through a clear definition of what the producer's role is, can the people be found whose abilities properly match that role.

Customer Service Representative

The term "customer service representative" can cover a relatively wide range of differing responsibilities. In some agencies, the customer service representative (sometimes called the "senior customer service representative") is virtually indistinguishable in responsibilities from the producer who is primarily responsible for maintenance of business. This customer service representative, like that producer, is essentially given the responsibility of maintaining existing business. It is often this customer service representative who takes over when the new business producer closes a sale. Thus, the personality attributes needed for this role are virtually identical to those of a producer as defined by some agencies.

Such a customer service representative, like the producer primarily responsible for maintaining and expanding existing business, should have a fair degree of the five key sales dynamics—empathy, ego-drive, conscientiousness, service motivation, and ego-strength—since sales remains part of the job responsibility. The senior customer service representative, again like the producer with similar responsibilities, should not have extremely intense ego-drive. Also, he or she probably can get away with somewhat less ego-strength than can the producer. The reason is that the customer service representative, even if he or she has some expansion of business responsibilities, is still essentially filling that responsibility through servicing an existing customer. Therefore, the sale, whether it be a cross-sell or coverage expansion, must, of necessity, be a soft one and, again, one in a service context.

Thus, the likelihood of rejection is much smaller. It is also much easier to avoid rejection by stepping back than it would be in a cold-contact situation where a step back often means never seeing the prospect again. As a matter of fact, it is very easy for the customer service representative to step back where resistance is encountered and clue a producer about the potential business expansion if more raw servicing ability is needed to accomplish this.

Thus, while the senior customer service representative should clearly possess a sufficient degree of ego-drive and ego-strength and as much empathy and service motivation as possible, some compromise can be made in the first two areas if the other key customer service attributes are exceptionally strong.

For the more junior-level customer service representative, however, there is a real difference in the requirements. In such a case, the job becomes largely clerical. The customer service representative must answer questions, must provide information, and is sometimes even given minor underwriting responsibilities. However, he or she is rarely, if ever, held responsible for following up on an account, keeping tabs of the x-date, or playing other roles in which sales ability or assertiveness is really necessary. This customer service representative must possess, first and foremost, a strong service motivation. What we mean is that people in this job must be strongly motivated to be liked. It is important for them to please someone, and so they will work hard to ingratiate themselves with the customers they are servicing. They want to do a good job because they want to be appreciated for doing that job; they want to be thought of as coming through.

Tied in with this motivation to please is patience, thoroughness, a strong sense of responsibility, and strong inner controls. They must be self-motivated; they must have a taskmaster within themselves, pushing them to work hard so that they can receive the approval that they crave.

Of course, customer service representatives must have the kind of detail ability and organization skills to allow them to do the needed detail work, and they must possess sufficient language, math, and underwriting skills to do that work and communicate properly with the customer. Most often, junior-level customer service representatives are not particularly assertive, and tend to be, if anything, overcautious; they are not quick decision makers and certainly, more often than not, do not possess strong ego-drive. For the role, however, these weaknesses are not real drawbacks. Customer service representatives do not typically need to be strongly assertive, although some assertiveness is certainly helpful, and their responsibilities do not call for a great deal of decision making on their own. Thus, the overcautiousness that is a serious drawback in a salesperson, or in a manager, and perhaps even in a senior customer service representative, is not a problem in the junior customer service representative's role, and if anything, some agents might prefer it.

Ego-drive, moreover, could be a drawback because if there is too much need to persuade, the patience to perform the customer service representative role would likely not be there. In effect, pleasing customers must be the primary motivation of customer service representatives.

Getting back to assertiveness for a moment, that quality could be extremely important to the customer service representative and, perhaps in addition to the possibility of some sales dynamics, could mark the difference between those who could move into a senior position and those who must stay at the junior level. In a senior service role, it is sometimes important to be assertive enough to say no to a customer. If a customer demands an unrealistic decision, it is far better for the customer service representative to deny the request and assertively explain why than to promise something that cannot be delivered. It is important that the senior customer service representative be assertive enough to shine the light of reality on a situation so that he or she can really come through as promised, and not offer the "pie in the sky," which, in the long run, does great damage.

Underwriter

In viewing the underwriter's role, most people would ask, "What on earth does underwriting have to do with sales?" Unfortunately, in selecting underwriters the response of "nothing" to that question all too often determines who is hired for the position. The reality is, however, that sales is, or should be, an important part of the underwriter's role. Of course, the underwriter must have outstanding detail ability, extraordinarily good self-discipline and personal organization, and financial competence. But if we only look at these qualities, how would the underwriter be differentiated from the actuary, the statistician, or, for that matter, the junior accountant?

The difference is that an underwriter must be assertive and should possess at least some degree of the central sales dynamics. This should be understood by simply recounting the underwriter's role in an agency. The underwriter takes an order produced by the salesperson and works to fill that order by placing it with one or a combination of companies with which the agency is working. As part of the underwriter's role, however, he or she is frequently faced with the need to say to the producer, "No, that cannot be placed in that way," or "No, this person cannot get a nonsmoker's rate," or "With this individual's driving record, it would be impossible to place the policy with any of our companies. It has to be placed in assigned risk." Thus, very often the producer and the underwriter are in adversarial positions, even though, theoretically, they are both working toward the same end—producing business for the agency.

On the other side of the coin, it is not, or should not be, the underwriter's role to find reasons why not to do business. Rather, he or she should be on the producer's side and try to find ways to place the business, even in the face of some difficulties.

From this description it should be evident that the underwriter must be assertive enough to say no to the producer when no is the only realistic answer, and he or she also must be assertive enough to push companies when that push could mean placing an important piece of business with a potentially important account. Anyone can write the simple policy, but only the really effective agency can write the creative ones, and the underwriter must play a key role in doing so.

Both of these functions also require, in addition to assertiveness, plain and simple sales ability. The underwriter could simply say no to the producer and begin a pattern of ongoing warfare with that producer. On the other hand, by saying no and successfully persuading the producer, as much as the producer may not like it, that no is indeed the only realistic answer, the two can work together more effectively and essentially pull in the same direction, which is critical to agency success. Similarly, though agencies can sometimes use assertive muscle with a company, it is much better if they can persuade the company that it is in its interest to place this unusual business, and that persuasion essentially must be carried through, at least in many instances, by the underwriter.

In short, the underwriter must possess all the obvious qualities—detail ability, thoroughness, personal organization, and financial competence— but also must have the toughness and the assertiveness to negotiate and the basic sales ability to persuade if that underwriter is to carry through his or her responsibilities at the highest level. If an underwriter in an agency lacks the sales dynamics—if the underwriter is simply not suited for the kind of tough negotiations or push necessary—he or she should at least have the courage to involve the agency head or some other appropriate manager.

Claims

When viewing the claims department of an agency, we can say virtually the same thing we did for the underwriter, and virtually the same qualities are required. Perhaps the biggest differences might relate to the degree of empathy and the level of service motivation needed. The claim is, after all, the reason why the insurance was purchased in the first place. Every customer is totally convinced that his or her highest possible claim is fully justified and that that claim should be met virtually without question. The claims person must deal with that perception, must please the customer, and yet again, given the dual representation of the agency, must also be fair to the company the agency represents. That balance does indeed require both outstanding empathy in relating to the customer and outstanding service motivation so that the claim will be actively processed and fairly met. Still, an underwriter must have enough ego-drive and ego-strength to persuade customers if they are being at all unreasonable, and, of course, to persuade the company when persuasion is required. An effective claims person can often mean the difference between a customer being lost or saved by the agency, and perhaps even more important, the difference between a quickly satisfied claim and costly, dragged-out litigation. The claims person should not simply be someone who writes up the paperwork on a claim, but should be an effective functionary who handles the claim for the claimant and the company and, it is hoped, resolves it to everyone's satisfaction. As in underwriting, to accomplish this often means plain and simple selling.

We began by expressing our view that the independent agent and the independent agency system present a fine example of capitalism working at its best. The best elements of capitalism—the opportunity for the entrepreneur, the need to compete effectively in order to survive, and the need to produce in order to compete effectively—are all present in the independent agency system. We have worked with thousands of agents and with national and state organizations of agents, and have found that the leadership in the industry indeed represents all these fine elements. We hope that we have made the point, however, that there are many highly effective organizations competing very successfully for new business and also working very hard to take agents' existing business away from them. Thus, to compete, the agency must be certain that every person in every position we touched on here is effective enough to be the one person with whom the insurance customer has come in contact. As we have said, to the prospect or customer, the agency is that one individual with whom the person has had an experience. If the experience is good, sales can be made and customers kept. If, however, the experience is with an individual inappropriate to his or her job, and thus producing a negative situation, the result is a non-sale, a potential loss to the independent agency system itself, and a customer who is ready to be taken away at the first temptation. An agency's employees, regardless of how good a story the agency itself has to tell, must indeed be its bottom-line advantage.

28

What It Takes to Succeed in Life Insurance Sales

The life insurance industry of today can no longer be thought of, in its pure sense, as an industry unto itself. The life insurance industry positions itself correctly as one involved in overall financial and estate planning. With existing tax laws, it is difficult to think of a proper estate plan that does not in some way integrate life insurance as a key part, if for no other reason but to avoid substantial estate taxes. We know of few, if any, benefit packages offered by industry that do not include life insurance and, of course, accident and health insurance. Increasing numbers of businesses use life insurance to ensure perpetuation and business continuity, and as important cornerstones of their pension and/or profit sharing plans. The life insurance industry has been progressive and creative in developing products such as "minimum deposit" and "universal life" to meet the consumers' changing needs and to better fit into its increasing role as part of a broad financial picture. The industry has also moved aggressively toward reducing overall life insurance costs, adjusting these costs to the changing mortality table.

With all this, the life insurance agent of today is, or at least should be, a key player in helping both the consumer and business to develop an integrated financial plan. The life insurance agent is, or again should be, an ultimate example of consultative selling.

Yet with all the progressive changes made by the industry, and with the objective importance of life insurance as it exists today, there is still an enormous gap, perhaps as wide as it was three decades ago, between what the life insurance agent should be and the perception of what the life insurance agent is.

This gap is perhaps best exemplified in Woody Allen's movie *Sleeper*. After being frozen as a medical experiment, Woody Allen awakens centuries later to a drastically changed world. The curious scientists ask, "What was it like to be dead for several centuries?" After pausing, he answers, "It was kind of like spending an evening with an insurance salesman."

It was, in fact, a life insurance company that in early 1958 asked us to do the research study that eventually led to the development of our psychological test—and to the founding of our company. The insurance company had been suffering a 55 to 60 percent turnover of agents during their first year and an 85 to 90 percent turnover over the first 3 years. The company indicated that, despite all its efforts, that turnover figure had not changed in more than two decades. At this writing, the industry turnover rate continues to be 55 to 60 percent in 1 year and 85 to 90 percent in 3 years.

With the enormous progress in technology and the major advances that the industry has made in the quality and diversity of products it offers, how can the absolute failure to reduce turnover be explained? We can offer three possible explanations:

First, the life insurance industry continues to cling to the belief that if a person has the proper connections—markets—and, of course, is given good training and has the desire to succeed, that person can sell life insurance.

Second, some companies convey to the job applicant their need to sell the applicant on joining the life insurance company, rather than, as in most industries, having the applicant work to sell himself or herself to the company.

And, third, many life insurance executives feel, and often state openly, that high turnover in life insurance sales is endemic to the industry and that such turnover must be accepted as an unavoidable cost of doing business.

Let us take a closer look at the three reasons, which, in our view, go far to explain why the insurance industry has such a difficult time reducing turnover and increasing productivity and professionalism.

Markets

In the past, life insurance agents were hired if they had a "market" they could sell to—even if this meant selling to their grandmothers, first cousins, or even buying a policy themselves. Though not readily admitted to, companies today still use a job applicant's market as a key reason for hiring. If an individual is a member of a country club or comes from an old, respected, and influential family, the assumption is that the person's contacts can be converted into life insurance sales. If that were so, and given the enormous income potential in the life insurance industry, why haven't the companies been able to hire people with such a market and permanently eliminate the turnover and productivity problem? The answer is that when an individual has the ability to sell, and has these ready markets, he or she will cash in on many opportunities. Absent that sales ability, however, the markets become an unfulfilling tease, and the non-salesperson rapidly begins to be viewed as a pain in the neck, a leech, or a cipher, rather than as a respected member of the community that theoretically was his or her market.

We recall the case of a man who had completed 20 years in the military. He retired with a colonel's rank, so was able to live on a fairly adequate retirement pension. This gentlemen, whom we will call "Mr. Townsend," was very much part of the "old-boy network." He was a graduate of the "right" prep school and college, was a member of all the "right" clubs, and definitely was friendly with all the key business and political leaders in the area. He, in fact, had a perfect market. Naturally, he was an excellent target for recruitment by several life insurance companies, one of which hired him.

Mr. Townsend was introduced to us by one of our clients, who asked if we could work with him to determine why, despite all his obvious advantages, he was not succeeding in life insurance sales. After testing and interviewing him in depth, we were able to determine that he clearly lacked the dynamics of a salesperson. He was an excellent leader, but was not a persuader. As a colonel in the army, he could tell people what to do; but as a life insurance agent, he had to sell them on what to do, and that simply was not him.

When we explored other possibilities with Mr. Townsend, the fact emerged that he had bought and sold stocks quite successfully for many years. He had family money to invest and did so quite successfully. His personality, moreover, was very much that of an effective money manager. He enjoyed following stocks and loved the trading game and was very good at it. It was decided that he would leave life insurance sales and seek a position as a portfolio manager, which he did obtain, and in which to this day he is very successful. We might add that he has recovered most, though not all, of his friends.

It is important to reemphasize here that markets certainly are of value. Everything else being equal, which it rarely is, we would certainly suggest to all our life insurance clients that they hire an effective agent with a market rather than one without one. However, we would suggest even more strongly that if the choice is between a non-salesperson with a market and an individual with tremendous sales talent but lacking a market, we would urge the hiring of the second individual without any hesitation.

Selling the Applicant on the Industry

A feeling of inferiority pervades some life insurance companies, leading them to seek individuals who may possess only the most superficial qualifications but who would be willing to work for them. The belief is that if the companies are too selective, they simply will not have enough people to fill the positions. Given the potential income of successful life insurance agents, this feeling is, to say the least, ludicrous and extremely costly.

Many successful life insurance salespeople become millionaires. Many others earn an exceptionally good income, and that income typically grows over the years. The life insurance agent, even more than most salespeople, is able to run his or her own show, work his or her own hours, and really be an independent businessperson without many of the inventory and other obligations that it normally takes to start and run a business.

The very fact that a life insurance policy not only produces excellent income at the sale but also continues to produce income for the agent over 10 years, or even a lifetime, makes the industry unique. With all this going for it, why should the life insurance companies have to persuade someone to join them? The opposite should be true. People should be knocking on the doors of the life insurance companies trying to break into an elite field of high earners. The reality, however, is that they are not, and the industry is forced to continually look for large numbers of people who might be persuaded to try to sell life insurance.

The reason goes back to the question of image. The very people who the life insurance industry would like to attract are likely to resist being tarred by the same brush as the old debit collector. Yes, the income potential may be great in theory, they reason, but, "It doesn't seem possible that 'so and so' (a life insurance salesperson they know) could be making that kind of income." In other words, the income potential and the image do not go together, and so people resist the industry. Another reason for resistance relates to the ease with which an individual can become a life insurance agent in some companies. "If the job is so easy to get, and the life insurance company is so eager to get me, how good could the job possibly be?" The old Groucho Marx line, "I wouldn't belong to a club that would have me as a member" applies here.

Is High Turnover Endemic?

Our research indicates the high turnover in life insurance sales is not endemic to the industry. In fact, with proper selection, the life insurance industry, given its potential for high income, can substantially reduce its turnover rate and greatly increase its productivity.

The costs of the revolving door are all too well known, though rarely are they openly quantified. According to an industry report, it costs high-productivity companies with high turnover (approximately 83 percent after 3 years) $190,000 per retained agent. On the other hand, for high productivity companies with better retention (66 percent turnover or 34 percent of the agents retained after 3 years), the cost is reduced to $90,000 per retained agent. In other words, the cost of that additional 17 percent turnover is $100,000 per retained agent over a 3-year period, and these figures do not include interest costs.

In addition to these measurable costs are the hidden, but all-important, costs of burnt territory and destroyed image that result from the public's exposure to life insurance agents who should not be. The image of the debit life insurance collector coming to the door each week is as negatively vivid to an entire generation as is that of the tire-kicking, fast-talking used car salesman. Even today, as often as not, life insurance agents choose to call themselves financial consultants or financial planners rather than accepting the label of "life insurance salespersons."

What is unfortunate about the image is that life insurance should indeed play a key role in nearly everyone's financial planning, as we said earlier. The life insurance industry provides an enormous service, the proper use of which could make the difference between financial stability and catastrophe to millions of people. As the industry develops increasingly sophisticated products, and as the mortality tables permit lower and lower percentages of the premium dollar to go into the coverage of mortality costs, life insurance products become more and more a part of living and not simply a hedge against dying. Given this fact, and the key role that life insurance must play in estate planning and pensions, why should the life insurance agent not be at least as well respected as the accountant, the lawyer, and the financial planner?

To us, there is a great irony here. Of all the industries we have studied, life insurance in theory should have one of the lowest turnover rates. The very structure of the compensation within the industry works to avoid turnover. Given the normal contract, the agent makes a percentage of the first-year premium and then receives a renewal each year that the policy remains in force. It is these renewals that build income that often exceeds, after a number of years, the income produced by first sales. When an agent leaves the company, these renewals generally are lost. Thus, unlike most jobs, when you leave, you are giving up not only money you earned through working but also guaranteed income in which you are vested because of your past work. This is a classic golden handcuffs situation, and yet the turnover rate is catastrophic. Clearly these golden handcuffs cannot be on very tight if the turnover is that high. It is as simple as the fact that the people hired are so unproductive that the few dollars in renewals makes no difference as an incentive to continue on. It is the good salespeople who are locked into the golden handcuffs because they produce the sales that produce the high renewals, and it, of course, is they who represent the some 15 percent who stay on, earn the big money, and become the professional career life insurance agents.

What Is the Solution?

The cure in each of these three cases is the same. The industry must hire more selectively; it must hire people who have the ability to be effective life insurance salespeople. If the industry hires more selectively, the job will immediately become more desirable. If it hires more effective professionals, the image will slowly turn around, and people will be more willing and even anxious to be identified with the industry. And if it hires more productive people, these individuals will earn the kind of income that will lock them into the industry and automatically reduce the ghastly waste that is the life insurance industry's revolving door.

How to Do It

Life insurance companies have to begin by scrapping both the notion of hiring on the basis of only superficial qualifications—the warm-body approach—and, the old, invalid hiring criteria: age, sex, race, experience, educations, and markets. They have to replace these incorrect approaches to hiring with a selective process based on whether or not an individual possesses the real potential to sell life insurance packages in a consultative way for the specific company, given the specific markets and the specific product mix.

The Basic Dynamics

In the August 1996 issue of *Best's Review*, we published a study identifying the key personality qualities that distinguished the 142 top performers from Allmerica, Equitable Life Assurance, Knights of Columbus, Jackson National Life, Jefferson Pilot, John Hancock, Life Investors Insurance Company of America, Life of Georgia, Lutheran Brotherhood, Mass Mutual, Metropolitan Life, Monumental Life, Mutual of New York, Northwestern Mutual Life, New York Life, Prudential, the New England, Principal Financial, and Transamerica. We found that the most successful life insurance agents have an extremely strong ego-drive, above average empathy, a high level of assertiveness, a strong sense of urgency, and enough ego-strength to allow them to ask for an order without fearing rejection.

First and foremost, they must have the empathy that allows them to read a prospect and to judge what the prospect's real needs are that might be met by one or a combination of the product's the agents have to offer. Particularly when dealing with life insurance, those needs can involve a multitude of hidden agendas. Fear of death is one of the great obstacles, and working around that fear to meet the client's needs requires great empathy as well as great sensitivity. Getting the right sense of the client's real purpose and real needs, regardless of what is actually said, can, in life insurance sales more than in most, make the difference between the beginning of a long-term relationship with an important customer and total failure. In today's market, a canned approach is virtually out, while the empathic response is the ultimate key.

Yet, again, as in many sales situations, empathy is not enough. Once the agent has picked up the cues and clues and fully understands the hidden agendas, and the prospect's real motives, he or she still must have the persuasive motivation (ego-drive) to use the feedback as a tool for persuasion. Understanding can develop friendships, but ego-drive makes sales. Yet there could be many situations in which too much ego-drive could be counterproductive. Again you are dealing with very important feelings, fears, and needs that the potential customer may not even recognize. Too hard a push at the wrong time or too much of a demand for an immediate decision could succeed in alienation rather than closure. What is needed is the right balance of ego-drive and empathy, depending on the customer and the product mix.

As life insurance products become more and more complex, and as they become more and more integrated into an overall financial plan, consultative skills and service motivation become increasingly critical elements for success in life insurance sales. The need to do a good job, the desire to come through, and the strong sense of responsibility, along with the need to be appreciated, which are all involved in service motivation, can make the difference between success and failure. The life insurance salesperson cannot close a sale and leave, because he or she is often viewed as the consultant who solves problems, looks at programs, and plays an ongoing, continuing role in the financial life of the customer. This is of enormous value, because it provides the salesperson with continual opportunities to cross-sell, to sell increasing amounts of a product, or to add other products into the customer's product mix. Yet the salesperson cannot be an individual who is only talking to the customer with an eye toward another immediate sale. He or she has to genuinely convey to the customer, and be assured that the customer most often senses this, that the agent wants to be of service. The successful agents enjoy doing a good job for the customer and being appreciated for the help they provide as much as they enjoy closing a sale in the first place. That combination, together with empathy, is certainly not the old debit image, but provides the kind of consultative image that the successful representative of the life insurance industry must convey today.

As for ego-strength, there can be no lack in this area, even with an abundance of the other three qualities. Again, we are dealing with enormous sensitivities and fears relating to death. Thus, regardless of the need for the product, and regardless of the ability of the life insurance agent, rejection is going to be a fact of life. There are precious few life insurance agents who can honestly say they close one in two contacts, and we include the insurance millionaires in that statement. So along with sensitivity, empathy, drive, and service motivation, the life insurance agent had better be able to take the rejection, deal with it for what it is, and go on to the next presentation with increased motivation to close that sale.

The first thing life insurance companies must do if they are to close the wasteful hiring revolving door is to seek people with these central dynamics, again, regardless of their markets or experience. Then companies should look for individuals among those people who have the other qualities necessary to sell their particular products. The possession of those additional qualities can make as much of a difference to success or failure as the possession of the central dynamics themselves.

One of our life insurance company clients provides a good example of the need for these additional qualities. As a training ground, the company's new agents were assigned the after–5 p.m. business. In that market, the possession of empathy, ego-drive, and ego-strength alone could mean success, since in most of these sales situations, the sale is made or not made on the first contact. However, a problem developed in the third year, when the company began to lose large numbers of previously effective people. We found that the reason for this loss lay in the change of responsibilities at the end of the second year.

What occurred was that, after 2 years, the company would take their most successful salespeople—that is, successful in the small-product market— and move them into what they termed "full career agent status" with the responsibility of selling estate planning, pension plans, etc., from 9 to 5. What was clearly the problem, as confirmed in our research and testing of the people attempting to make the transition, was that though they invariably possessed the empathy, ego-drive, and ego-strength to sell the small-policy buyer and get quick closes, many lacked the other vital attributes required in the consultative sell involved in the larger-product business market. So they soon dropped off.

Our research indicates that as life insurance products become more complex and integrated with other financial products, the need for consultative selling will increase. Consultative selling involves the selling of solutions, not mere products. The facts are that the old rules of selling no longer spell success in the life insurance industry.

The successful life insurance salesperson will have to be that unique individual who has the technical knowledge to understand the product's possibilities, the empathy and conceptual ability to interpret the client's needs, and the drive and wherewithal to seize opportunities. The prototype of a life insurance salesperson, the quick closer of the past who needs instant gratification, cannot be successful today. What is needed, in addition to the five dynamics of sales which we have discussed thoroughly, is a strong sense of personal responsibility, a high level of conceptual intelligence and persistence, and enough assertiveness combined with empathy to ask for a decision without being thought of as being too pushy or too much the bully. The ability to think on one's own feet—and a balanced sense of urgency to get things done are also key qualities often not thought about in the selection process.

The Job-Matching Solution

We have said in the strongest possible terms that the life insurance industry can reduce turnover, increase per-agent productivity, and substantially upgrade the industry's image by replacing its current hiring approaches with one involving the hiring of people possessing the personality attributes to sell successfully in the company. In other words, the old haphazard hiring approaches should be replaced by one which we term "job matching."

We have compared the productivity and turnover of people hired the old way with that of people who have been hired using the job-matching approach. As we present these comparisons, keep the industry norm in mind—55 to 60 percent turnover in 1 year, and 85 to 90 percent turnover in 3. Also keep in mind that 20 percent of the life insurance agents are selling 80 percent of what is sold. With this as background, here are the comparisons: Of those individuals hired using the job-matching approach— their personality effectively matched to the company and to the products being sold—61 percent are in the top half of their sales force after 14 months on the job, while of those hired the old way, only 7 percent are that successful. Looking at turnover, 28 percent of the job-matched individuals are no longer with their company after 14 months, though many of these remain in the industry but with another company. Of the individuals hired the old way, on the other hand, there is a very typical 57 percent turnover rate at the end of 14 months, with a vast majority of these leaving the industry because of poor productivity.

It should be clear that it takes a very special human being to successfully sell life insurance in today's market. If the industry continues hiring thousands of people on the basis of its inappropriate criteria, the results will be increasingly negative, given the needs in today's market and with today's products. At the very least, it can be safely said that if the approach to hiring does not change, the problem of the revolving door will continue to be discussed 25 years from now. On the other hand, if the industry is willing to institute objective, sound, and proper job-matching methods, a major impact on turnover and agent productivity can be achieved.

29

Locking the Real Estate Revolving Door

The turnover rate in the real estate industry is as high today as it was half a century ago. Each year, 55 percent of all real estate salespeople continue to leave their companies, either to go with other real estate firms or to leave the industry entirely. Over the course of 3 years, more than 85 percent of associates are no longer with their original company. This incredibly high turnover rate continues to exist primarily because of what we have termed the "warm body approach" to recruitment and selection.

Many owners and managers of brokerage companies have been lulled into erroneously believing that a high turnover rate costs them little or nothing. They argue, "If we contract salespeople who have paid for their own licensing, and we do not pay them a salary, we have nothing to lose. We simply provide them with a desk and a telephone. So if they sell even one property, we are that much ahead of the game." Those who believe this myth simply fill spaces with bodies and feel they have recruited successfully if every desk for which space is available is filled by one of those bodies.

There is another fallacy that relates to this fill-all-the-desks-with-warm-bodies concept. It is a fallacy that is perpetuated by the industry and bought by many individuals. It goes something like this: Everybody has had the experience of buying homes, and there is a literally limitless supply of people buying and selling homes, land, etc. So if someone is intelligent enough to get a license, and is presentable and interested in a good career, even part-time, he or she could and should sell real estate.

This fallacy is an open invitation to the dabbler and creates an endless drain on the time and effort of a real estate firm's principals or managers. This anyone-can-sell-real-estate myth, which has characterized the industry too long, must be shattered. Managers should recruit selectively. That is, they should choose only those salespeople who possess personality characteristics that match the requirements of the position and who are capable of achieving maximum productivity. The hidden costs of indiscriminate recruiting and selecting are just too high.

Counting the Costs

To begin assessing the costs, consider the results of our studies of more than 25,000 corporate clients, including nearly 3,000 real estate firms. These studies have proved that more than four out of five people attempting to sell in the real estate industry seriously lack the appropriate personality dynamics to indicate that they would have any chance for real success in the industry. Why does this matter if they do not cost the company anything, anyway?

First, consider advertising. When managers are asked why they advertise, they invariably answer, "to make the phone ring." Advertising, by itself, does not sell a property. Successful advertising creates enough interest to cause prospects to call your company. Then the ball is in the salesperson's court.

So what happens when that precious prospect, produced at great expense, contacts one of the four out of five salespeople who are unsuited for selling real estate? The odds are that the prospect will not become a buyer. To see the evidence in clear numerical terms, apply the formula shown in Figure 29-1 to your company. First, fill in the dollar volume sold by your best producer during the past year. Next, enter the number of salespeople who worked for your company during the same period. Multiply those two figures together and subtract the actual volume sold by your company during the past year from the product. The result is the minimum amount of money your company lost because all your prospects did not contact your best producer.

The fact that your top salesperson sells that many properties and that dollar volume, given your economic conditions, competition, and so on, means that every salesperson in your company could generate that sales volume. It could be done, because it has been done. Consider the possibility that your less capable salespeople are driving away the prospects who contact them, thereby losing business that could be converted into profit by

(A) Dollar volume sold by best producer during the past year	_____
(B) Number of salespeople working for company during past year	_____
(C) Multiply (A) x (B)	_____
(D) Volume sold by company during past year	_____
(E) Subtract (D) from (C)	_____

Figure 29-1

true professionals. The telephones and desks you provide the "no-cost" salespeople actually are costing you a great deal.

In addition to this cost, assess the cost, or profitability, of each salesperson by examining his or her conversion ratio. That is, compare the number of calls to which a salesperson responds with the number of sales he or she closes. A good conversion ratio means hard dollars for the real estate firm.

In fact, the cost of unproductive salespeople may be even greater than these numbers indicate. Your salespeople convey an overall impression of your company to prospective buyers and sellers. To the average consumer, your company is the salesperson with whom he or she has contact. If the experience with the salesperson is good, a sale is more likely, and your company probably will also gain referrals and the intangible benefit of a good reputation. However, an unpleasant experience can create a negative ripple effect that extends far beyond one lost sale and can adversely affect your company and the entire industry.

Ultimately, what is sold in the real estate industry is professionalism. If consumers fail to encounter true real estate professionals, it is easy for them to say to themselves, "I'd rather buy or sell a house myself than deal with someone like that."

If you agree that every salesperson should represent your company in the most professional way possible, and should have the potential to achieve a high conversion ratio, it stands to reason that you should stop believing that people "cost you nothing." If your company and the real estate industry are to move forward as you would like, the notion of the no-cost associate must be totally scrapped. We have told many real estate groups that, in our view, the lack of salary creates perhaps one of the greatest disservices to the industry, because it makes the hiring decision so easy, and, again, the costs are so great. What we suggest is doing away with this haphazard, costly method of filling desks and replacing it with real selectivity. Bear in mind that the real estate salesperson is selling the largest item that virtually anyone ever purchases on the residential side; and on the commercial side, the real estate salesperson is often dealing with high-powered people who must respect the salesperson; otherwise it is unlikely they will ever do business with that person or that company again. Thus, in this industry more than in many, careful selection of people capable of doing the job is vital and must be instituted if the profession is to reach the level of respect its importance deserves.

How to Do It

As we have suggested for all sales jobs across industry, the key to selecting productive people in the real estate industry involves matching the personality strengths and weaknesses of an individual to the functional requirements of the specific real estate job. There is no way in this chapter to deal with all the permutations and combinations involved in real estate selling. To match an individual to a job you must look at the size of the real estate firm, its geographic location, its management structure, the level of property sold—custom houses, tract houses, and so on—whether it has both a commercial and residential branch, and much more. With these enormous variations in mind, however, what we can do here is look at the three major categories of real estate sales: listing, residential presenting, and commercial sales. If we understand that within these categories the variations are enormous, an overview, at least, could prove helpful to understanding how job matching can bring more effective people into the industry. There is no doubt that if firms hire or contract with an individual who is suited to residential presentations (if that is the position) or is suited to listing, and so forth, a huge step forward can be taken. Let us look at these broad categories in the hope that this can be a start for refinements to follow.

Listing

The very nature of the work involved in listing clearly defines the personality attributes required to do that job. The lister is the closest thing in the real estate business to the pure salesperson. The job involves the persuasion of a seller, not only to convince the seller to allow a real estate firm to sell his or her property with the intended 6 or 7 percent commission (a loss of profit to the seller), but also to allow the salesperson's firm to have an exclusive on the property for a specified period of time. Thus, the listing salesperson not only has to convince the seller that it is worth paying the commission but also has to persuade the seller that the saleperson's firm is the best one to do the job of selling the property at the best possible price, and in the most prompt manner possible.

What is clearly indicated by the nature of this task is that the listing salesperson must have a good deal of ego-drive—the inner motivation to persuade and convince as a key means of gaining personal gratification—if she or he is to have any hope of securing a good share of listings. Such salespersons are very likely to have one opportunity to close the listing prospect, and if they do not succeed, the likelihood of eventually making the sale reduces substantially. Yet as much as they need the strong drive to close, they also must have good empathy to temper that drive. If they do not have the ability to sense the reactions of the prospect, and to deal with those reactions sensitively, they are likely, if they have ego-drive, to barge ahead and be thought of by the prospect as some kind of a pushy bulldozer with whom the seller would not think of doing business. Such bulldozers, though they might secure an occasional listing, are not likely to secure the majority of them and may burn territory permanently for their firm by offending the prospect.

Thus, what is needed to succeed in listing sales is an individual who can sense the reactions of other people and use the feedback from those people as a tool with which his or her persuasive ability can be used most effectively. Such individuals also must have a good sense of self to deal calmly with the inevitable rejections. They must not personalize those rejections and, when rejected, must be stable enough to leave prospects with a good feeling and with enough openness that they may become prospects again at some later time.

Finally, the lister has to be assertive enough, all the sensitivity issues notwithstanding, to ask for the order, and where appropriate, the lister has to be persistent enough and personally well organized enough to follow up. Though they may be in the minority, there are situations where a second or third call could be appropriate. Sometimes, with proper follow-up, a lister could notice the same ad for a private sale 3 months later and use that opportunity to again contact the prospect who has not as yet sold the property to see if now the prospect might be more open to talk about a listing. Again, this requires sensitivity, but it also requires sufficient tenacity and personal organization to enable the salesperson to be aware of that ad.

Residential Presenting

The presenter, by contrast, does not require the same level of ego-drive as does the lister. In fact, there is some evidence that an overly strong need for the immediate close could constitute a negative in many presenting situations. People normally cannot be sold a house in any manner even resembling hard sell. The word "presenting" really describes the process, although it quickly should be added that salesmanship still plays a vital role in achieving the end result.

Given the fact that selling plays a role, there definitely is a need for ego-drive on the part of the successful presenter; but this ego-drive ideally should be moderately strong, not of the intense variety needed by the lister. The presenter should enjoy the close, but also should be motivated in other important ways as well, particularly toward providing service.

What the presenter must possess is an exceptionally high level of empathy. Buying a property, whether it is a piece of land or a house, is an enormously important and emotionally charged process for buyers. They are most often making the largest single purchase that they ever have made and, beyond the money, are ordinarily making an enormous commitment to that purchase. They not only are buying a home, but are also buying an area, a town, a school system, a transportation system, zoning requirements, a tax structure, and much more. Thus, empathy on the part of the presenter is critical if he or she is to read the needs and requirements of the prospect and present the products that really meet those needs. We have had enough experiences as real estate consumers to attest to the fact that all too often people are shown properties that are totally irrelevant to their real needs, and often even opposite to their expressed requirements. What has happened to us, and to many people we know, is that real estate salespeople trot out their inventory, trying to push properties that they happen to have exclusives on, instead of focusing on the prospects' requirements. This not only fails to sell a property, but often so offends the prospects, and literally tires them out, that even when they are shown a more appropriate property, they tend to resist it and probably will not buy. That is why presenters must have outstanding empathy along with at least moderate drive, and extremely strong service motivation. As much as they may want the close, they must be motivated to receive the "Thank you," "You did a good job," or "I appreciate that." In other words, to go along with their need to sell, they must, if they are to be successful, have an extremely strong need to please the prospect.

Regardless of the selection offered, however, a prospect is still not necessarily going to buy the first or second property presented. Thus, the presenter must have extraordinary patience, persistence, and the ability not only to stay with a prospect but also to set up presentations in a systematic, organized, efficient manner designed to maximize his or her time and to respect the time of the prospect. We have seen real estate salespeople make prospects wait around for a key, crisscross town inefficiently (spending more time in the car than viewing properties), and, in general, waste an inordinate quantity of time. Such inefficiency can be just as destructive to the sale as all the other areas we have just discussed.

Another critical personality quality that many presenters should have is conceptual ability. This does not mean that these salespeople have to be architects or interior designers, but they should have sufficient ideational and conceptual skill to be able to talk with the prospect in these areas and help the prospect visualize the potential of the property. Along the same lines, though they need not be zoning or tax experts, they must have sufficient detail ability and, of course, knowledge to deal in these areas since these issues frequently occur.

Finally the presenter probably does not need the same level of ego-strength as does the lister. The lister is exposed to frequent rejections because he or she is trying to make a quick sale. The presenter with the empathy and other abilities we just discussed is really providing a service requested by the buyer. The prospect wants to find a house or a piece of land, and so the presenter is perceived by that prospect as providing an important service. Even when the prospect does not buy a particular property presented, it is the property that is not exactly right as opposed to the salesperson being rejected. Thus, though obviously presenters must have some ego-strength—they cannot be totally down on themselves—they can get away with a little less ego-strength than the lister who is exposed to constant rejection.

Commercial Sales

In this era of computers, industry is constantly consulting statistics to guide the development of management policy. One of the most important, yet rarely used, statistics is what we referred to earlier as the conversion ratio. This is the percentage of contacted prospects that are converted to customers. This conversion ratio is critical at all times, in that the company has invested enormous time, money, and effort to develop prospects. Lost prospects represent wasted time, money, and effort and, of even greater importance, business permanently lost to the company. In these highly competitive times, the conversion ratio is even more critical.

In commercial as well as residential real estate, advertising alone does not sell the product. Successful advertising creates prospects. However, it is the salesperson representing the company and dealing directly with the created prospect that creates the sale. It is critical, then, that the individual responsible for converting prospects possess the ability to do just that. For a start, the commercial real estate salesperson must possess three of the key personality qualities essential to sales success: empathy, ego-drive, and ego-strength. Yet in commercial real estate sales, more than in many other fields, other qualities can be as important to success as the possession of these central dynamics. Perhaps the primary one among these is detail ability.

If an individual possesses the three critical dynamics, but is unable to cope with detail, success in commercial real estate is unlikely. The commercial salesperson must be able to cope with detail and use data as an integral part of the sales presentation. Details, ranging from the simple ones like price per square foot to the complexities of write-offs on partitions in an open-space environment, are part and parcel of the commercial real estate sale. If the salesperson's ability to utilize detail is anything but top-notch, all the sales ability in the world is not likely to result in a sale.

On the other hand, many commercial salespeople rely totally on the shuffling of data but forget, largely because of their lack of ego-drive, that the data still have to be presented persuasively in order to demonstrate the benefits to the potential customer. Thus, just as the person with good sales dynamics but little detail ability cannot succeed in commercial real estate, neither can the detail-oriented individual succeed without the basic dynamics of empathy, ego-drive, and ego-strength. Unfortunately, too many commercial real estate salespeople rely purely on details, and thus perform poorly. Being enmeshed in detail, and so focusing on detail for its own sake, can be as negative to the sale as total lack of detail ability. When detail ability is integrated with the basic sales dynamics, the details involved in the situation can be used as a tool to help make the sale; it is through that integration that commercial property can be sold.

The commercial real estate salesperson must be shrewd in order to judge or have insight into a situation. He or she must be a tough negotiator, be personally well organized, be assertive in interpersonal relationships, have good conceptual ability, and be able to think on his or her feet. The individual must be persistent, patient, thorough, and a good communicator. Also, in comparison with many listing or residential situations, commercial sales are unique in that the commercial salesperson must be comfortable dealing with people on the highest levels. This is a characteristic lacking in many people, including many salespeople. Some people may have strong sales dynamics but can be in awe of people in positions of power. We have seen many individuals who have empathy and ego-drive totally freeze when confronting the president of a company or a public official in high office. This power block cannot exist in effective commercial salespeople. They must deal with the chairman of the board of a large corporation as comfortably as with an office manager, and that comfort must be real and not feigned. People read discomfort very accurately and do not respect it. Typically, buyers in positions of power will not want to do business with someone who stands in awe of them, but they will want to do business with a peer in a relationship of mutual respect. Thus, that ability to be a peer, regardless of the position of the individual, is critical.

Of course, many of these qualities are helpful and even necessary in many sales situations, but all of them are really essential if an individual hopes to sell commercial property successfully and particularly if the individual hopes to sell at a high level.

Finding Qualified People

The question could be asked, where might these highly qualified people be found? Do these paragons, capable of selling listings, making residential presentations, or selling commercial property, or, even more problematic, some combination of these, really exist?

The answer is that people with the ability to do the job exist in some abundance. The problem is that real estate firms do not look for these people in the right places. Typically, brokers will try to pirate a competitor's salesperson or manager. Rarely do they ask themselves why these people wish to change companies. If they were really successful with a competitor, why would they be willing to change jobs? The answer might be that they were not really that successful. They may have blamed lack of success on everything but their own ability and be joining you to find some elusive pot of gold at the end of a nonexistent rainbow. The result of pirating in this industry, as in many others, is most often the recirculation of mediocrity.

As we said earlier, many real estate firms use the warm-body approach, literally hiring or contracting with anyone who is capable of being licensed. Others, especially many of the commercial brokerage firms, continue to use the old criteria, particularly age and experience, which all of our studies have proved have no validity as predictors of success.

The reality is that while only some 20 percent of people now selling in the real estate industry have the ability to sell, one out of four individuals walking or driving by your office also possesses that ability, regardless of what the person is currently doing. A good percentage of people possess the ability to sell real estate, in either listing, presenting, or commercial sales. What this provides is a virtually limitless source of talent, if the old preconceptions can be scrapped. There is no question that if individuals possess the dynamics suiting them to the appropriate sales job, and, of course, are given appropriate training and supervision, they will succeed.

The answer, then, to recruiting and selecting effective people for the real estate industry, people who will provide the professionalism that the industry needs and deserves, is to open up the recruiting efforts to the broadest possible population. Select carefully from that broad population those one in four who have the ability to sell, and select from among those the individuals who have the ability to sell a particular real estate product for a specific real estate firm. If training and effective supervision are provided to those appropriate individuals, the real estate revolving door will indeed begin to be locked and your advertising dollar will begin to pay off far better because of the increasingly higher conversion ratio produced by an increasingly higher level of professionals.

30

Automotive Sales: Then and Now

While it was a life insurance company that asked us to do the research that led to the founding of our company Caliper, in 1961, it was the auto industry that provided us with the first opportunity to put our theories into actual practice. A large manufacturer contracted us for a study of 30 of its dealerships across the country. The results of that study were published in the *Journal of Psychology*, July/August 1964 issue, and were written about less formally in other publications such as *Automotive News* and *Sales and Marketing Management*.

It was, in fact, the work we did with those 30 dealerships and the referrals stemming from that work that effectively launched our company. This work also convinced us, if we still had any lingering doubts, that sales success could be accurately predicted using the test we developed and utilizing our job-matching process as a replacement for the old, haphazard hiring criteria that industry typically used. Parenthetically, all too often these same haphazard, invalid criteria continue to be used today.

Since the publication of this initial study, we have worked with literally thousands of auto dealerships, and, over a span of years, the National Automobile Dealers Association. This work, together with projects with a number of manufacturers, has allowed us both to know the industry well and to chart its evolution, at least from a sales and management personnel perspective, over four decades.

From the perspective of what is takes to succeed in sales, the auto industry, second only perhaps to banking, has changed most markedly. Any discussion of what it *really* takes to succeed in auto sales today would read very differently from the same discussion in 1961.

This difference can be summarized rather simply, though the implications of this difference are enormous. When we wrote about the auto industry in the early 1960s, we were able to discuss sales success in the auto industry quite accurately, primarily in terms of an individual's possessing empathy and ego-drive. If an individual was able to get good feedback from a prospect, was able to really sense the prospect's needs and reactions (empathy), and was motivated to use that feedback as a persuasive tool (ego-drive), by and large, that individual would succeed in auto sales. Even then there were some regional and product differences and some differences related to the dealer's system, but fundamentally the possession of the qualities of empathy and ego-drive made for success, and the lack of same allowed a confident prediction of sales failure.

Today, a discussion of what it takes to succeed in auto sales would center more on consultative sales than the very comfortable, simplistic realities of the early 1960s. The reason for this evolution relates largely to the enormous change of attitude of the buying public. Through the 1960s and into the early 1970s, our love affair with the automobile flourished. Perhaps the deprivations of World War II, when new cars were unavailable, still lingered in the hearts of the automotive consumer. Perhaps the automobile was the one symbol of success, of freedom, of status that could be grasped by many people with modest means. We could speculate forever about the cause, but for whatever reason, the automobile was indeed the passion, pride, and identity of so many of us.

The result of this love affair provided the auto industry with the happy situation of prospects entering a dealership really wanting to buy an automobile. The sale still had to be made, as evidenced by the gross failure of salespeople lacking empathy and ego-drive, but the process was made easier by the fact that the prospect wanted to be a customer if he or she could be properly sold. Also, the issues involved in the sale were frequently as simple as the appearance and/or power of the automobile and its affordability. What also made it easier for the industry, and, of course, for the salesperson, was the 2-year mentality. Customers would return 2 years later, when they were ready to trade the car for the new, beautiful styles of 1967, or the new model just brought out in 1969. Newness and disposability made for a nearly endless supply of customers, and, again, the desire to buy made for relatively easy sales, especially for a good salesperson.

Some automotive experts began talking about changes in the late 1960s and early 1970s, and spoke long and loud about the need for Detroit to change some of its thinking to get ready for changes. Their voices, by and large, were cries in the wilderness, and it was not until the trauma of the Arab oil embargo that the reality of the need for change was brought home to the industry and to the buying public. That change totally altered, probably forever, the nature of what it would take to succeed in automotive sales.

The Oil Crisis

So much has been written about the impact of the Arab oil embargo of 1974 that a great deal need not be reiterated here. Suffice it to say that for the first time in postwar America, people had to begin thinking about the practicalities of driving. Whether dealing with gas lines, the odd or even days on which gas could be purchased, and/or the rapidly accelerating price of gasoline, the automotive buying public had to view the automobile in a very different way. Suddenly gas mileage became more meaningful than chrome or fins; and efficiency, rather than bigness and power, became the key selling point. The result of Detroit's lack of foresight was the immediate acceleration of import sales and the rapid increase of the market share of those imports. Add to all this the increasing complexity of automotive technology, including onboard computers and other components, previously thought of only for large jetliners, and you end up with a product that is sold or not sold based on a multiplicity of often complex issues.

The sales situation was made still more difficult by the rapid attitudinal change away from the notion of a new car every 2 years. People became very interested in how many Volvos were still on the road with a million plus miles on the odometer, or how many 10-year-plus Volkswagens were still running around. This interest in durability with a concomitant sales value, in long warranties and in 24-hour road service, has been accelerating as the price of the automobile, both foreign and domestic, has increased exponentially.

The major impact of these factors also relates very much to the question of what it takes to succeed in sales in this industry. Many dealers, primarily marginally successful dealers or very small dealers, either have gone out of business or have been acquired by or merged with bigger, more successful operations. The megadealer, the chain, the multiple-brand showroom, and the Internet are increasingly becoming the name of the automotive retail game. As a result, the small dealership, unless run with great skill, will have a great deal of trouble surviving.

Automotive Sales in the New Millennium

What, then, does it take to succeed in automotive sales today, and how has the industry responded to the changed requirements? The profile of what is takes to succeed in auto sales today much more closely resembles the profile of the consultative salesperson than it does that of the successful automobile salesperson of the 1960s. More than ever, the auto salesperson is selling the consumer the second largest ticket item he or she will ever buy. What is being sold is not only transportation, but also status, and what is included is economy, financing, high degrees of technology, warranties, lease programs, and so much more. The automotive salesperson has to be competent to deal with all these components and to provide the kind of consultative sale that meets with the customer's needs through a balanced integration of components focused on those specific needs. Of course, empathy and ego-drive are still essential because, as in any other kind of sale, the word "sale" is still the essence, and without empathy and ego-drive, few people can succeed in any kind of sale.

Today, however, ego-strength becomes a far more important component. With all the complexities and the enormous multiplicity of alternative product options, the potential for rejection is greater than ever. Just as salespeople have to use empathy to understand the customer's needs, and to try to meet those needs, salespeople must also have the ego-strength to understand that, despite all their best efforts, the customer could say no. If that no is too devastating to a salesperson's sense of well-being, he or she is simply not going to be ready for the next customer, who, if approached properly, would be ready to say yes.

Where the automobile salesperson used to be typical of the hard-driving, detail-hating salesperson, today he or she must have at least a decent tolerance of detail to succeed. Of course, no one can be everything; and so, more often than not, an individual with enough ego-drive to close effectively does not like handling detail. Yet, like it or not, the automobile salesperson, particularly as you go upscale, had better be able to handle detail with effectiveness. These salespeople must, at least, be able to deal with warranty issues, put together a lease package, and discuss details of the technology of the automobile. Of course, they can bring in help when issues get beyond their capability, but they had better be able to go to a certain point or they will lose credibility with sophisticated customers.

Similarly, while so many sales earlier could be generated by in-showroom traffic, so much today must be generated, as in so many other industries, through customer follow-up, referrals, and the process of going out prospecting. This, of course, varies enormously from region to region and even from big city to rural area. But the overall reality that prospect generation is a much more important component of automotive sales than it ever was cannot be denied. In order to generate these prospects, the salesperson cannot simply stay in the showroom waiting for the inevitable flow of traffic, but must be a sufficiently good self-starter to go after the prospects, and organized well enough to keep records, to follow up on customers, and to ask for and follow up referrals, if real success is to be achieved.

The sheer complexity of what is being sold also often necessitates a team approach to sales. Even if the salesperson possesses enough detail ability, self-starting ability, and personal organization to do the bulk of the work, there are still going to be many situations in which other people will have to be brought in to put a particular deal together. Being able to work with a team to bring in resources and to gather information when necessary is probably as critical to today's automotive sale as anything we have discussed. Nobody can be everything and know everything, and so long as the salesperson can bring matters to a certain point and not look incompetent to the buyer, bringing in expert help looks good to customers because they know they are dealing with an organization and not simply a salesperson. This component of being a good team player is often lacking in the typical hard-driving salesperson and certainly was lacking in many of the auto salespeople of the 1960s.

Communication skills are another important area of difference. Obviously, to sell anything, some ability to communicate is necessary. But today in automotive sales, it is not enough just to know the technology and financing and have a desire to sell them. Rather, it is critical to be able to communicate this knowledge intelligently, in a way that is comprehendible to the prospect. The best way to offend and drive away customers is to make them feel inept or incompetent by talking over their heads.

Communication is also critical in another respect. As prospects have to be generated, it becomes more and more important for the auto salesperson, like the insurance agent, real estate person, and banker, to become an integral part of the community. Being in the Rotary or Kiwanis or chamber of commerce and taking other leadership roles in the community become very important. To achieve this in a positive way, communicative skills and, for that matter, some leadership ability must play an important part.

We can add to this recipe such obvious elements as intelligence, flexibility, shrewdness, and the ability to think on one's feet, and we are still only beginning to describe the kind of complex individual who will be truly successful in today's automotive market.

The need for the auto salesperson to be an engaging expert is particularly important as more and more buyers are looking to the Internet for their auto purchases. If people can sit at home and select an automobile at very little over cost, and even have their new automobile delivered to their home, why should they go through the trouble of shopping from dealer to dealer? Automotive salespeople have to bring a true added value to the purchase; otherwise they will become superfluous.

Differences within the Market

After having said this, it is still important to emphasize that enormous differences still exist within the industry in terms of who will or will not be successful in a given situation. Since no one can be everything, matching the right person to the job still becomes a key to predicting whether or not an individual will succeed in a particular dealership. There still is no doubt that an individual in a large urban dealership who possesses empathy, ego-drive, and ego-strength can probably get by with somewhat less of the other elements than he or she could if in a relatively small dealership in a rural area where virtually no in-house traffic could be counted upon. The need to be a participant in the community is obviously more critical in a small or medium-sized town than it is in a large metropolitan area where such participation would hardly be noticed. The need to be fully skilled in all the complex areas of the auto sale is far more critical in the small dealership than it would be in the larger dealership blessed with lease specialists and the like. The need for fine intellect, sophistication, and outstanding presentation skills is still probably greater at these higher levels as well. We will not take the time here to fully break down the subtle differences in what it takes to succeed in selling Chevrolets or Cadillacs, Volkswagens or Mercedes, Plymouths or Porsches. We hope a few of these more general comments convey the concept, but as you look at individual salespeople and how they fit into a specific dealership, you still must look at product, region, dealership size, sales system, organizational structure, and more to really determine how that individual salesperson might fit into that dealership and to which level of success he or she might aspire in that context.

Before leaving this issue, one other element should be touched on as a dealer and a prospective salesperson attempt to make a decision about whether or not they are well matched: the sales system employed by the dealership. There are, of course, many such systems, and variations within each of these, but suffice it to say here that there is a critical difference between a system that fundamentally expects the salesperson to carry through a deal from beginning to end, and other systems in which the salesperson brings the sale to a certain point and then involves other people, typically an assistant sales manager or a sales manager. There are also important differences between systems where each salesperson takes his or her turn as prospects come in the door and other more laissez-faire systems where every customer is up for grabs. Similarly, the dealership must make up its mind about what percentage of time an individual is in the showroom or is expected to be outside, prospecting. All these elements obviously relate to the personality required for success. If, for example, a salesperson is not really expected to close, but is expected to bring a prospect to a certain point after which the sales manager really closes the sale, one could give up some ego-drive in assessing the potential effectiveness of that salesperson, but would probably not compromise on empathy, presentation skills, and even assertiveness. Similarly, that sales manager should have a great deal of ego-drive in addition to other attributes. As well, if there is a regulated system, superaggressiveness might not be necessary, because the salesperson has his or her turn with the customer; but in a laissez-faire situation, survival could depend on being very aggressive. In a final example, where the system primarily calls for showroom activity, one could compromise in the area of self-starting or personal organization, but, again, this is becoming less and less realistic. On the other hand, where prospecting is key, no compromise can be made in these areas.

Service and Parts

Before discussing how the industry has dealt with the increasingly complex nature of the auto salesperson, let us look at two frequently neglected areas involving sales productivity: service and parts.

The problem here relates to the very names employees in these departments are given: "service writer" and "parts counter person." These job titles imply that all that might be expected of a service writer is to take service orders, write them up, and give customers a date when they can pick up their cars. The job description is "someone who writes up service orders." Similarly, the job description of a parts counter person might be "maintain inventory of parts and give the customer the part he or she requests, and, of course, collect the money or write up the credit card." Unfortunately, the reality in too many dealerships is that people in service writer or parts counter positions function exactly according to these job descriptions, and so take a great deal away from the bottom-line potential of the dealership. Let us first take a look at the service writer and discuss why this job description is wrong—and where the potential really exists.

Service

When customers bring their cars in for service, unless it is purely routine maintenance service, it is tantamount to going to the dentist. You know you need to go to the dentist, but you certainly do not do it because you want to. Similarly, you know your car needs service, and so you go for that service, but it is really the last thing you want to do. What people in their right mind enjoy paying money simply to keep their car going properly? What makes it worse is, not only are you paying money, but your car is unavailable for a period of time; and, of course, you have to invest your own time, money, and effort to get it to and from the dealership. So when a customer meets the service writer, there is an immediate built-in resistance. At least when the customer pays money for a new automobile, he or she is deriving a desired benefit. But service is a troublesome annoyance, a painful necessity in the mind of the customer. The question then is how do the service writers deal with that problematic relationship? They can, as they often do, simply ask, "What is wrong with your car?" and then write down what the customer says and give a completion date. What this does, of course, is leave the relationship on this disgruntled level; and it results in, at most, selling the customer only what the customer thinks he or she needs. How much better it would be if the service writer, or what we hope is the service salesperson, probed a problem with a customer. How much better for the overall relationship between dealership and customer it would be if the service salesperson asked how long the problem had existed, asked questions about other functions that might be related to the problem, explored with the customer whether somehow the problem might be placed under warranty, and generally looked at problem solving rather than at simply writing up the order. Most sophisticated dealers will state emphatically that this kind of approach by a service writer not only can turn an adversarial relationship into a positive one, but also frequently can result in increased sales by the service department.

What we are suggesting is that a service writer should have all the dynamics necessary to function in a good service role, but also must be sufficiently sales-oriented to view each service contact as a potential sales opportunity. If that service writer possesses the right dynamics, he or she might even contact new buyers after a certain period of time to make certain that the car is running well, to remind them of their 1,000-mile service, and, perhaps near the end of a year, to remind them that the time in which they might buy the extended 5-year warranty is nearly expired. These are all sales, whether the word "service" is attached to them or not, and so sales dynamics should be part of the service writer's makeup. Obviously the single most important dynamic that a service writer must possess is empathy. Only with empathy can a service writer understand why customers might be angry, what their needs are, and how the service writer can meet those needs sufficiently to alleviate any anger. On the other hand, you probably would not want a service writer with overly intense ego-drive. Yes, the service writer must have enough persuasive motivation to look for sales opportunities, and for that matter to close. But service motivation must still be the more dominant force within the person's dynamics. The service writer must want to make a sale, but even more importantly he or she must want to please the customer. As a key means of gaining personal gratification, the service writer must need to hear: "Thank you," "You did a good job," or "I appreciate that."

Along with these qualities, the service writer must be reasonably assertive, which is the dynamic most often lacking in service writers we have evaluated in hundreds of dealerships. The customer is going to demand same-day delivery or insist that a particular job is covered under warranty even though the warranty expired 3 years ago. In such cases, the service writer must be sufficiently assertive to kindly and sensitively, but still firmly, say no. As in any other service situations, the unkept promise is the worst negative, and so the ability to say no with reason, and empathy, and ego-drive, is critical. The service writer further has to have all the other attributes of the service person—a good sense of responsibility, excellent detail ability, and sufficient coordinative and follow-up skills—to process a service order and see to it that the service department does its job in doing quality work in a timely manner. In other words, the service writer must deliver as promised. The quality of the relationship between the service writer and the customer more often than not can make the difference between the potential for repeat or expanded business and the permanent loss of that customer. The service station is always an alternative once the warranty expires, and if the auto dealership is to maximize its bottom line, that alternative should not be made too tempting by a service writer whose job is simply to write up the order.

Parts

The parts situation is not nearly as complex as that of the service writer, but still should involve some sales ability, which it most often does not. Certainly there is an order-taking and inventory aspect to the parts counter job. But when a customer is at the counter, a sales opportunity is presented. If the parts counter person is polite, is competent, and provides the product, the dealership is not hurt. Still, many opportunities do exist in the parts department that are not taken advantage of, but that could, in a simple, most cost-effective way, add considerably to the dealership's bottom line. Many a part has been bought in an after-market store or in a service station that could have and should have been purchased from the dealership if someone had bothered selling that part. In today's competitive world, it is simply too good an opportunity to be lost through mislabeling a potentially valuable function.

Has the Industry Adjusted?

We have talked about the enormous changes that have taken place in the industry, and how they have impacted on what it takes to succeed in sales within the retail auto industry. While the industry has reacted belatedly to the new product requirements, it has largely failed to react to the people implications of these requirements. With some dramatic exceptions, dealerships today are still examples par excellence of the warm-body approach to hiring. They pay minimal starting wages and will hire most people who are "willing to work hard," are "willing to put in the hours," and "like automobiles." Many consumers still hold a built-in fundamental contempt for the individual who is charged with the responsibility of selling that very high-ticket, very complex automotive product. In a perfect example of this, a large manufacturer asked us to do a study of a number of its dealerships to develop a salary-based compensation plan. This study was designed to determine whether dealers would be receptive to paying salespeople salaries if they could be provided with carefully selected, potentially productive people.

The proposed salary plan involved a base of $20,000 per year with incentives, and the reaction from most dealers, even with many built-in factory supports, was negative. Is it any wonder that most of the people entering the industry continue to be way below par, and the turnover rate continues to be at a staggering 60 percent per year?

What is amazing to us is that virtually any dealer we speak to in a seminar or one on one articulates his or her belief that hiring top professional, productive salespeople and retaining those people are essential to their success. Yet those same dealers continue to insist upon the minimal salary, open-door hiring process.

Dealers have to adjust to the fact that they need consultative professional salespeople—and that these people are not likely to be found by offering $700 monthly starting salaries, even with the use of a car. People meeting today's needs in the auto industry do exist and can be found through proper recruitment, selection, and, of course, compensation. But they need to be sought out, and in doing so, many old attitudes need to change as radically as the products themselves have. The dealers who do this will not only survive but thrive. The others will be gobbled up or go out of business, perhaps to the long-run benefit of the industry and the buying public.

Can Better Selection Really Work?

Earlier in this chapter, we mentioned our initial study of the auto industry which was published in the *Journal of Psychology* in 1964. That study proved that even through simply measuring empathy, ego-drive, ego-strength, and a few additional qualities, automotive sales success could be predicted. Ten years later, we completed a far more ambitious study, the results of which were published in the October 1974 issue of *Automotive Executive*.

Of particular interest in that study was how automotive salespeople who were job-matched performed significantly better than those whom we identified beforehand as not having the qualities needed to succeed.[*] This study was later included in our September–October, 1980 article in the *Harvard Business Review*, "Job Matching for Better Sales Performance."

---

[*](This study compared the performance of individuals whose particular personality dynamics matched the specific sales job against those individuals hired for other reasons, but whose dynamics did not match the job.

In essence, of the 421 automotive salespeople who were job-matched and still on the job after 14 months, 86 percent were in the top half of their sales force. On the other hand, of the 254 salespeople who we said were not job-matched, only 26 percent managed to perform in the top half after this length of time. These findings are illustrated in Table 30-1.

In 1998, we conducted a study for *Automotive News*, in which we assessed the potential of 320 top salespeople in 139 dealerships around the country. The goal of this joint study was to develop an "ideal profile" of the best salespeople, which dealers could use as a standard for future hiring.

We explored several variables to determine whether particular personality qualities were needed to sell automobiles in specific dealerships. For instance: What is it that distinguishes the very best salespeople in automobile dealerships today? Are they driven to persuade others? Or are they more service-oriented? Have cars and peoples' buying habits changed so much over the past few years that the old rules no longer apply? Or is selling automobiles a game of persistence and bucking the odds, the same as it always was?

We set out to explore these questions through a joint study conducted with *Automotive News* in which we assessed the makeup of 320 salespeople who were identified as "the best" by their managers in 139 dealerships throughout the country. In the process, we explored several variables to determine whether particular personality qualities were needed to sell automobiles in specific dealerships. For instance, we differentiated the best salespeople in terms of the size of the dealership they were working for, region of the country, and make of cars sold. We also looked for variances among top salespeople in dealerships where the price was fixed as opposed to the more traditional negotiative approach; and we also took into account whether the salesperson closed the deal, the sales manager was brought in for the final stage of negotiation, or the sales process was a combination of both approaches. Each of the participants was assessed by administering the Caliper Profile, our psychological test, which has been utilized to evaluate the potential of over 1 million applicants and employees.

Comparative Performance of "Job Matched" vs. "Not Job Matched" Automotive Salespeople After 14 Months		
	Top Half of Sales Force	Bottom Half of Sales Force
Job Matched *421 individuals*	86% *364 individuals*	14% *57 individuals*
Not Job Matched *254 individuals*	26% *65 individuals*	74% *189 individuals*

Table 30-1

If the 320 top-performing salespeople were merged into a composite picture of one person—with one collective personality—the news is that this composite defies the stereotype of the hard-driven, arm-twisting, tire-kicking, won't-let-you-go-until-you-sign-today salesperson.

The best salespeople in dealerships today are, not surprisingly, above average in ego-drive (the need to persuade). They also have a slightly higher than average level of ego-strength (the self-confidence to bounce back from rejection). They are assertive enough to ask for an order, and urgent enough to want to get things done now. As one of the top salespeople at a dealership in Philadelphia, Pennsylvania, said, "My style is low pressure and subtle, yet persuasive. If I don't close the first time, I'll close the next time. I try to give as much information as possible to our clients to help them make a decision. My advice to someone just starting out in this business is: Don't stop calling until a client says he or she is no longer interested. Don't let the rejection affect your outlook. Instead offer your future assistance and move on."

Interestingly, as an aggregate, the best automotive salespeople today, while having the classical qualities needed to succeed in sales, are not as extremely driven as our studies show salespeople to be who sell insurance or stocks and bonds. In fact, we found through this study that salespeople who had too much of a need to persuade did not last long at certain types of dealerships. Some of the very best salespeople were clearly more driven than others. But too intense of a level of ego-drive could be a drawback in some sales situations. So being in the 70th percentile of ego-drive is fine, but the 88th percentile could present some difficulty in some situations.

One interesting, and unexpected, finding was that this group's level of empathy was surprisingly below average when compared with other sales professionals. In virtually every other study we have conducted across other industries throughout the years, we have universally found that empathy, the ability to sense the reactions of another person, is central to sales success. Higher levels of empathy traditionally enable salespeople to fine-tune their persuasive nature, letting them home in on the needs of a prospect.

One of the top salespeople with a dealership in Moberly, Missouri, defined empathy succinctly as "knowing when to talk and when to shut up." Salespeople with low empathy might barge ahead when they really shouldn't.

While one of the purposes of the study was to describe the best salespeople, so that dealers have a model for future hiring, we feel compelled to insert here that seeking future automotive salespeople with higher levels of empathy will improve productivity and reflect well on the profession as a whole. As a fleet and lease manager for a dealership in Seattle, Washington, underscored, "Good salespeople are good listeners. You can see this in how they react to a question; they can keep the process moving along."

Still, this study uncovered that the majority of top automotive salespeople are not particularly open to new ideas, they don't necessarily listen well to others, and it is relatively hard for them to break out of the rules they use to drive their sales pitch. This is not to say that they are not "people people." They just like their routine. They are also slightly above average in terms of their gregariousness, and they have an average level of helpfulness.

The best automotive salespeople, we have found, are also what we call "externally structured." These individuals respond well to the dealership environment, in which the sales manager sets the tone and goals and expectations are clearly defined.

These patterns held true in dealerships wherever they were located in the country. And there were fundamentally no differences found between the best salespeople representing different makes of automobiles.

One variation in the makeup of the best salespeople that is worth noting is that those who excel in smaller dealerships (with under 30 employees) are significantly more gregarious and accommodating than the best salespeople in large dealerships (with 130 or more employees). The implication here is that the best salespeople in smaller dealerships cannot just rely upon the name and reputation of the dealership to attract customers. Instead, they have to be a bit more outgoing and approachable and go out of their way to be more helpful to sustain the intimacy and hometown feeling of a smaller dealership. As one of the top salespeople with a dealership in Norwich, New York, said, "We are dealing with local customers who know us, and this requires more of a caretaking approach. We want our customers to come back again and again."

Some Differences

Next we looked at who closes to see if there was a fundamental difference in personality attributes. We broke the group into three categories. There were 16 top salespeople for whom the sales managers actually did the closing, 67 who closed by themselves, and 108 who closed with assistance at times from the sales manager. The only significant difference we uncovered was that the ego strength (the ability to handle rejection) was higher (64%) for salespeople who sell by themselves compared with salespeople who sell with help from their managers (50%). Such a finding might be expected since people who sell by themselves have to be able to handle the rejection that comes with the sales territory.

We also focused on whether there was a difference between people who sell at a fixed price versus those who negotiate. There were 261 top salespeople representing 112 dealerships where traditional negotiating is involved, and 10 top salespeople selling at fixed prices for 6 dealerships, including Saturn, Ford, Chevrolet, Pontiac, Mitsubishi, and Subaru. While there were not enough fixed-price dealerships to make a definitive statement, we were surprised to uncover no significant differences between the two groups. This is interesting considering the advertisements for certain fixed-price dealerships, which claim that you can't tell the difference between their customers and their salespeople walking the floor. Their salespeople, they imply, are simply there to service your needs and answer your questions.

One of the more striking findings was that women clearly exhibited a higher level of empathy than did their male counterparts. This is consistent with our findings in other professions and industries. When we broke out the most successful salespeople by gender, we found that 88% of our respondents were males and 12% were female. Among the differences worth noting overall are that top-performing female salespeople in our study were significantly more flexible, outgoing, accommodating, and energetic than top-performing male salespeople; and they were less cautious and rules driven. One of the top salespeople at a dealership in Los Angeles noted, "Over the past few years, I've become more confident, particularly with customers who may not prefer a female salesperson. I can handle them more flexibly and comfortably now."

Another interesting finding is that nearly half of the best salespeople we surveyed had no previous automotive sales experience. This confirms our long-held belief that prior experience is not necessarily a predictor of success in sales. There can be a myriad of reasons for someone succeeding in one position, which may have nothing to do with succeeding on another job. When trying to determine whether someone has the qualities needed to succeed in automotive sales, or any other position for that matter, we have found that it is much more effective to assess someone's potential than it is to concentrate on his or her former accomplishments.

Time on the Job

Over time, the best salespeople, we have found, bring different strengths to their profession. They've learned what works for them, depending upon their fundamental personality attributes.

Rather than uncovering just one ideal profile, we have determined there are, in fact, two distinct profiles that characterize top automotive salespeople. Understanding the strengths and limitations of these two profiles can have enormous implications for hiring automotive salespeople in the future.

Essentially, when we broke the group of top performers down into those who were there for a relatively short period of time (less than 2 1/2 years) and those who had been there for a comparatively long period of time (over 8 years), we came up with two strikingly different profiles.

As can be seen in Figure 30-1, the higher-tenure group (comprising 52 top performers) were more thorough, accommodating, and sociable than their peers. They were also less persuasive, assertive, and aggressive. This group of veterans, a number of whom had been with the same dealership for over 20 years, built their business through repeat customers and referrals. But it must be emphasized, they don't start out on top. It generally takes them several years to hit their stride.

As the owner of a dealership in McLean, Virginia, said about one of his top performers who had been there a long time, "He is consistently one of the dealership's top salespeople. It took him 3 years to develop, but now, 14 years down the road, he has established a loyal core of customers whom he services to the hilt." And the president of a dealership in Salisbury, Maryland, agreed that his 11-year veteran "eased into it, rising to the top after a few years with us, and now she just continues to grow." On average, we found it takes just shy of 5 years for top producers with this more conscientious, responsible, service-oriented profile to hit their stride.

The style of these consultative, high-tenured, topflight salespeople was summed up by a top-performing, long-tenured salesperson in Roscommon, Michigan. He noted, "Clients today are more educated and particular. As a result, it is much harder to close than ever before. It's usually not a 'same day' sale. I need to be able to tell each client everything they want to know about the car. Then they are likely to shop around, so I'll call the next day to answer any questions they might have. After that, I'll keep in touch every day or so until they make a decision. Clients don't want to be pressured. They want to have access to solid information, and to know they can trust you."

On the other hand, there is a distinctly different profile for high performers who have been at a dealership for less than 2 1/2 years. These top salespeople are decidedly more driven to persuade others. In fact, their level of ego-drive is more than 20 percentage points higher than their high-tenured counterparts. As can be seen from Figure 30-1, top-performing salespeople who have been at a dealership for a relatively short period of time also have slightly more ego-strength (the ability to rebound from rejection), and are definitely more assertive and aggressive. They also have more of a tendency to set their own rules and are a bit more confident. And as a group, they are less thorough and cautious than, and not nearly as sociable or accommodating as, top performers who have been there a longer period of time.

To sum up, what emerges are two distinct profiles: those who are more classically driven and hit the road running, but—if they are overly driven—do not last for the long haul; and those who can take several years to hit their stride, but then keep up their book of business by establishing a solid, reliable reputation.

Automotive Tenure Comparison

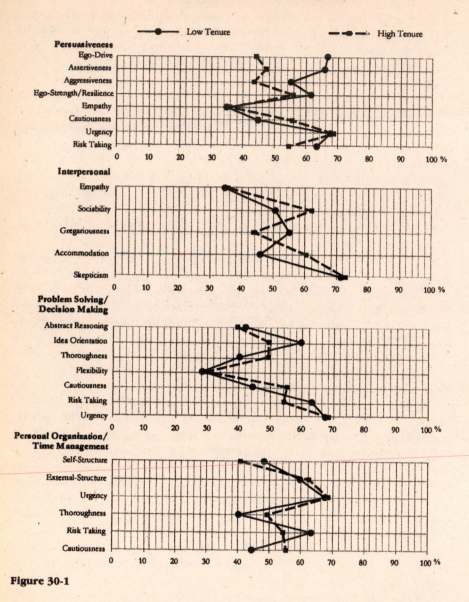

Figure 30-1

The Dilemma

This poses an interesting dilemma for owners and sales managers who are trying to hire salespeople with the potential to build their business. Do you bring on hard-driven salespeople to convert sales quickly? Or do you invest the time necessary to hire salespeople with more of a consultant's demeanor, who will not necessarily bring in new business immediately, but may, over time, set new records?

If you lean toward the more thorough and accommodating model, how do you know that such individuals will be able to survive through the first several years that it typically takes for them to build their base of business? Or if you are looking for the more classically driven salesperson, you have to ask yourself, "Why is it that so few of them are with the same dealership for the long term?"

The ideal would be to find someone who is a combination of these two profiles. The perfect applicant would be empathic, driven to persuade, assertive, able to bounce back from rejection, and thorough, conscientious, sociable, and accommodating. Such an individual will be able to close sales early on and will know how to build long-term relationships.

But we are rarely faced with the best of both worlds when trying to make quick hiring decisions. So while you may want to set your sights on finding individuals who are a combination of these two ideal profiles, the truth of the matter is that you will usually have to decide on someone who fits either the more consultative or the more driven profile.

How do you decide which profile is best for your dealership? Coming up with just the right mix of sales talent depends upon first determining the specific needs of your dealership and then assessing the potential of your sales candidates. You can start out by asking yourself, "What is most important? Selling more units? Increasing profit? Satisfying customers? Or bringing in repeat business?" The order in which you place these goals will point the way toward defining the profile of the next salesperson you are seeking. Other questions to consider are: Does the location of your dealership require an enormous amount of prospecting? Do you have too many of one kind of salesperson? And are you trying to alter the public's perception of your dealership?

As a corporate training officer at a dealership in Addison, Texas, said, "For us, the key question is, 'How do you know who is the right person to hire?' In the past, we only cared if someone had proven sales ability. And that's led to a revolving door. In reality, if a person doesn't have the character and attitude to make full use of their sales talent, then they're not going to stick around and be successful."

So the question we endeavored to answer—what is the "ideal profile" of the best automotive salespeople?—turns out to have a different solution for each dealership. A new mix of talents and abilities might, in fact, be the most appropriate answer for attaining your business goals. Hiring the best salespeople for the future is no longer as simple as trying to clone your top salesperson.

Ultimately, our study identifies two top sales profiles—a driven top performer for the short term and a more consultative model for the long term. Somewhere in between is the possibility of trying to uncover those rare individuals who possess the qualities of both ideals.

Determining whom to hire for the future is a matter of matching an individual with the best-suited profile to your dealership's particular needs. Combining the drive and resilience of a top salesperson with the empathy and conscientiousness of a consultant (whether on your staff or the next individual you hire) will go a long way toward building a sales force of highly productive, career-oriented professionals.

31

Banking on People: The Key to the Bottom Line

A few years ago, a bank asked us to do a study aimed at determining the reasons for a pattern of increasing job dissatisfaction among its employees. As the bank described the problem, it became apparent that not only was there increasing job dissatisfaction, but there was also a related problem of increasing turnover, particularly among long-term employees.

The first step we took was to conduct an attitude study, the results of which provided us with an early clue to the nature of the problem. Many long-term employees, particularly loan officers, complained, "When I was hired years ago, it was to do one job. Today they are asking me to do something entirely different." This led us to conduct an extensive job analysis, focusing particularly on the loan officer function, and then to do a series of interviews. It became clear that the employees felt that changes were happening all around them in the bank—but that they were not a part of those changes.

What had in fact occurred was that the loan officer's job had evolved dramatically from a purely financial, decision-making capacity to a heavily sales-oriented function. Individuals who were doing an outstanding job, given the early job definition, felt like they were standing still as their jobs changed around them.

The bank's management had taken on a new, aggressive marketing approach in the community. It recognized that this was necessary to survive in today's competitive financial marketplace. But it had not prepared its loan officers for all the changes that were needed. It had not assessed the inherent abilities of its current loan officers, nor had it developed new job descriptions, offered training and coaching for those who were enthusiastic about the new possibilities their jobs offered, or developed alternative career paths for those who saw their careers going in a different direction. So while the management of this particular bank grasped the importance of

249

sharing with its customers that the bank had become more market-driven, it had neglected to prepare its employees for the changes.

A new advertising campaign had been designed to focus on making the institution more competitive. New services were introduced to differentiate the bank from its competitors, such as:

- No minimum balance required for free checking
- Lower auto loan rates if you have more than $400 in your checking account
- Overdraft protection line of credit
- Your own private business banker
- Automatic transfer of funds from checking to savings
- Ready credit if you set up a "special" account
- Automatic teller machines capable of dispensing cash, making deposits, and transferring funds at any hour
- An open door to the president
- Home equity loans
- No-points mortgages
- Special focus on small and medium-sized businesses
- Discounts on auto loans for depositors

While the bank seemed geared to enter a new era, it was leaving its employees—particularly its loan officers—in the dust.

We advised management that the bank's new market-driven image, through its new advertising campaign, would become meaningless unless it reflected reality. And the reality it had to reflect was in the people who worked in the bank.

After all, advertising, no matter how persuasive, rarely sells a bank. At most, a successful advertising campaign can only bring potential customers into a commercial bank or a thrift. Whether or not prospects developed through advertising are converted to customers is directly dependent upon the quality of the people within the institution to whom these prospects are exposed. It is important to understand that few customers have any real idea about the structure, policies, or financial strength of their bank. The bank, even to more sophisticated business customers, is the teller, the loan officer, or the vice president with whom that customer happens to deal. Too often, the enormous amount of time, money, and effort devoted to bringing a prospect in is undone in the first 30 seconds if that prospect deals with the "wrong person."

Unfortunately, as Robert Frost wrote, to many people, "A banker is someone who will give you an umbrella when the sun shines and takes it back when it rains." Advertising can help set aside this negative image, but one bad contact with a rude, discourteous teller or a loan officer who acts more like a computer than a human being will quickly reinforce a negative view that could have been turned around by a smile or just a bit of empathy.

Although seemingly inconsequential, a personal example might make this point. We were in Florida recently and received papers from our office which had to be notarized and immediately returned by overnight mail. So we walked into a nearby bank, where a notary told us there would be a $2 charge, then asked for our account number. We explained that we did not bank in the area, to which she explained that she could not offer us this service, as it was provided only to bank customers. We offered to pay an additional fee for the service, but she adamantly refused to provide us with her signature because we were not currently customers.

The end of the story, of course, is that we walked across the street to another bank, which gladly went to the *enormous trouble* of providing us with a notary stamp. The fact is that we will be opening a bank account in the area next fall, and we leave it to the reader to figure out which bank will receive our account.

This personal, rather insignificant incident brings home the importance of service orientation to successful banking. Why, in good sense, would a bank deny a simple service such as notarizing one document, even with payment for the service, if there were even one chance in a hundred that offering such a service could lead to a future account? There is, of course, no rational marketing answer to that question. It has more to do with a bank employee being caught in some sort of policy-driven, rules-oriented mindset, which treats the customer as an inconvenience, and ultimately will leave the bank lobby empty.

People Give the Edge

If an institution wishes to develop and maintain a competitive edge, the key to that edge is the people working in that institution.

Part of the problem that a commercial bank or thrift faces by definition is that its people need to be financially oriented. A teller must be able to handle money. A good loan officer must be able to judge credit and be comfortable with figures. Often, these fiscal abilities run counter to the skills required to perform people-oriented job responsibilities.

In order to understand this point, let us backtrack and look for a moment at the psychology of occupational choice. A young man or woman becomes an accountant or financial analyst often because he or she is not comfortable with the pressures and ambiguities of human relationships. That accountant or finance person derives enormous ego-gratification from balancing the books, developing financial plans that work, effecting cost savings, and the like. If that person is properly matched to a job requiring these financial skills, he or she will be happy and successful in that job.

At the other end of the continuum is the individual who is far too restless to cope with numbers and detail. This individual has ego-drive and so derives his or her gratification from the successful persuasion of another human being. The ego-driven individual wants and needs the victory of a successful persuasion as a powerful enhancement of his or her ego. Financial planning would require too much patience and attention to detail for an ego-driven individual.

Can these two ends of the continuum be found in the same person? The answer is, to some degree in some cases, but certainly not in most. The first type, the financially oriented individual, has traditionally dominated bank staffs. The need for the teller to have good people skills, the loan officer to have excellent persuasive skills, and the bank's staff to include people with financial, persuasive, and people skills has only of late begun to be realized, and the problem is that all too many employees are simply incapable of doing all of what today's banking job requires. They view their position as primarily, if not solely, a financial one. In many cases, this view is reinforced by tradition and by management, as employees receive promotions for their success strictly on the basis of the financial aspect of their work. Yet no deposit will be made unless an individual agrees to make that deposit. No loan will be made unless someone chooses to borrow. And no mortgage will be provided unless the borrower chooses that institution to provide it. The bank's need, then, is clearly for people who have not only financial skills but people skills and persuasive skills as well.

Combined Skills Are Rare

This is not an easy task we are describing. Based on our research across industry, we have determined that about one in four individuals possesses really good detail ability, i.e., very good potential as a finance person. About the same number, one in four, possesses good persuasive skills. But in less than a third of the cases do the combinations overlap. Thus, as a bank recruits tellers, loan officers, commercial call personnel, and the like, it has to begin by selecting people with certain competencies in terms of their financial abilities; it also has to be willing to eliminate at least three out of four of these financially competent people who do not possess the needed people and persuasive skills.

This means that a financial institution would probably be able to successfully hire one really good teller or loan officer out of ten superficially qualified applicants. Is this expensive? Of course it is, but how much less expensive is this rigorous hiring than the loss of one customer with the multiplied effect of that loss? How much better is it to concentrate just a little more effort on bringing in the right people for the right jobs to begin with, and spending the necessary time and money to train and supervise these appropriate people, than to spend the enormous money and efforts required in continually recruiting and firing—and continually losing customers?

Costs of the Wrong People in the Wrong Job

A simple method by which the costs can be measured is to compare the productivity of the top loan or outside call officer and that of a person near the bottom. The difference between those numbers represents pure cost in terms of reduced revenue. Clearly, what a banking institution's top people produce can be produced by others, and if other individuals are not doing so, they are literally throwing revenue away.

Another major cost stemming from the lack of effective salespeople in banking institutions relates to cross-selling. A recent study disclosed that 75 percent of the people who opened an account or took out a loan at a financial institution within the past year were not told about any additional services that might benefit them. Beyond this, 25 percent of those who said their financial institutions did attempt to cross-sell a product indicated that the product was an IRA; and only 10 percent of those approached actually opened an additional account. With the enormous and rapidly increasing array of products and services offered by banking institutions, this failure to cross-sell has an enormous negative impact on a bank's bottom line and, so, on its ability to compete.

A Sales Culture

For a banking institution to maximize sales opportunities, even on one product, and certainly for it to take full advantage of cross-selling opportunities, a sales culture must exist within that bank, which, as we have discussed earlier, is often lacking in tradition-bound organizations. What will it take to create this new sales culture in an institution?

First, for there to be a sales culture, there must be sales-oriented individuals within the institution. Also, a culture has to be developed which fosters, promotes, and rewards successful cross-selling. Management can set the tone for whether the employees of a commercial bank or thrift will possess:

- An understanding and problem-solving approach toward each customer's needs;
- An attitude that selling is mutually beneficial to the bank and the customer;
- A team, rather than an individual, effort toward completing a sales transaction; and
- A feeling that the institution is special and worthy of a superior effort.

Sales can only flourish if goals are clearly spelled out. The simpler and clearer the goals are, the greater the likelihood that a culture can develop around those goals.

Setting these goals is probably more difficult in the banking industry than in many others because of the duality of the banking relationship. When an individual discusses a possible loan with a loan officer, a sales goal would obviously be for that loan officer to make the loan—to sell the loan. On the other hand, the loan officer's fiscal responsibility includes making a judgment about the efficacy of the loan. Simply put, not every loan should be made. Clearly, the goal is not simply to put as many loans as possible on the books, but rather to sell loans that are good for the bank.

This duality even exists for outside call officers. Although the goal is obviously to establish as many accounts as possible, there are many accounts that simply may not be worth having. Here again, good business judgment and fiscal sense must balance the sales goal. Thus, as the banking industry increasingly recognizes the sales and marketing aspects of its overall function, it also must develop a valid performance appraisal system that can include balancing sales with the very necessary fiscal responsibility to make top sales realistic and profitable.

To be truly effective and to enhance the development of a sales culture, sales goals need to be followed up with periodic performance appraisals. If performance criteria are clearly defined and transmitted to employees, the potentially productive individuals will respond positively to periodic objective measurement of their performance. Personally motivated, driven salespeople want to be recognized. Knowing that a system for appraising performance is in place will serve as real, positive motivation for persuasively motivated professionals.

Implications for the Future

Whether discussing commercial banks or thrifts, it is safe to say that the banking industry has undergone tremendous change in the last couple of decades. And this change is likely to continue at a rapid pace well into the new millennium. An industry that was marked by regulation, simply defined products and services, and clear separation of services among the various institutional categories is now rapidly becoming deregulated, with multiple product offerings and enormous overlap in services, not only among banks, but between banks and other financial services institutions. Even a few years ago, it would have been unthinkable to read in the newspaper or see on television a savings bank ad proclaiming itself as a one-stop financial shopping center.

The intense competition resulting from these factors has led to the demise of many institutions, including some very large and well-respected ones; the acquisition of others; and the bankruptcy and restructuring of still others. And the competition among banks and between banks and competing industries is only going to get more intense.

So we return to the beginning. With the evolution of the industry has come the evolution of the job, though the latter evolution has not always been well recognized. Where the job of the loan officer might some time ago have been described as simply approving loans, today few would deny that a loan officer needs some sales ability. Although some elements within the industry still look down their nose at sales, viewing banking as above the need to sell, most, perhaps reluctantly, now recognize that to succeed, they had better sell; and many have even set up sales forces to do just that. There are even positions in some banks called "sales," and while others might be called "outside call officers" or even "branch managers," their job descriptions prominently include sales. The casualties are the individuals who were suited to their jobs 10 years ago, as they were then described, but who are, through no fault of their own, rendered ineffective by their new job description. They are the same people, but what they are now expected to do is radically different. What can be done for these people?

Perhaps there are other jobs within the institution that still fit their motivations and strengths. It is hoped that if they have provided loyal service to their bank, they would be offered the opportunity to fill those positions. Others, of course, may retire. But it is critical to a bank's survival that jobs requiring persuasion be filled by individuals who possess the dynamics of a salesperson. While a banking professional must certainly have detail ability, organizational skills, and good financial orientation, he or she must combine these skills with the ability to sense the reactions of others, the motivation to persuade them, and the sense of confidence to be rejected where necessary. The banking salesperson must also have the motivation to provide service since that is what banking, after all, is still all about.

Though they are not easy to find, people with this combination of abilities do exist, if the industry will actively seek them. The challenge is to turn traditionally unaggressive financial institutions, which may have prospered in yesterday's highly structured, rate-protected marketplace, into lean, hungry, professional sales organizations that provide outstanding service.

32

High-Technology/Consultative Sales: The New Breed

As our economy shifts from producing products to delivering services, the nature of selling is changing dramatically. To meet the challenges brought on by selling intangible services, a new breed of salespeople is emerging. Such salespeople come across as consultants. Rather than being perceived by their clients as product suppliers, consultative salespeople are viewed as problem solvers and profit improvers. These new, emerging salespeople are particularly evident in high-technology sales, but are now being seen in new and old industries alike.

What is occurring in high technology is condensed into a shorter period of time than any other development in history. High technology has already permeated every aspect of our lives and changed the way we do things, from paying our bills to preparing a marketing strategy.

All this is occurring at head-spinning rates. Today's high technology will be tomorrow's state of the art, and merely commonplace the day after. Along the way, our future is reshaped. Certainly, the nature of sales is changing. And there is much the sales profession at large can learn from those who are on the frontier of new developments.

That is why, some time back, we undertook a study of sales forces in client companies selling new technologies, i.e., microcomputers, minicomputers, and mainframe computers; telecommunications and office automation; computer time-sharing networks; applications software; and biotech and medical equipment. This study immediately preceded the dot-coms, but in our recent work with several of these companies we have found that the results of our earlier work apply directly to these emerging organizations. Among successful salespeople of such high-tech products, and they are a rare breed, we found some striking differences from salespeople who thrive in almost every other field. These distinctions have important ramifications for everyone trying to sell in today's marketplace.

As the president of a software developing firm put it: "When it comes to high-tech products, the old rules of selling no longer apply. This is because successful high-tech salespeople are not really selling products or services. What is actually sold are solutions—solutions which have to be customized to meet the unique needs of each client."

In most sales situations, as we have described elsewhere in this book, the need for persuasive drive cannot be overemphasized. Enough is never too much. However, for someone selling high-tech, information, or professional services, we found that if the need to persuade is too intense, it can be a hindrance rather than an asset. The reason involves the very nature of the consultative sale. In consultative selling, the salesperson must be willing to build the sale in a slow, step-by-step process.

The intensely ego-driven salesperson wants the close right now. He or she wants the instant gratification that the close brings and will have difficulty delaying that gratification. It certainly is impossible to convey the image of the concerned consultant when the need to close immediately is too intense.

We want to be clear here: Successful high-tech salespeople must have some ego-drive, or else they will never close a sale, but their drive must be tempered. Ultimately, a high-tech sale takes time—which means it takes patience, follow-through, persistence, empathy, and the ability not to take rejection personally.

What evolves is an individual who is extremely attentive to a client's needs and totally intent upon seeking an ideal solution to each client's unique problems. Since each client has unique needs, each high-tech product or service must be tailored to meet those needs completely, or else the sale will be lost to a competitor.

The consultative sale is the classic example of "the sale beginning after the sale is made." Once the system, service, or program is installed, the salesperson's job has just begun. The sale forms the basis for a continuing, long-lasting relationship in which the salesperson troubleshoots any problems that might arise and implements new facets of the system as needs expand.

Clients are keenly aware that they are not simply buying another piece of equipment. In fact, in many ways they are acquiring an ancillary employee. The ability to develop a trusting, long-lasting relationship is essential to success in high-tech sales since additional products and services will be expected by a client for a long time to come.

To provide solutions to problems, an individual must convey the solid, stable, reliable image of someone who has credibility, exhibits keen intelligence, and can be trusted to alleviate problems and concerns and really help to come up with the best possible solutions. The qualities that we uncovered which most differentiate the successful high-tech salesperson from the rest all add up to this solution-oriented consultant's image.

"There is an enormous amount of consulting involved with every high-tech sale," confirms a vice president of sales for a company that provides clients with a computer time-sharing network. "Each client has unique needs—there is no one widget for all problems—and our service must be tailored to meet those needs completely, or we will lose a sale to one of our competitors." Clients ask informed questions, and the salesperson who does not know his or her product and understand the client's needs inside out is going to be perceived as being poorly prepared, and will reflect negatively on the product and the company.

We have found that most productive high-tech salespeople are also extremely well organized. They have to be able to handle details well and organize their work effectively. This personal organization gives them the capacity to keep many things in mind simultaneously, including the technical aspects and capabilities of a wide spectrum of products and services.

High-tech salespeople also need to be bright, articulate, and confident enough to deal with key executives in major corporations. Since the purchases are substantial and the products will have tremendous impact on the overall effectiveness of an entire company, the sale is generally made at the highest level of an organization.

To excel, high-tech salespeople must have the ability to get their point across strongly and confidently without appearing pushy or overly aggressive. Such individuals should also be unpretentious, because of the diversity of people encountered. There is a precarious balance between presenting a professional consultant's image while simultaneously being open to meeting with people in all types of corporate situations.

High-tech salespeople must have the flexibility to adjust their communication style to the particular individual with whom they are dealing. As a manager from one of the first manufacturers of minicomputers put it, "High-tech salespeople do not have to convince just one individual, such as a purchasing agent, within a firm." They have to convincingly speak the language of programmers, systems analysts, and controllers, as well as CEOs and boards of directors.

Our research findings underscore that people who excel in high-tech sales are excellent communicators, both verbally and in writing. They must have the ability to compose letters, proposals, and reports clearly, concisely, and convincingly. This is distinct from salespeople in almost every other field, who, for the most part, view paperwork as drudgery and an obstacle to closing additional sales.

Over time in this kind of selling, one has to be technically oriented to succeed. The problem is that not all people who are technically oriented can sell. In fact, from the point of basic personality characteristics, the successful salesperson and the successful technician are almost polar opposites. So simply moving people from the technical side to the sales side would be corporate suicide.

Still, a technical background is a necessary starting point, as noted by an IBM marketing manager. He describes a scenario where one's technical credibility is being challenged all along the way. Innocently enough, a high-tech salesperson starts out by asking, "What kind of collection basis are you using?" But as the prospect responds with a curt "10-bit BCDs," the sale could come to a grinding halt—unless the salesperson could say something like, "Our binary code decimal base ranges from point one to point zero, zero one, which could significantly increase your capabilities." But what does the salesperson say when the technician responds, "The floating exponent range of my calibration is more than your system can handle"?

At this point, most salespeople would have to excuse themselves, saying something like, "Well, this is a very good point. Let me get back to my technical people and I'll have an answer for you first thing in the morning." But, of course, the next morning the prospect may be hard to find. You can see why the successful high-tech salesperson is a rare breed.

Such salespeople must be long-timers, because the firm's investment will not be recovered in 6 months or even a year. He or she must have enormous perseverance. Attention must be paid to the slightest detail or solutions will not be complete. And such an individual must be thoroughly knowledgeable about his or her company's products as well as the business world. Meanwhile, the high-tech salesperson needs persuasive ability, but as we said, it must be tempered.

Where do you find this new breed of salespersons? Short of hiring twins, one adept in technology and the other in sales, and working them as a team, it is difficult to uncover someone who can stand out in the technical as well as the sales end of the business world.

Most good people who have both attributes are not looking for new jobs. And even if they were, there are not enough of them to go around.

So where do you look for those who are not looking? One of the most overlooked places for finding high-tech salespeople is in a company's own backyard. A potentially record-breaking salesperson might be working in the company, doing something completely different, wasting his or her natural ability.

One recent study found that nearly 90 percent of scientific programmers and analysts are interested in exploring new computer jobs. Certainly some of the these technical wizards will also have the innate ability to sell. Many of them may be at a dead end, with no clear path for advancement from their present positions. Selling might give them a fresh start. Once you have identified those who have the requisite technical background and the desire and ability to sell, sales training can be effective.

Now, we have just described a unique individual—the successful high-tech salesperson—and from the start we said that by getting a clearer understanding of what it takes to succeed on the leading edge of new developments, there would be lessons for all of us in sales. What are those lessons, and how can they be translated into other sales situations?

The common thread winding through the field of high-tech sales is that clients are becoming increasingly sophisticated and knowledgeable before making purchases. Studies in numerous other industries show that this trend in consumer awareness is having far-reaching consequences throughout the entire sales profession. Well-thought-out and researched questions are being asked before even the most minor acquisitions are made, and there is little patience with the salesperson who tries to gloss over any concerns or objections.

Just as high technology has affected all aspects of our lives and made consumers demand quality, value, and high performance in everything they buy, so the high-tech, consultative salesperson appears to be the first of a new breed. Ultimately, we can all learn from those who are succeeding on the frontier of new developments.

7

The Successful Salesperson in Today's World

From a business perspective, the boundaries of countries have disappeared. What does this mean for those who are trying to succeed in selling? Our studies show that the profile of the successful salesperson is essentially the same in America as it is in Japan, Sweden, England, Brazil, Canada, Hong Kong, or virtually anywhere else in the world. It all comes down to motivation.

It's All Motivation

Fish gotta swim.

So here's the scoop. Not everyone is cut out to be a salesperson, and not every salesperson is cut out to be a sales manager and/or a leader. Moreover, those people who are most successful and most productive in their careers have managed to satisfy all the different motivators: activity, *material, social,* and *growth* at the same time.

I Love This Game

First and foremost, people who are the most productive over a long period of time have found a set of activities and tasks to engage in that are consistent with their skills and their basic personality dynamics. As a result they really like what they're doing or at least most of what they're doing most of the time. If you find a job that's consistent with who you are, you'll never *work* another day in you life.

Selling is a rewarding role for people who are outgoing, ego-driven, empathic, confident, reasonably conscientious, and willing to take risks. If that's you, there are plenty of opportunities and a lifetime of rewarding experiences for you to engage in. As an occupational category, sales continues to grow. Moreover, unlike some professions, it exists in virtually every conceivable industry, working with every conceivable product in nearly every location throughout the world. There is nothing under the sun (including the sun for that matter) that does not in some way have a sales role associated with it. Think about it. If you've got the skills and the inclination, you could be selling almost anything. Making a killing. And having an incredible amount of fun while you're at it.

Show Me the Money

Material rewards, like money for example, provide people with both a basic ability to survive and an unlimited opportunity to excel or, if you will, strike it rich. Perhaps the single most obvious motivator for working, money is a great equalizer that allows people the freedom to exercise their individuality and express their personalities. From a business perspective it enables an organization the ability to fine-tune and focus its efforts by systematically "reinforcing" behaviors the organization needs to have accomplished in order to attain important goals and outcomes: "If you do this, I'll give you that. And if you do it better, I'll give you more!"

In no other occupational category is the opportunity for individual material success higher than in sales. For those people who have the talent (a combination of the right skills and the right personality), the sales profession offers a nearly limitless ability to be rewarded for doing what comes naturally. Can you imagine getting paid a bonus for going out and meeting new people, convincing them that this or that great product will really make a difference in their lives and then having them thank you for it? And you get your expenses paid while you're at it? It must be too good to be true. Getting a bonus for doing what comes naturally? Quick, pinch me—I must be dreaming. On the other hand, if you're not suited to doing those tasks, the material reinforcers (money included) will never be entirely satisfying no matter how great they are.

You Like Me ...You Really Like Me

Social and status rewards nurture our soul. Hey, help us quell the fleeting, lingering, or sometimes deep-seated and often significant doubts we all have about our self-worth. While many of us have developed a high degree of confidence and wouldn't admit to needing to be recognized, there's nothing quite like a meaningful pat on the back from someone respected, a promotion, a public accolade, or a lifetime achievement award to make us feel just a little bit better about who we are. If someone else recognizes our value, it must be true. In any occupation we all crave recognition of our value and contribution beyond the material reinforcement that money provides. It's great to be doing something you like. It's better if someone notices. As Woody Allen so aptly put it in his classic film *Annie Hall*, "We all need the eggs."

The sales occupation provides many opportunities for social recognition and status rewards—perhaps more so than any other occupational group. Every day these gutsy people put themselves and oftentimes their financial security on the line. Through their individual, highly visible efforts, they contribute to the organizations they work for in the most measurable way possible: the creation of revenue. Without the efforts of salespeople, the lifeblood revenues of the organizations they are part of would dry up. These are the heroes who allow the rest of us to play the game.

So if it's social reinforcement and recognition you crave, look no further. There are many forms of social and status recognition made available to this occupational group (oftentimes to the dismay of others in the organization who may not be eligible): salesperson of the month, salesperson of the year, the president's club, the chairman's circle, a Rolex watch for a lifetime of sales achievement. It goes with the territory. So enjoy the sunlight; its warmth goes right to the soul and will make you feel good about who you are.

On the other hand, if you're not cut out to sell and fail to achieve a level of performance consistent with the needs of the organization or the peer group, be prepared to be left out in the cold. Those same social rewards that are heaped upon those who are so visibly successful are just as quickly withdrawn or even worse applied in the negative. There's nothing worse than not performing in a sales position where the generation of revenue is so easily counted and counted upon. And the sting of "negative status" merely adds insult to injury. As Joe Lewis once said, "You can run but you cannot hide." Find something else to do if your ego-strength can't take the heat of the kitchen and the ongoing challenge of the competition. It is not for the faint of heart.

The Sun Will Come Up Tomorrow

So here's this person doing exactly what she likes to do best...*for a living*. Let's say she's been setting sales records for your company for the past 5 years. She's getting great material reinforcers (money, bonuses, cars, Rolex watches, etc.). And to make it even better, everyone knows her name. She gets lots of recognition and has lots of status. What else could she possibly want? What is this voice inside her head that keeps saying in a nagging way, "The grass is greener somewhere else; the grass is greener somewhere else"? Depending upon the events of the day, or the week, or the year, that inner voice is either really quiet and unobtrusive or so loud little else can be heard.

We all have an inner voice that keeps us looking to the future. Sometimes the voice says: "I gotta get out of this place." Sometimes the voice says, "I like what I've got, but I could have so much more, if I only..." Sometimes the voice is loud and insistent; sometimes it's on really low volume and barely audible. But it's there inside, waiting for a moment of external opportunity or internal dissatisfaction to raise the volume. You know what we're talking about.

Aside from activity reinforcers that allow us to do what we want to do (at least, most of the time), material reinforcers (like money) that sustain us and focus our effort, and social reinforcers that nurture us and make us feel better about who we are way down deep, we all have a need, even for those of us who are pessimistic, to believe, to wish, and to hope that the future will be better than today; that there's more to be had, even if what we have already is great.

It's not a job match made in heaven until all four of the motivational reinforcers are firing on all four cylinders. Nobody likes feeling like they're at a dead-end job, not even people who are nearing the ends of their careers. We all have a need to feel that there's something more to be had.

So here's the good news for both talented individuals who need jobs that are fulfilling and for organizations that have an ongoing need to retain a talent pool: A really good job match for both parties is one where individuals are doing what they're best suited to do, where the money is good and the material incentives are focused, where there is recognition and status provided for the contributions being made, and where there is a mutual investment in retaining, developing, and promoting the talent pool.

For salespeople and companies that realize this, it can be smooth sailing. For those who don't, the seas will be choppy.

Ultimately, this gives salespeople an incredible amount of security and freedom. Just consider this: Selling is the ultimate transferable skill.

First and foremost, it's completely and entirely transportable. It travels very light. As we noted, the profession of sales, in one way or another, is an important function in every industry and in every company, for every product line and for every concept imaginable. With the right knowledge and interest, the skills of selling transcend the company and the product and can be adapted and fitted to suit the individual's special interests and unique capabilities. You want to work for a different company? It's yours! You want to sell air? No problem. How about the sun? Solar energy, we're told, is a hot commodity. Or perhaps you prefer selling freedom, or truth, or a trust in the divine. These are all selling roles, and with a little knowledge and passion about the goods, a talented salesperson can make it anywhere.

Aside from transportability across product lines, industries, and companies, the sales profession is also transportable across borders. It exists everywhere in the world. And here's the really good news: Our research in the Americas, Europe, and the Far East supports the notion that despite a few cultural differences, there is a unique and recognizable sales personality that cuts across all cultures.

Successful salespeople in New York City share similar personality strengths with the best salespeople in Tokyo, once we adjust for a few stylistic and cultural considerations. In our studies, we have found that the best Japanese salespeople are just as motivated to persuade as their counterparts in the United States. The only real difference is that they tap into their empathy and adjust to the subtler, more refined approach needed to be effective in Japan. While the cultural differences may appear striking between Japan and the United States, they are equally strong between midtown Manhattan and rural Texas. In both cases, our studies have proved that top salespeople are able to succeed by playing to their strengths and adjusting their approach to the needs of each situation.

Another quick, interesting finding from our studies is that the best salespeople in various countries sometimes defy stereotypes. For instance, the top British salespeople are a bit more freewheeling and aggressive than the best salespeople in the United States. These differences, while intriguing, take into account that the best salespeople around the world are all driven to persuade, empathic, able to bounce back from rejection, conscientious, and motivated to come through for their clients. When these basic, underlying sales dynamics are in place, success will follow. This is all very good news for top salespeople and the organizations that need them.

And as if that weren't enough, if you have what it takes to succeed in sales, your career path is wide open. You may have additional strengths and motivations and be able to adapt to roles in sales management or entrepreneurial leadership. Some of our best leaders started out as salespeople, and some of our best coaches and managers were only fair players themselves. Or you also have the freedom to continue succeeding in sales, as you have been doing, setting new personal achievements and charting new territory—either within your company or elsewhere.

At the end of the day, it's all about recognizing your talents, skills, and personality strengths and then doing what comes naturally. The winners in this world, we have found, are those individuals who know who they are, know what they are after, and know how to play to their strengths.

Here's the final word: If your talents lie in sales, or in sales management or entrepreneurial leadership, the world is your oyster—so shuck it!

Index